R.H.

D1373346

Introductory MUSIC Theory

JOYCE DORR

University of North Carolina at Asheville

Wadsworth Publishing Company

I(T)P™ An International Thomson Publishing Company

Belmont • Albany • Bonn • Boston • Cincinnati • Detroit • London • Madrid • Melbourne •
Mexico City • New York • Paris • San Francisco • Singapore • Tokyo • Toronto • Washington

To three powerful influences —

my husband, my daughter, my mother.

Music Editor: *Katherine Hartlove*
Editorial Assistant: *Janet Hansen*
Production: *Greg Hubit Bookworks*
Production Services Coordinator: *Debby Kramer*
Print Buyer: *Karen Hunt*
Permissions Editor: *Bob Kauser*

Text and Cover Designer: *Cloyce J. Wall*
Copy Editor: *Carole Crouse*
Signing Representative: *Mike Dew*
Compositor: *TBH/Typecast, Inc.*
Text and Cover Printer: *Malloy Lithographing, Inc.*

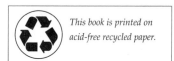

This book is printed on
acid-free recycled paper.

Printed in the United States of America

1 2 3 4 5 6 7 8 9 10—01 00 99 98 97 96 95

For more information, contact Wadsworth Publishing Company:

Wadsworth Publishing Company
10 Davis Drive
Belmont, California 94002, USA

International Thomson Publishing Europe
Berkshire House 168-173
High Holborn
London, WC1V 7AA, England

Thomas Nelson Australia
102 Dodds Street
South Melbourne 3205
Victoria, Australia

Nelson Canada
1120 Birchmount Road
Scarborough, Ontario
Canada M1K 5G4

International Thomson Editores
Campos Eliseos 385, Piso 7
Col. Polanco
11560 México D.F. México

International Thomson Publishing GmbH
Königswinterer Strasse 418
53227 Bonn, Germany

International Thomson Publishing Asia
221 Henderson Road
#05-10 Henderson Building
Singapore 0315

International Thomson Publishing Japan
Hirakawacho Kyowa Building, 3F
2-2-1 Hirakawacho
Chiyoda-ku, Tokyo 102, Japan

Library of Congress Cataloging-in-Publication Data

Dorr, Joyce.
    Introductory music theory / Joyce Dorr.
      p.   cm.
    Includes index.
    ISBN 0-534-18858-3
    1. Music—Theory, Elementary—Programmed instruction.
MT7.D708   1995
781—dc20   94-47259

CONTENTS

8. Ledger Lines and *8va* 28
9. Half Step and Whole Step 30
10. Black Keys 31
11. Accidentals 32
12. Enharmonics 33
13. Dynamics 34
14. Timbre 34
    Summary 35
    Chapter Review 37

4 Notation: Duration, Rhythm, and Tempo 41
1. Introduction 41
2. Note Types and Names 41
3. Note Values 42
4. Rest Values 44
5. Beats, Pulses, Accents 45
6. Measures and Bar Lines 45
7. Meter (Time) Signature 46
8. Dots, Ties, Fermatas 47
9. Upbeat (Anacrusis) 49
10. Tempo / Metronome 50
11. Repeat Signs 51
12. Legato and Staccato 53
    Summary 54
    Chapter Review 56

C. Organizational Element: Melody 60

5 Scales 61
1. Introduction 61
2. Diatonic Scale 61
3. Modes of the Diatonic Scale 62
4. Blues Scale 65
5. Chromatic Scale 66
6. Whole-Time Scale 68
7. Pentatonic Scale 69
8. Octatonic Scale 71
9. Tone Row 72
10. Synthetic Scales 73
    Summary 74
    Chapter Review / Aural Skills Exercises 76

6 Major Scales and Key Signatures 79
1. Introduction 79
2. Design and Construction 80
3. Transposition 82
4. Key Signatures 83
5. Staff Location of Key Signatures 87
6. Circle of Fifths 88
7. Scale-Degree Names 90
8. Syllable Names 91
9. Tonality 91
   Summary 92
   Chapter Review 94

iv   *Contents*

Part Two
RHYTHM 217

Accompanying Materials

Workbook
Compact Disc
Instructor's Manual

We all know that music is a form of communication. It is different from numbers or words in that it communicates feelings rather than facts. But still, music uses real mathematical relationships among sounds to get its message across. For instance, a melody is a succession of intervals set in a rhythmic pattern, and intervals and rhythms are both defined by mathematical ratios. As listeners we hear these ratios, which our mind then uses to create feelings and emotions. As musicians we manipulate the mathematical relationships among sounds to deliver our message to our audience.

Thus, the changing tone color of a beautifully played note, the pulsating beat of a rhythmic pattern, and the solid sound of a consonant chord all arise from mathematical relationships. Scientists and engineers study these relationships in a field called *musical acoustics*, whereas musicians study the relationships through the concepts of *music theory*. These two disciplines use different ways of talking about sounds, but the principles underlying them are the same. Most important, however, is the fact that these principles are the universal tools of music making. They are the same for every musician, and for all kinds of music. What we do with the tools determines what our musical message will be.

I believe that it is important to understand that a skilled musician performs two tasks simultaneously. Using his creative power, he shapes the emotional effect of his musical message, while with his performance skill and his understanding of music theory (the universal tools of music making) he determines exactly what sounds he shall compose or perform. Very few musicians learn these tools without extensive study. Most music students become proficient musicians only after studying performance and theory with teachers who are skilled at showing how the tools of music making are used. This is true for all types of music, whether traditional or experimental, Western or Eastern, "serious" or "popular."

In this music theory text, Dr. Joyce Dorr clearly sets forth the principles of melodic and harmonic construction and shows examples from music of many idioms. She does this from the point of view of an experienced teacher who has taught a generation of music students and who has a clear vision of the importance of a good background in music theory to all people who would become proficient in any field of music.

Robert A. Moog

About the Book

This text is designed as an introductory study of music theory, a study that deals with the elements and fundamentals of music and with music literacy. An underlying philosophy dictating both content and approach is that students are better equipped and better motivated to deal with the abstract theoretical concepts and techniques of music if they possess a basic understanding (in layman's terms) of what music actually is and how it is composed. Thus, throughout the text, there is an attempt to provide a rationale and a historical framework for the concepts and techniques being studied and to approach each aspect of the theory of music from an aesthetic vantage.

Because music is an aural art, numerous exercises for improving aural skills are provided; for the same reason, a compact disc of musical examples accompanies the test. Because creativity is the essence of the art, opportunities for original composition are provided at appropriate points throughout the text. Because the learning of so much of the course material is dependent upon review, repetition, and practice, drills are included at the end of each chapter and numerous exercises are available in the Workbook.

About the Audience

Proficiency in the knowledge, techniques, and materials contained in this book is a prerequisite to the regular music theory sequence in a college music-degree program. In addition to the traditional majors in music, however, many students are now choosing careers in music-related areas such as music business, recording arts, sound reinforcement, mass communications, theater, film scoring, and commercial music. (See Appendix I for a listing of music and music-related careers.)

In general, then, this text is designed for a very diversified audience but specifically for the following types of students:

1. Music majors, or prospective majors, who lack the appropriate basic skills, knowledge, or music literacy to commence the required music theory sequence

2. College students who do not intend to major in music but who need this information and these skills to prepare for careers in any of the music-related professions

3. College students who are interested in this course as an elective to expand their general knowledge and expertise or to fulfill general education requirements

4. High school students who are preparing to audition for acceptance into a college music-degree program and who want either a formal course in this subject or a "refresher" self-study course in preparation for college placement tests

5. Students preparing to be teachers in the elementary schools or teachers who want or need this type of course for enhancement or for certification

6. Private instructors in applied music, persons in adult education enrichment programs, directors and members of musical performance groups, and amateur performers, as well as others interested in the art

About the Design

A flexible design makes this text adaptable to a variety of course formats (semester or quarter terms, correspondence course, and so on) and to a varied number of class sessions and credit hours. Likewise, the chapter sequence can be rearranged to suit individual pedagogical preferences.

Part One focuses on the basic concepts of music, music literacy, and the organizational elements of music. It is divided into six sections with the following categories and chapters.

A: The Art of Music—Chapters 1 and 2

B: Music Notation—Chapters 3 and 4

C: Melody—Chapters 5 through 8

D: Harmony and Texture—Chapters 9 through 12

E: Form—Chapters 13 and 14

F: Timbre—Chapter 15

Part Two focuses on rhythm and is divided into seven units. It is designed to be interspersed throughout the course, commencing after study of rhythmic notation in Chapter 4.

I: Simple Meters

II: Compound Meters

III: Subdivision of the Beat in Simple Meters

IV: Subdivision in Compound Meters

V: Triplets

VI: Syncopation

VII: Asymmetrical Meters

The Workbook combines an abundance of drill material for the acquisition of techniques and skills with a variety of musical compositions that can be used to emphasize specific music concepts. (Pages in the Workbook have been perforated for tear-out and are three-hole-punched so that the student can retain corrected assignments.)

The compact disc of musical examples is an intended asset. Too often music is talked about and looked at on the printed page but is not heard, or at least not heard sufficiently. But music is an aural art, and for that reason, the majority of the musical examples included in this text are performed on the accompanying compact disc.

Conclusion

This text attempts to couch the arid facts and fundamentals of music in a musically artistic setting. It was written from a basic premise that the comprehension of the *art and essence* of music is the underlying rationale for studying its significant, albeit abstract, theoretical concepts and techniques.

Note: An earnest attempt has been made to use musical examples that most likely will be familiar to students. In many cases, these have texts to aid the student in recalling the material; thus, the student will, perhaps, be better able to grasp the concepts and techniques being discussed.

Acknowledgments

I am indebted to numerous people for their help and support in the completion of this project: my brother Wayne, who financed my earliest ventures into music; my students, particularly the class of 1995; my colleagues Russell Schmidt, for his critique of the manuscript; Wayne Kirby, for his assistance in the area of electronic timbre; and Robert Moog, for his vision and insights.

I am grateful to my first editor, Suzanna Brabant, for her early guidance and confidence in the project and to my current editor, Katherine Hartlove, for her direction and counsel and for seeing the manuscript through reviews, revisions, and publication. I appreciate the assistance of Rebecca Deans and Sheryl Gilbert for their work with the ancillary components of the text; Robert Kauser, permissions editor; and Debby Kramer, Greg Hubit, and Carole Crouse for their care in production.

Finally, to the following three powerful influences—Thelma, my mother, for her constant and continual inspiration; Maria, my daughter, for her careful scrutiny of the manuscript and numerous suggestions for refinement; and Laurence, my husband, for his love, help, support, strength, patience, inspiration, and daily encouragement—*no words of gratitude could ever be adequate.*

Joyce Dorr

Part One

BASIC CONCEPTS OF MUSIC

The

Art

of

Music

*I*ntroductory theory is designed to help the student acquire a basic music literacy and an understanding of at least some of the basic organizing principles and techniques used in music composition. Before beginning the study of this central subject matter, however, we should spend some time thinking and talking about music in general terms.

Music can do many things and serve many purposes. It can evoke emotions, create moods; it is used for entertainment, social events, religious functions, and the like. Its techniques and styles are so diverse that we need to look at some of the commonalities. To do that, we must answer some fundamental questions: What is music? What are its materials, its elements, and its components?

Section A deals with philosophical and aesthetic ideas, such as, What is music? What are its components? What are its elements? and What are some of the basic organizing principles involved both in the creation of a musical work of art and in a critical listening and analysis of the work?

Music

1 Definition of Music

*I*t is generally agreed that **music,** in its most fundamental meaning, is *sound organized in time,* or simply *organized sound.* The term implies an *art.*

Essential to the meaning of art, and thus to music, is that it is fashioned by a human being. Sounds that exist in the environment, however orderly or interesting they may be, do not automatically constitute *music.* Nature produces sound but no symphony, no song. On the other hand, environmental sounds may be incorporated into a musical context by the composer. A composer is free to choose any sounds and to organize those sounds in any way.

This deliberate organization of sound in time, by humans, is precisely what constitutes music. It will be music whether or not we like it, whether or not it makes musical sense to us, and even whether or not it is regarded as significant art by those who hear it.

The definition ("sound organized in time") is all-encompassing. Those who say that any music they do not like, or do not understand, is not music at all are simply stating a preference. It does not alter the fact that what they are hearing or referring to is indeed music. Liking or not liking is irrelevant to the intrinsic or real meaning of the concept.

It is also important to differentiate between *what music is* and *what it can or might do.* Music has been defined broadly as a universal language, a basic social and cultural phenomenon of mankind, a conveyor of emotion, an expression of religion, and so on, but such statements are more descriptive than definitive.

That music can affect us in many and perhaps significant ways is not disputed, but it is generally agreed that we cannot predict with absolute certitude what that effect will be. The general consensus is that music cannot be counted on to communicate anything more specific than the music itself.

Imagination is a powerful tool in the composer's creation of the artwork. Likewise, imagination plays a significant role in the listener's reception and perception of the artwork. The artist imaginatively/creatively organizes his or her experience into a work of art; the recipient listens to the work of art and imaginatively/creatively organizes it into an experience.[1]

ARTIST

EXPERIENCE   ORGANIZATION   WORK OF ART   ORGANIZATION   EXPERIENCE

RECIPIENT

2   Components of Music

To make music, then, we need two basic components: sound and time. The sounds and their organization will determine the essence of the musical message. They will also define the genre, type, or style of music, as well as the quality of the music. Thus, the *art* is in the *organization*.

Some propose that space and silence are also components of music. In this text, however, we will focus essentially on what are generally considered the integral components of music: *sound* and *time*.

3   The Meaning of *Sound*

Vibrating objects set air in motion, which in turn causes the air to move in *sound waves*. **Sound** is the sensation perceived by the mind when the sound waves reach the ear. In another sense, the sound source itself is frequently referred to as sound. Sound has four *properties:*

1.   **Pitch:** The *highness* or *lowness* of a sound

2.   **Intensity:** The *loudness* or *softness* of a sound

3.   **Duration:** The *length* of a sound

4.   **Timbre:** The unique quality of the sound (*tone color*)

Each of these four properties presents a myriad of artistic options to the composer.

4   The Meaning of *Time*

Time, unlike sound, is not easy to define. Some regard it as one of the greatest mysteries confronting man. To deal with this obscure phenomenon, human beings

[1] The *performer* of a musical work also plays a powerful role in imparting a composer's artistic message.

have developed ways of measuring its quantity. We speak of the interval of time between an event and its repetition, or between an event and the next event.

This is analogous to what happens in music. The composer either repeats a musical idea (musical event) or follows it with another idea. In so doing, the composer is ordering or measuring time. In turn, the listener can recall what came *before*, can experience the *now*, and can even anticipate or speculate as to what might be coming next. The composer is effectively filling up, using up, or measuring time for us.[2]

Music is a *temporal* art. Unlike a painting or a sculpture, which can have an immediate impact, musical information requires time to be heard and to be assimilated by the mind.

Summary   To make music, a composer combines two components—sound and time—and organizes them in such a way as to make a musical statement. The overall significance of the musical statement is dependent upon the creativity of the composer. The secret of success lies in the creative/artistic organization of *sound* in *time*. In the next chapter, we will look at some of the organizational elements and techniques commonly used by composers.

The following table summarizes the facts presented in this chapter.

Music	Sound organized in time
Components of music	Sound and Time
Sound	Sensation perceived by the mind when sound waves reach the ear
Properties of sound	Pitch, Intensity, Duration, Timbre
Pitch	Highness or lowness of the sound
Intensity	Loudness or softness of the sound
Duration	Length of the sound
Timbre	Quality of the sound (tone color)
Time	Indefinite, unlimited duration (past, present, future)

---

[2] Leibniz (1646–1716), the philosopher-mathematician, is said to have referred to music as "counting performed by the mind without the mind knowing it."

Chapter Review

Terms/Concepts

1. Music
2. Sound
3. Time
4. Pitch
5. Intensity
6. Duration
7. Timbre

Review Questions

1. What are the two essential components of music?

2 Why is it not accurate to refer to music simply as a "universal language"?

3. Comment on the difference between what music *is* and what it *can do.*

4. Comment on the role of the imagination in the creative process.

5. What are the *properties* of sound?

6. Why is the word "organized" an essential concept in the definition of music?

7. What is meant by the statement, "Music is a *temporal art*"?

Elements of Music

2.

1   Introduction

*I*n music, as in all art, *organization* is vital to the creative process; and as with all information, musical information has to be presented in a logical and coherent manner for communication to occur. The composer's design and organization of the basic **elements of music**—melody, rhythm, form, harmony, texture, timbre, tempo, and dynamics—should make it possible for the listener to follow and to understand the musical composition.

The remainder of this chapter is devoted to a brief study of these eight elements of music.[1]

---

[1] These eight elements of music are defined and analyzed briefly in this chapter and will be studied in detail throughout the remainder of the text.

2 Melody

Melody is a series of pitches (or tones) that conveys a musical idea or thought. Sometimes referred to as the *tune*, melody is frequently the most memorable element of a musical experience.[2]

Although a virtually limitless variety of melodies exists, we will restrict our study to melodic contour and melodic patterns.

Contour

A composer creates a melody by selecting and arranging pitches, in consecutive order, analogous to the way a writer selects and arranges words to make sentences. The particular pitch arrangement yields a certain overall **contour** or shape, which in turn gives character to the melody and helps reveal its musical meaning.

Contours can vary widely from melody to melody. In some, the pitches gradually climb higher and higher (or lower) to a certain focal point. Others start on a low pitch and *leap* to a high pitch, or vice versa. Some melodies arrive at a high (or low) pitch only once in the musical sentence, whereas others exhibit a seesaw effect. Still others are relatively static, with little ascending or descending motion.

To illustrate various types of melodic contour, we will introduce two symbols used to notate music: the *note* and the *staff*. We will study both of these symbols in Chapters 3 and 4 and although there are several types of notes, the one we will use here is called a *whole note:*

The *staff* is a type of grid, consisting of five lines and four spaces:

Notes placed either on the lines or in the spaces of this staff designate pitch. (Another musical symbol, called a *clef*, is necessary to designate specific pitches, a concept that we will study in Chapter 3.) When notes are placed on the staff in an *ascending order*, they indicate pitches that are rising; in *descending order*, pitches that are getting lower.

Ascending   **Descending**

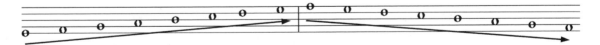

---

[2] The concept "melody" implies that the pitches are presented in a *rhythm*—a concept that we study after our discussion of melody. Melody is an interaction between pitch and rhythm.

The following six examples illustrate a variety of melodic contours. Each of these examples can be heard on the compact disc that accompanies this text.

2-A (CD)   **Melody with minimal variation in pitch**

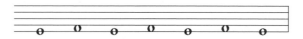

2-B (CD)   **Melody with no variation in pitch (static)**

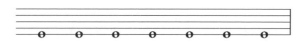

2-C (CD)   **Melody arriving at the same high point several times**

2-D (CD)   **Melody arriving at the high point only once**

2-E (CD)   **Melody starting on a high pitch and gradually descending: "Joy to the World" (Handel)**

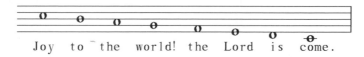

2-F (CD)   **Melody gradually climbing to the highest note of the entire piece after descending three pitches: "The First Noel" (French)**

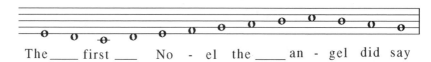

WORKBOOK 2-1 and Aural Skills 2-1 are recommended here.

Notice that, in the preceding melodies, no lines or spaces were skipped as the notes ascended or descended the staff. This is called stepwise or **conjunct** melodic motion. The opposite of this—a melody that skips some pitches as it moves from one pitch to another—is called **disjunct** melodic motion.

Obviously, there are degrees of disjunct melodic motion. Melodies can be entirely conjunct, mildly disjunct, extremely disjunct, and so on. Except for some twentieth-century music, melody in Western music generally has tended to be more conjunct than disjunct.

This is particularly true of popular songs and folk music. Skips, where they do exist in these genres, are usually few and small for the simple reason that conjunct melodic motion generally is easier to follow and to perform.

In the next three examples, notice that the skips often are placed in a strategically significant location for effect, for emphasis, or for both.

2-G (CD)   **A large skip at the beginning, plus two other significant leaps: "Over the Rainbow" from *The Wizard of Oz* (Arlen-Harburg)**

Some-where   o - ver   the   rain - bow, way   up   high

2-H (CD)   **Stepwise motion and small skips take the melody to the highest point at the very end of the phrase: *Auld Lang Syne* (traditional).**

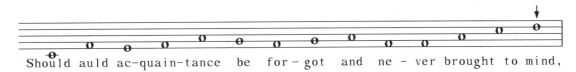

Should auld ac-quain-tance be   for - got   and   ne - ver brought to mind,

2-I (CD)   **Two ascending skips in the first line seem to prepare for the highest skip, at the beginning of line 2: "Happy Birthday" (traditional).**

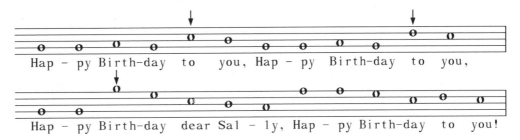

Hap - py Birth-day   to   you,   Hap - py   Birth-day   to   you,

Hap - py Birth-day   dear Sal - ly, Hap - py   Birth-day   to   you!

See *Workbook*, Score #7, "I Believe" for an example of conjunct melody.

Another important aspect of melodic contour is **range**: the distance from the lowest to the highest pitch. Human voices as well as all musical instruments have limits to their respective ranges, and the human ear can hear sounds only within a certain limited range. Composers have to work within those limits.

WORKBOOK 2-2 and Aural Skills 2-2 are recommended here.

Melodic Patterns

Melodies are either motivic or through-composed. A **motivic** melody is composed with a small unit of pitches, called a **motive.** The motive is repeated, either exactly the same way or with some variation, for as many times as is appropriate until the melodic idea is complete. (*Note:* A motive generally includes a repetitive rhythmic pattern as well as a pitch pattern.) A **through-composed** melody is not dependent upon a repeating pattern. It consists of one continuous line of pitches that simply evolve.

The next examples all begin with the same four pitches. In the first two, however, these four pitches constitute a motive from which the entire melody derives, whereas in example 2-L, a pattern is not repeated.

2-J (CD)   **Motivic melody (based on first 4 notes of example 2-L). Motive is repeated identically 3 times.**

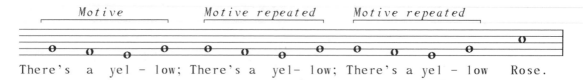

2-K (CD)   **Motivic melody (based on first 4 notes of example 2-L). Motive is heard 3 times, each time higher.**

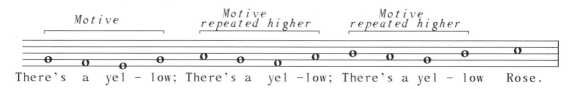

2-L (CD)   **Through-composed melody (no repeating pattern): "The Yellow Rose of Texas" (Don George)**

WORKBOOK 2-3 and Aural Skills 2-3 are recommended here.

3   Rhythm

Rhythm has to do with *time*, that is, the *temporal* aspect of music. Musical events, which include sounds and silences of varying lengths, occur *in time*. Musical information is communicated, and the meaning perceived, through a temporal process.

Perhaps because it is a common physical phenomenon (we each have a pulse, a heartbeat), most people have a natural reaction to rhythm. In music, rhythm is heard and felt as beats or pulses, some longer or shorter than others, some more accented than others.

The beat is what we are feeling when we tap our foot to music or snap our fingers. The particular arrangement of the long and short pitches and the accented and unaccented pitches can alter the effect of the music.

In the following four examples, the pitches remain identical, but the rhythm changes. With each rhythmic variation, you will hear the melody acquire a different musical character. The first is simply a series of descending pitches, which you may recognize as a descending scale—along with performance syllables shown under the notes. (*Note:* Notational symbols introduced in this chapter will be studied in Chapters 3 and 4.)

2-M (CD)   **Descending scale; each pitch given equal length**

Do   Ti   La   Sol   Fa   Mi   Re   Do

2-N (CD)   **With the new rhythm, the tune can now be heard as "Joy to the World" (Handel).**

Joy   to   the   world!   the   Lord   is   come.

2-O (CD)   **Same pitches with another rhythmic change**

2-P (CD)   **Same pitches with yet another change in rhythm**

WORKBOOK 2-4 and Aural Skills 2-4 are recommended here.

4   Form

Form refers to the design and structure in music. Melodies can be combined to yield an overall form in a musical composition, comparable to what happens in literature where sentences are joined to form paragraphs and chapters as the story unfolds. The composer does the same thing in music but with sounds instead of words, giving the musical information a coherence and a logic so that the musical meaning may be perceived. One way of discerning the form is to note the partial and full closures, analogous to commas and periods in language.

Composers rely on various techniques (which we will study more thoroughly in Chapters 13 and 14) to enable the listener to follow the musical phrases and "sentences." In example 2-Q, the text helps clarify the musical phrase and sentence structure. Notice that at the end of the first *phrase* we sense a slight pause (or comma), and the melody then proceeds to complete the musical thought.

2-Q (CD)   **"Oh! Susanna" (Stephen Foster)**

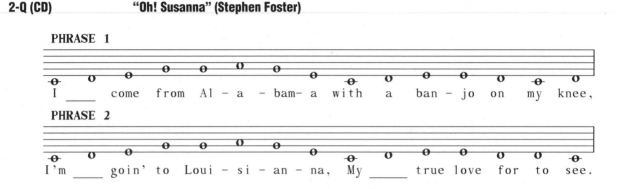

WORKBOOK 2-5 and Aural Skills 2-5 are recommended here.

5   Harmony

Harmony can be defined narrowly as the sounding of two or more pitches simultaneously. Harmony provides musical depth, somewhat analogous to perspective in paintings; thus, it is allied closely with musical *texture*. Melody provides the *linear* aspect; harmony, the *vertical*.

The effect is obvious—for example, when a vocalist sings a melody with harmonic accompaniment provided by guitar or when a pianist plays a melody with the right hand and accompanies it with other tones in the left hand. When two or more people sing the exact same pitches at exactly the same time, they are singing in *unison* and there is no harmony.

It should be noted, however, that the term *harmony* generally connotes a broader concept, that is, the whole *succession* of combined pitches (chords) in a composition. Also, although harmony can add an interesting dimension, it is not an essential element of music. In fact, harmony is a relatively late phenomenon in the evolution of music, appearing in the Western world about A.D. 900.

In examples 2-R through 2-U, a tune is shown first as *melody only* and then with varying layers of harmony. Listen to these examples on the CD to hear how the addition of harmony can change the overall musical effect.

2-R (CD)　　　　**Melody only: "Down in the Valley" (traditional).**

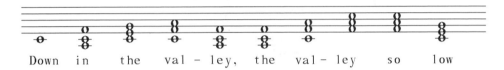

Down　in　the　val – ley,　the　val – ley　so　low

2-S (CD)　　　　**Two-part harmony: "Down in the Valley"**

Down　in　the　val – ley,　the　val – ley　so　low

2-T (CD)　　　　**Three-part harmony: "Down in the Valley"**

Down　in　the　val – ley,　the　val – ley　so　low

2-U (CD)　　　　**An arrangement for piano: "Down in the Valley"**

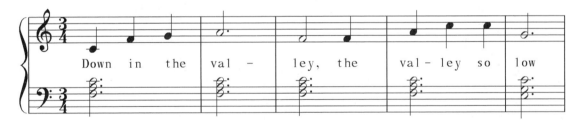

Down　in　the　val – ley,　the　val – ley　so　low

WORKBOOK 2-6 and Aural Skills 2-6 are recommended here.

6　Texture

Texture refers to the *density* of the music or the particular "weave" that results from the layering of the various melodic and harmonic "threads" throughout the composition. (See examples in Chapter 12.)

All music has some type of texture. Where there is only a single melodic line, with no harmonic accompaniment (as in example 2-R), we have the thinnest of all possible textures. With each additional layer, the "fabric" becomes "thicker" and, in some cases, "coarser." Just as fabric will change depending on the type and the number of threads interwoven, so too will the music. Listen to examples 2-R through 2-U again to hear the differences in texture.

WORKBOOK 2-7 and Aural Skills 2-7 are recommended here.

7 Timbre

Timbre (pronounced "tamber"), sometimes referred to as tone color, is the unique quality of a particular sound—that quality which makes one sound different from another.

Each sound, each musical instrument, each voice, has its own unique quality. A violin does not sound like a flute, an oboe sounds different from a trumpet, and so on. Although groups or "families" of instruments, such as the strings (violin, viola, cello, and so on), have certain similarities, each instrument has its own tone color. Likewise, each person's voice possesses its individual timbre.

Listen to the performance of example 2-V, in which the melody is played first on a flute, then on a saxophone, then on a piano. With each change of instrument, the timbre is altered and the overall effect is different.

2-V (CD)   **"Amazing Grace" (1. Flute;   2. Saxophone;   3. Piano)**

Any variation in the combination of instruments can change the effect of the musical message. Listen to example 2-W. It is performed first by four stringed instruments, next by four voices, then by four brass instruments, and finally by four woodwind instruments. Each time the timbre is changed, the overall musical effect is different.

2-W (CD)   **"Amazing Grace"**

1.   Strings—Violin, Viola, Cello, Bass

2.   Voices—Soprano, Alto, Tenor, Bass

3.   Brass—Trumpet, Horn, Trombone, Tuba

4.   Woodwinds—Flute, Oboe, Clarinet, Bassoon

8 Tempo

Tempo, which is the speed or pace at which the music is performed, can be a significant factor in the effect the musical information will have. Often the tempo will be dependent upon the amount of musical information contained in the melody and the harmony, as well as on the complexity of the rhythm, and so on.

The particular mood or the particular desired effect will also dictate the tempo. For example, a march for a sports event will generally have a faster, more upbeat tempo than a funeral march.

9 Dynamics

Dynamics refers to the intensity of the sound, that is, the level of loudness or softness. This is a concept so familiar to everyone that it needs little explanation.

Dynamics can play a significant role in communicating a specific musical message. Sounds can increase tension and excitement as they increase in volume and, conversely, decrease tension as they diminish. On the other hand, no change in volume whatsoever can also have its own peculiar, even hypnotic, effect.

Summary In this chapter, we have attempted to note some general facts about the organization of *sound and time* into music. We noted that sound and time can be organized with *melody, rhythm, form, harmony, texture, timbre, tempo, and dynamics.* These are known as the elements of music. We also pointed out that the art of music is in the organization.

This preliminary study of these very basic introductory ideas should make the learning and understanding of the material in the remainder of the text more comprehensible and meaningful.

The following table summarizes facts and definitions contained in this chapter.

Elements of Music	Organizational approaches to *sound* and *time*
Melody	A series of pitches that conveys a musical idea
Rhythm	Arrangement of the pitches (and silences) of varying lengths (durations)
Form	Design and structure of the music
Harmony	Two or more pitches sounded simultaneously
Texture	The density of the music resulting from the melodic and harmonic content and interrelationships
Timbre	The unique quality of a sound (tone color)
Tempo	The speed of the music
Dynamics	The relative loudness or softness of the sounds

Chapter Review

Terms/Concepts

1.	Elements of music	8.	Tempo
2.	Melody	9.	Dynamics
3.	Rhythm	10.	Melodic contour
4.	Form	11.	Conjunct/Disjunct
5.	Harmony	12.	Range
6.	Texture	13.	Motive (motivic)
7.	Timbre	14.	Through-composed

Review Questions

1. What is *melodic contour*?

2. What is the difference between *conjunct* and *disjunct* melodic motion?

3. For most of its history in the Western world, has music been more conjunct or more disjunct?

4. Why must the composer be conscious of *range* in music?

5. What effect can *rhythm* have on a melody?

6. Approximately when does the element of harmony appear in music in the Western world?

Aural Skills

(Aural Skills Exercises noted throughout the chapter, which require the instructor's assistance, are located in the Instructor's Manual. The following can be done by the student without the instructor's assistance.)

1. Sing the first line of "America" and for each pitch indicate whether it is H (higher than), L (lower than), or S (same as) its preceding pitch.

   My coun - try, 'tis of thee, Sweet land of li - ber - ty, Of thee I sing.

   1st   S   __ __ __ __   __   __ __ __ __   __ __ __ __ __

2. Listen to "When the Saints Go Marching In" (Chapter 14, example 14-K) and decide the following:

   a. Is the melody ascending, descending, or fairly static in the first phrase?

   b. Does the melody seem to reach the high pitch only once, or frequently?

c. Where does the high pitch occur (early in the phrase, at the middle, at the end, or throughout?)

d. Does the melody seem to move in stepwise (conjunct) motion, does it have small skips (mildly disjunct), does it have large leaps (very disjunct), or is it a combination?

e. Does the melody stay within a range that is comfortable for you to hum or sing?

f. Does the melody look or sound motivic, or through-composed?

g. Is the melody heard alone, or is there harmony?

h. What is the timbre of the piece?

Chapter Drills

(Solution to the first question is provided. Answers can be found in Appendix A.)

1. Indicate whether the second pitch is A (higher than), B (lower than), or C (same as) the first.

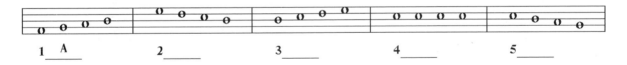

2. Indicate whether the pitches are A (ascending), B (descending), or C (static).

3. Indicate the number of times the highest pitch appears.

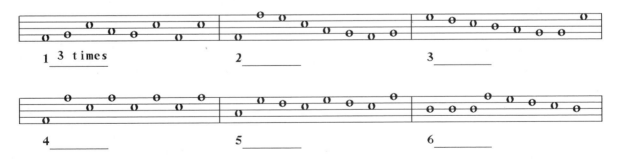

4. Indicate whether the pitch arrangment is A (conjunct), B (mildly disjunct), C (extremely disjunct), or D (static).

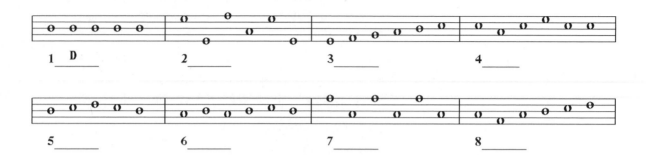

1 __D____   2_____   3_____   4_____

5_____   6_____   7_____   8_____

5. Consider each entire line of notes separately and indicate whether the melody is A (motivic) or B (through-composed).

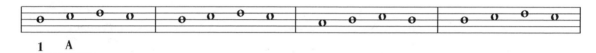

1__A____

2_____

3_____

Music

Notation

*M*usic generally is dependent upon someone other than the composer to perform it, or to bring it to life, so to speak. For this reason, a set of symbols has been devised that communicates to the performer the composer's chosen sounds and their *time* arrangement. These symbols constitute a communication system called **music notation.**

Until about A.D. 900, there was no precise notational system. Melodies simply were transmitted orally, taught by one generation to the next. Obviously, in this type of communication there exists a potential for misrepresentation.

To assist in more accurately recalling the liturgical melodies of the church, musicians (about A.D. 600) invented a type of notation (called *neumatic* notation) that could at least hint at—and thus serve as reminders for—the *rise and fall* of the particular melodies. This system could not specify precise pitch, nor did it indicate the duration of the pitch. It acted merely as a memory-aid and served to facilitate the teaching and learning of melodies.

Between A.D. 900 and 1000, a more precise notational system began its long evolution. Symbols were devised that made it possible to indicate *specific* pitches. Durational, or rhythm notation, however, had to wait several more centuries for its development.

For much of its history, music was essentially vocal—people were singing songs, songs had a text, and the rhythm derived from that text. With the addition of the element of harmony, music became more complex. When two or more singers were attempting to perform jointly and to sing different words on different pitches at different times, it became necessary to communicate exactly how long a pitch should be held in relation to any other pitch. Thus, between 1200 and 1300, new symbols were introduced to provide definite durational information.

Although the traditional notational system has its limitations, it has enabled countless composers to communicate their particular *organizations of sound in time.* With this system, it is possible to designate each of the properties of sound and to denote the organizational elements of music: melody, rhythm, harmony, form, timbre, texture, tempo, and dynamics.

The system has been refined over the centuries and continues to evolve. Some contemporary composers have resorted to inventing new symbols and personal notational systems to communicate the many new sounds and sound combinations they have created. Others have resorted to recording their own music directly on tape so as not to be dependent upon a still somewhat imprecise or perhaps not totally reliable system.

Section B of this text deals with a study of the traditional and commonly used notational system, and then proceeds to examine some of the basic organizational techniques used by composers of music in the Western world. (See Appendix B for more historical detail.)

Notation: Pitch, Dynamics, Timbre

1 Introduction

*E*ach of the four properties of sound (pitch, intensity, duration, and timbre) can be notated, thus providing a visual image of the composer's musical work of art and enabling another to read and perform it. In this chapter, we will study the **notational system** for the first three of these properties. Chapter 4 will focus on the fourth, duration.

2 Music Alphabet

Pitch refers to the *highness* or *lowness* of one particular sound as it relates to other sounds.[1] The first seven letters of the alphabet (A–G) are used to designate pitches, making it possible to refer to each specifically and to be able read and write them.

Because, in most music, pitches descend as well as ascend (in the *rise* and *fall* of melodies, for example), musicians need to know the music alphabet backwards and forwards.

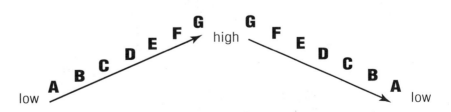

[1] Pitch is determined by *frequency,* which is the number of vibrations per second produced by the vibrating object.

3 Piano Keyboard

The standard piano **keyboard** (which has a total of 88 black and white *keys*, each producing a different pitch) provides a visual image of the pitch names.[2]

The lowest pitches are at the left side of the keyboard. Proceeding to the right, the pitches become progressively higher. The name of the lowest white key is *A*, the next *B*, the next *C*, and so on. After *G* we start over again, calling the next white key *A*, and continue in this fashion all the way to the highest pitch on the keyboard.

3-A　　　　　　　　　　**Piano keyboard with letter names**

WORKBOOK 3-1 is suggested here.

4 Staff, Notes, Clefs

To indicate specific pitches, composers use three symbols: the staff, notes, and clefs. The **staff** is a type of grid consisting of five parallel horizontal lines and four spaces. See example 3-B.

3-B　　　　　　　　　　**Staff**

　　　　Notes are placed on the staff to indicate pitches. The basis of a note is the *notehead* (white or black), to which may be added a stem, as seen in example 3-C.

3-C　　　　　　　　　　**Three note types**

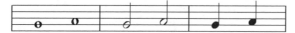

(Notes can be placed on lines or in spaces.)

(All note types and their durational values will be discussed in Chapter 4. In the present chapter, however, we will use only the stemless white note known as a whole note.)

---

[2] This is about the extent of the range of pitches generally used in Western music.

The location on the staff shows the *relative* highness or lowness of the pitches. The higher a note is on the staff, the higher the pitch indicated; the lower the note, the lower the pitch.

3-D   **Notes ascending/descending the staff**

The staff and notes alone cannot designate *specific* pitches. When combined with a **clef,** however, each line and each space acquires a definite pitch name. The two most frequently used clefs are the **treble clef** (also known as the **G clef**) and the **bass clef** (also called the **F clef**). Both are evolutionary results of Gothic letters for "G" and "F," respectively.[3]

3-E   **Treble clef and Bass clef**

Treble Clef
(G Clef)
(Used for pitches ranging
from medium to high)

Bass Clef
(F Clef)
(Used for pitches ranging
from medium to low)

Placed on the staff, the treble clef indicates where pitch G is located (which is why it is called the G clef) and labels this the **treble staff.** It designates the second line from the bottom as G by encircling it as shown in example 3-F.

3-F   **Treble staff**

The bass clef indicates where the pitch F is located and labels this the **bass staff.** It marks the fourth line from the bottom of the staff with a large dot, and two additional dots, one on each side of the fourth line, as shown in Example 3-G.

3-G   **Bass staff**

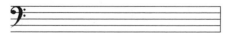

WORKBOOK 3-2 is suggested here.

---

[3] See the Glossary for another, less commonly used clef sign, known as the C clef. Also see WORKBOOK 3-35 for drills involving this less commonly used clef sign.

5 Name of the Lines and Spaces

Once you know the staff location of one pitch, you can name the others by proceeding up or down alphabetically.

3-H **Treble and bass staff pitch names**

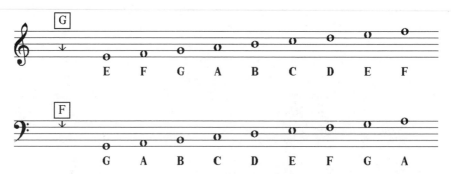

Memorize the names of the lines and spaces for each clef, starting with the first line or space. (Note that the first line and the first space are at the bottom of the staff, not the top as you might expect.)

Line 5 →
    Space 4
Line 4 →
    Space 3
Line 3 →
    Space 2
Line 2 →
    Space 1
Line 1 →

Use example 3-I as a guide for memorization.[4]

3-I **Names of treble and bass lines and spaces**

TREBLE LINES: E G B D F   TREBLE SPACES: F A C E

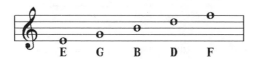

BASS LINES: G B D F A   BASS SPACES: A C E G

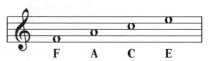

WORKBOOK 3-3 through 3-8 are suggested here.

---

[4] Reading from the bottom line to the top, some like to use mnenomic aids:

Treble lines: **Every Good Buddy Does Fine**	Bass lines: **Good Buddies Do Fine Always**
Treble spaces: **FACE**	Bass spaces: **All Cows Eat Grass**

The first line of the treble staff designates pitch E. The top space also designates E, but this is the next higher E on the keyboard; the third space of the bass staff indicates the next lower E. The location of the note on the staff provides precise information concerning the highness or lowness of the desired pitch.

3-J   **Location of pitch E on staff and on keyboard**

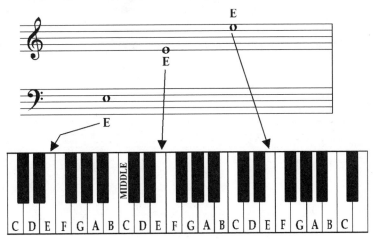

6   Octave

The distance between two pitches having the same name is called an **octave.** In example 3-J, the first E is one octave lower than the second; the third E is one octave higher than the second and two octaves higher than the first.[5]

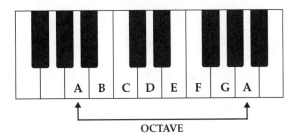

7   Grand Staff

The two staffs joined by a vertical line, called a *bar line,* and by a *bracket* or *brace,* constitute the **grand staff** (also referred to as the *great staff*).[6]

[5] The term *octave* means "eight." Every eight white keys, the pitch is repeated, *one octave higher or lower.* This results from the nature of the physics of sound. When an object vibrates as a whole, a string for example, it produces a certain number of vibrations per second (*frequencies*). When the string is divided exactly in half (shortened, that is), the rate of vibrations is doubled, emitting a sound that is heard as very similar to the first, but higher. See Appendix F for more detail.

[6] The term *staves* is also used for the plural of *staff.*

A short segment of a line (called a *ledger line*) is drawn between the treble and bass staffs to designate a pitch referred to as **middle C.** This is the centermost C on the keyboard. (Generally, when middle C is used, it is placed not exactly in the center of the grand staff but closer to the treble staff or the bass staff, depending on the musical context. Ledger lines will be discussed shortly.)

Notice in example 3-K that the space immediately *above* middle C is D; the space immediately *below* middle C is B.

3-K   **The grand staff and middle C (plus B and D)**

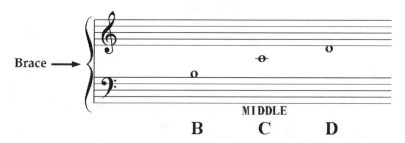

The treble staff designates pitches that are *above* middle C; the bass staff designates pitches that are *below* middle C. Music calling for a range of pitches too wide for a single clef will use the grand staff—for example, piano and most choral music.

Example 3-L shows the pitch names for each line and space of the grand staff, including the ledger lines and spaces between the two staffs.

3-L   **Letter names of the entire grand staff**

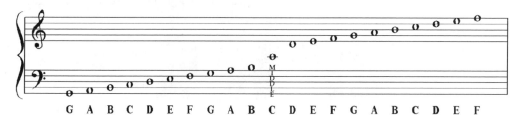

G A B C D E F G A B C D E F G A B C D E F

WORKBOOK 3-9 through 3-12 are suggested here.

8   Ledger Lines and *8va*

To notate pitches that are higher or lower than those which can be indicated on the staff, we simply add short segments of lines above or below, as needed. These are called **ledger lines** and **ledger spaces.** We have just discussed middle C, which is one ledger line below the treble staff and one ledger line above the bass staff.

3-M   **Ledger lines and spaces**

Numerous ledger lines can make reading difficult. For simplicity, the symbol *8va* is used. Placed *above* a note, it indicates that a pitch one octave higher than written should be played; placed *below* a note, it indicates one octave lower than written. See examples 3-N through 3-P.

3-N   **Seven octaves of pitch E with ledger lines**

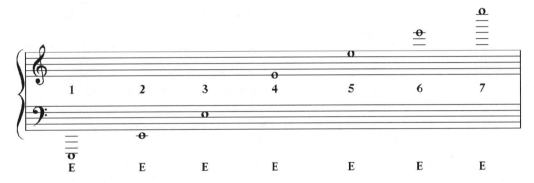

3-O   **Seven octaves of pitch E with symbol *8va***

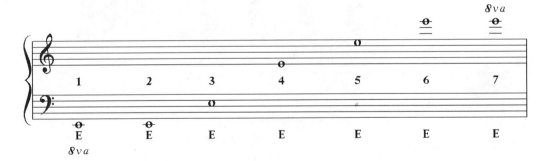

3-P   **Keyboard location of seven octaves of pitch E**

WORKBOOK 3-13 through 3-19 are suggested here.

3-Q   **View of the seven octaves of the keyboard—also shown on the treble and bass staffs. (The octaves are frequently referred to as follows, from lowest to highest: CC, C, c, c¹, c², c³, c⁴.)**

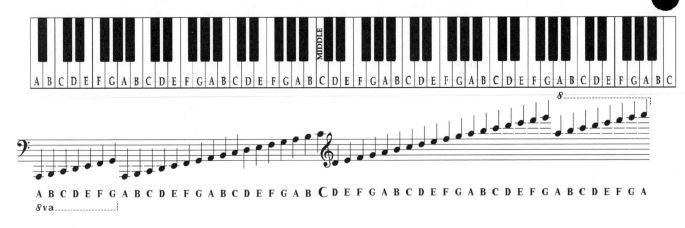

9   Half Step and Whole Step

The distance from one key to its adjacent key on the piano (white or black) is a **half step.**[7] If there is an intervening key, the distance from one key to another is a **whole step.** Example 3-R shows various possible whole steps and half steps on the keyboard.

3-R   **Half steps and whole steps on the keyboard**

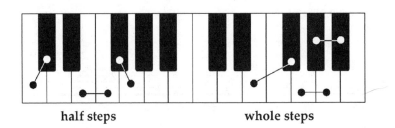

half steps   whole steps

WORKBOOK 3-20 is suggested here.

[7] The half step is sometimes referred to as a semitone. The octave, which was discussed in Section 6 of this chapter, is divided into twelve equal half steps. (It could be divided in numerous other ways, but for most Western music, the half step, or the semitone, is the division used.)

10   Black Keys

Thus far, we have named only the white keys of the piano keyboard. The black keys are divided into groups of *twos* and *threes*. Notice also that each white-key letter name always falls at the exact same place in relation to the black-key groups; for example:

C is always the white key to the left of the two-black-key group.

D falls between the two black keys.

E is on the right of the two-black-key group.

Refer again to example 3-Q.

The black keys aid in locating the white keys. Cover the black keys and all the white keys look exactly the same. On the other hand, the black keys take their names from their adjacent white keys. Each is referred to as either a *sharp* (symbolized by the sign ♯) or a *flat* (symbolized by the sign ♭), depending upon its relationship to the white keys surrounding it.

The black key one half step to the right of a C, is *C-sharp*. If we refer to it as one half step to the left of D, it is called *D-flat*.

In notation, a sharp sign placed to the left of a note means the note should be played one half step higher; a flat sign means it should be played one half step lower. Each black key, then, has more than one name.

3-S

Black keys shown on staff and keyboard

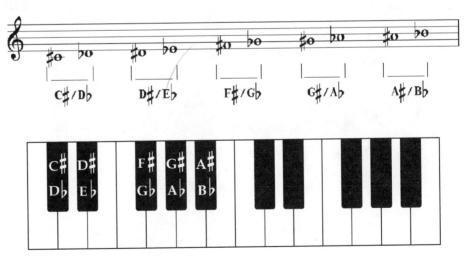

WORKBOOK 3-21 through 3-27 are suggested here.

The symbols we have been discussing (♯ and ♭) are called **accidentals.** Two other accidentals used in music notation are the double sharp (𝄪) and the double flat (𝄫). The **double sharp** raises a pitch a *whole step;* the **double flat** lowers it a *whole step.*

3-T   **Double sharp and double flat**

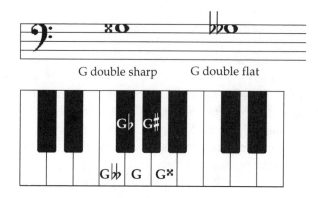

One final accidental, the **natural** (♮), cancels a previous sharp, flat, double sharp, or double flat. Once a sharp or a flat has been inserted into the musical notation, it remains in force until it is canceled.[8] (The natural sign is one way to cancel. A second method will be discussed later in the text.)

Accidentals

♯   A sharp raises a pitch one half step.

𝄪   A double sharp raises a pitch one whole step.

♭   A flat lowers a pitch one half step.

𝄫   A double flat lowers a pitch one whole step.

♮   A natural cancels a previous sharp, flat, double sharp, or double flat.

WORKBOOK 3-28 and 3-29 are suggested here.

---

[8] This is not the case in twentieth-century atonal music, where an accidental affects only the note with which it appears.

12 Enharmonics

Notes differing in notation and name but not in pitch—for example, C♯ /D♭, D♯ / E♭—are known as **enharmonics.**

Though written differently, they sound exactly the same. The black key between D and E is D-sharp or its enharmonic, E-flat. The purpose of these different names will become clear later when we study scales and chords.

There are two locations on the keyboard where two white keys exist without an intervening black key: between E and F and between B and C. The distance here is only a half step. To play E-sharp, then, we still move up only one half step, to the white key F. E-sharp and F-natural are enharmonics, as are F-flat and E-natural.

3-U   **Sharps and flats on white keys**

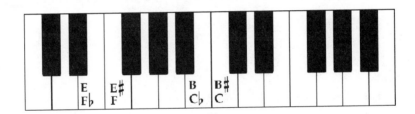

WORKBOOK 3-30 and 3-31 are suggested here.

13 Dynamics

Dynamics refers to the property of sound known as *intensity*. This has to do with the *loudness* or *softness* of a sound. (*Amplitude* and *volume* are other terms sometimes used as synonyms for *dynamics*, but each of these terms has its own distinct meaning.)

In music notation, various symbols are used to indicate whether the pitches should be played *relatively* loudly or softly.

The following is a list of terms and symbols used to denote dynamic levels. Although these are commonly used notations, some composers prefer to substitute the vernacular for the Italian terms. The use of abbreviations (or symbols) for these terms is standard practice. (See Appendix C for a more extensive list.)

Italian Word	Abbreviation/Symbol	Definition
pianissimo	**pp**	very soft
piano	**p**	soft
mezzo piano	**mp**	moderately soft
mezzo forte	**mf**	moderately loud
forte	**f**	loud
fortissimo	**ff**	very loud
crescendo	*cresc.* or $<$	gradually louder
decrescendo	*descresc.* or $>$	gradually softer
diminuendo	*dim.*	gradually softer

Although dynamics began to play an increasingly important role in music composition and performance around the mid-eighteenth century, its notation is still not an exact system. For example, just how loud is *f* and just how much louder is *ff*? Some contemporary composers have opted to put their music directly on tape, thus avoiding reliance upon a somewhat imprecise system of notation or upon another performer's interpretation of that notation.

WORKBOOK 3-32 is suggested here.

14 Timbre

Timbre is the *unique quality of a sound,* sometimes referred to as its *tone color* or *tone quality.* It is determined primarily by the object that produces the sound. Composers can specify the desired timbre by indicating the instrument(s) for which they are writing or simply by writing in a format that is a recognizable notational scheme for a specific timbre. The piano, as was noted earlier, uses the grand staff. A composition for an instrumental trio, for example, would use three staves, all joined by a brace, indicating that all the parts are played simultaneously. See examples 3-V, which is a piano score, and 3-W, which is a score for three instruments: two violins and a viola.

3-V   **Écossaise (Ludwig van Beethoven)**

3-W   **"Joy to the World" (Handel) for two violins and viola (original arrangement)**

Summary   We have now seen how a composer can communicate three of the four properties of sound: *pitch, intensity,* and *timbre.*

We noted that pitches are referred to by alphabet names from A through G. We related these letter names to the white keys on the piano keyboard and to the lines and spaces on another music symbol studied here: the staff.

We saw how the location of *notes* on the staff, accompanied by a *clef*, specify precise pitches. Other music symbols studied in this chapter (relative to the notation of pitch) are *octave, grand staff,* and *ledger lines and spaces*.

The concept of whole step and half step was introduced for the purpose of understanding *accidentals* (sharp, flat, double sharp, double flat, and natural signs) and enharmonically equivalent pitches.

Methods for notating dynamics and timbre were also studied in this chapter. The fourth property of sound, duration, will be addressed in the next chapter.

WORKBOOK 3-34 and 3-35 are suggested here.

The following table summarizes the facts and concepts contained in this chapter.

Notation of Pitch	
Music Alphabet	*A, B, C, D, E, F, G*
Staff	5 lines and 4 spaces, each capable of specifying pitch
Clef	Gives *specific* pitch names to each line and space of staff
Treble clef	Indicates where G is located All lines and spaces are *above* middle C
Bass clef	Indicates where F is located All lines and spaces are *below* middle C
Grand staff	The treble and base staffs joined by a bracket
Ledger lines	Individual lines/spaces added above or below the staff
Octave	The next higher or lower pitch with the same letter name
Half step	The distance from one key (pitch) to the very next
Whole step	The distance from one key to the next, with one intervening
Accidentals	
Sharp	Raises a pitch one half step
Flat	Lowers a pitch one half step
Double sharp	Raises a pitch a whole step
Double flat	Lowers a pitch a whole step
Natural	Cancels any accidental
Enharmonics	Pitches that sound the same but are named and notated differently
Notation of Intensity	Shown by a set of dynamic marks
Notation of Timbre	Shown by the type of score provided

Chapter Review

Terms/Concepts

1. Pitch
2. Intensity
3. Timbre
4. Notational system
5. Dynamics
6. Staff
7. Music alphabet
8. Keyboard
9. Clef
10. Treble clef (G clef)
11. Bass clef (F clef)
12. Notes
13. Noteheads/Note stems
14. Treble/Bass staffs
15. Grand staff
16. Octave
17. *8va*
18. Middle C
19. Ledger lines/spaces
20. Whole step/Half step
21. Sharp/Flat/Natural
22. Double sharp/flat
23. Accidentals
24. Enharmonics

Review Questions

1. Why is a notational system needed?
2. The *treble clef* indicates that all the pitches are above what specific pitch?
3. The *bass clef* indicates that all the pitches are below what specific pitch?
4. What is meant by *dynamics*?
5. What can a composer do to indicate the desired *timbre*?
6. What is the purpose of the *grand staff* and *ledger lines*?

Chapter Drills

(Solution to the first item in each drill is provided where appropriate. Answers to all Chapter Drills can be found in Appendix A.)

1. To acquire a familiarity with the keyboard, go to any piano and play all the two-black-key groups; then all the three-black-key groups.
2. Starting at the left, say the name of each white key; do the same starting from the right of the keyboard.
3. Randomly locate the various keys—for example, all the C's, G's, E's.
4. Locate the highest C and the lowest C on the keyboard, and so on.

5. In the following, give the names of the white keys indicated by the arrows.

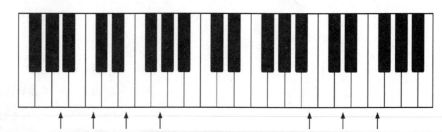

6. Identify and define the following symbols:

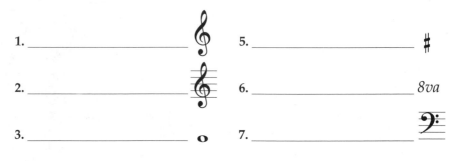

1. _____

2. _____

3. _____

4. _____

5. _____

6. _____

7. _____

8. _____

7. Practice drawing the treble clef sign and the bass clef sign on the staff.

8. Draw the treble clef and write in the names of the lines and spaces.

9. Draw the bass clef and write in the names of the lines and spaces.

10a. Add the appropriate symbols to make a grand staff of the following two staffs.

10b. Starting with the lowest pitch, write in the name of each line and space on the staff.

11. Write the letter names of the treble staff lines: _____

12. Write the letter names of the treble staff spaces: _____

13. Write the letter names of the bass staff lines: _____

14. Write the letter names of the bass staff spaces: _____

15. Draw a grand staff and draw a note to show each location of pitch A.

16. Place the treble clef on the staff and write the notes on the staff (in *any* location).

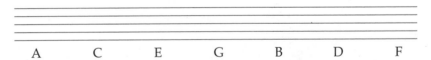

    A   C   E   G   B   D   F

17. Place the bass clef on the staff and write the notes (in *any* location).

    A   C   E   G   B   D   F

18. In each of the following exercises, write the letter name of the note.

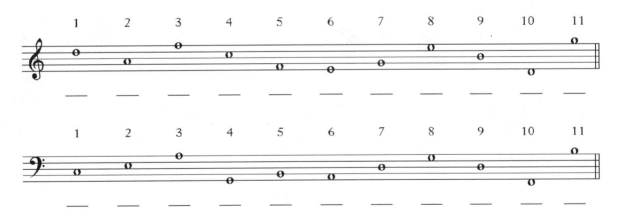

19. Show where the following would be played on the keyboard by writing the *number* of the pitch on the appropriate white key.

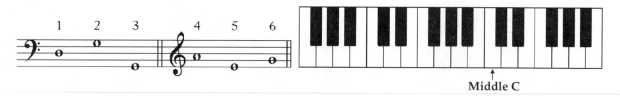

20. Write the name of each ledger line or ledger space.

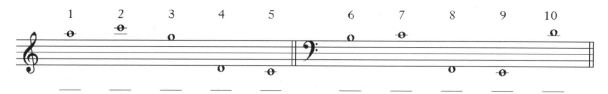

21. Show where each note would be played on the keyboard (sharps, flats, double sharps, and double flats).

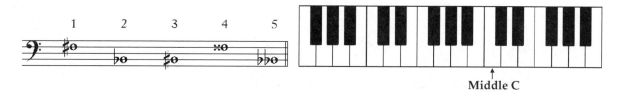

22. Give an enharmonic name for each of the following pitches.

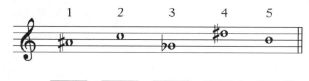

23. Beside each note, lower it one half step. Do *not* change the letter name. Add or delete accidentals as needed.

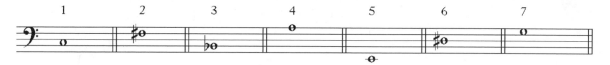

Notation: Duration, Rhythm, and Tempo

1   Introduction

*C*hapter 3 focused on symbols and devices used to notate three of the four properties of sound: pitch, intensity, and timbre. This chapter deals with the notation of **duration,** which is the *temporal* element of music, generally referred to as *rhythm.*

We have already discussed how notes are used to represent pitches. Notes also serve to specify the length of time a pitch is to be sustained and to indicate relative durations.

2   Note Types and Names

Notes are made up of an oval-shaped *notehead*, open or solid and with or without a *stem* or **a flag.**

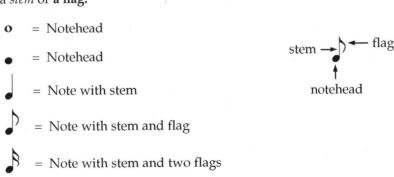

o = Notehead

• = Notehead

♩ = Note with stem

♪ = Note with stem and flag

♬ = Note with stem and two flags

When two or more flagged notes appear consecutively, the flags can be replaced by a **beam(s)**.

Example 4-A depicts the various note types and their respective names. It also shows those notes that can be beamed.

4-A   **Note types and note names**

Types		Names	(with Beams)
𝑜	Open notehead	WHOLE NOTE	
𝅗𝅥	Open notehead and stem	HALF NOTE	
♩	Solid notehead and stem	QUARTER NOTE	
♪	Solid notehead, stem, and flag	EIGHTH NOTE	♫
♬	Solid notehead, stem, and 2 flags	SIXTEENTH NOTE	♬
♬	Solid notehead, stem, and 3 flags	THIRTY-SECOND NOTE	♬
♬	Solid notehead, stem, and 4 flags	SIXTY-FOURTH NOTE	♬

WORKBOOK 4-1 is suggested here.

3   Note Values

In the previous chapter, we saw that the particular location of a note on the staff specifies the precise pitch that is to be heard. Now we will see that the use of particular *types* of notes makes it possible to specify the precise length of time a sound should be heard and indicates relative durational values.

Note types and their relative values

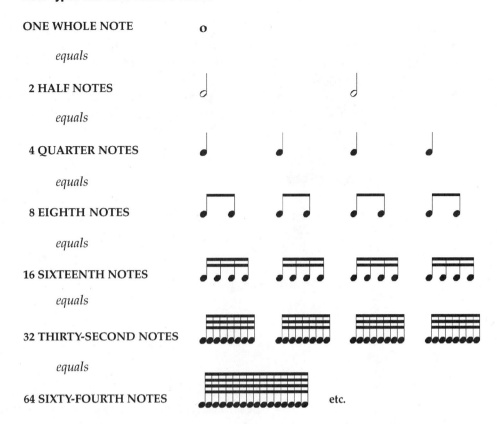

ONE WHOLE NOTE

   equals

2 HALF NOTES

   equals

4 QUARTER NOTES

   equals

8 EIGHTH NOTES

   equals

16 SIXTEENTH NOTES

   equals

32 THIRTY-SECOND NOTES

   equals

64 SIXTY-FOURTH NOTES   etc.

(The DOUBLE WHOLE NOTE [⨎], rarely used since 1600, equals 2 WHOLE NOTES.)

WORKBOOK 4-2 through 4-4 are suggested here.

Stem Direction

The stems go *up* if the note is *below* the middle line on the staff, *down* if *above* the middle line (the point being to keep as much of the stem on the staff as possible). If the note is on the middle line, the stem can go either up or down. In this case, the choice is determined by the context. (*Stems going up are located on the right of the notehead; stems going down are placed on the left.*)

Stem direction

Flags and Beams

When two or more consecutive flagged notes are to be heard as a group, it is common practice to replace flags with beams. (As you will note in the Rhythm Units, Part Two of this text, beams aid in communicating the rhythmic pulse of the music.)

The use of flags is generally reserved for single notes or, in some cases, to indicate a specific type of articulation, as demonstrated in example 4-D. (*Flags are always placed on the right side of the stem.*)

4-D   **Flags and beams**

WORKBOOK 4-5 is suggested here.

4   Rest Values

Silence in music (the cessation of sound) can be effective at times. Notes represent sound; **rests** signify silence. Like notes, rests have specific time values—shown here with equivalent note values.

4-E   **Rests**

WHOLE REST		=	WHOLE NOTE	
HALF REST		=	HALF NOTE	
QUARTER REST		=	QUARTER NOTE	
EIGHTH REST		=	EIGHTH NOTE	
16th REST		=	16th NOTE	
32nd REST		=	32nd NOTE	
64th REST		=	64th NOTE	

WORKBOOK 4-6 and 4-7 are suggested here.

Music is perceived as moving through time because of the rhythmic arrangement of the sounds and silences in a composition. Combinations and patterns of notes create the rhythm. (This will be explained more fully in the following sections and in the Units on Rhythm.)

5   Beats, Pulses, Accents

Most Western music possesses an underlying **beat,** which continues throughout the piece. The beat is marked by the recurring patterns of strong and weak pulses, which are designated by a recurring periodic accent. It is the beat that incites our foot-tapping or finger-snapping. We sense the musical time of a piece by the beat patterns.

The simple rhythmic patterns are *duple, triple,* and *quadruple,* shown here with beat one accented:

Duple: **One** two; **One** two; **One** two; etc.

Triple: **One** two three; **One** two three; etc.

Quadruple: **One** two three four; **One** two three four, etc.

Note: More complex patterns can result simply from the *combining* of groups of twos or threes.

6   Measures and Bar Lines

Starting with beat 1, each *repeat of the pattern* constitutes one **measure** of music. Measures are marked off by vertical lines, called **bar lines.** Single lines denote individual measures, and **double bar lines** designate either the end of a piece or the end of a major section of a composition.

4-F   **Bar lines and measures**

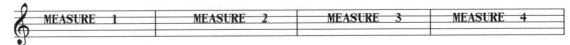

4-G   **Double bar**

7 Meter (Time) Signature

Meter is the system of regularly recurring patterns of strong and weak beats (pulses) of equal duration. Usually the patterns are marked off by a constant and regular accent. At the beginning of a composition, the meter is identified by a *meter signature* (also referred to as a *time signature*),[1] which consists of two numbers, one above the other—for example:

$$\frac{2}{4} \quad \frac{3}{4} \quad \frac{4}{4} \quad \frac{2}{2} \quad \frac{3}{8}$$

The time signature indicates how the rhythm is notated. The top number denotes the number of beats in the pattern; for example:

2 on top (*duple meter*) means 2 beats per measure.

3 on top (*triple meter*) means 3 beats per measure.

4 on top (*quadruple meter*) means 4 beats per measure.

The bottom number (in simple meters) indicates the note type that will get one beat. (*Note:* This is not the case in compound meters. Compound meters will be explained shortly.)

4-H

Various meters

2 = two beats to a measure
4 = quarter note gets one beat

3 = three beats to a measure
4 = quarter note gets one beat

4 = four beats to a measure
4 = quarter note gets one beat

3 = three beats to a measure
8 = eighth note get one beat

4 = four beats to a measure
2 = half note gets one beat

Once we know the meter, the other rhythm information is clear. For example, if there are two beats to a measure with the quarter note getting one beat, there can be only two quarter notes per measure, one half note, four eighth notes, and so on.[2]

---

[1] The time signature appears only at the beginning of the piece unless the meter changes during the course of the composition (unlike clef signs, which appear on each staff throughout the piece).

[2] This type of rhythm is known as *metric rhythm,* which becomes increasingly commonplace after 1600.

Four measures in $\frac{2}{4}$ meter

Four measures in $\frac{3}{4}$ meter

Four measures in $\frac{4}{4}$ meter

Four measures in $\frac{4}{2}$ meter

WORKBOOK 4-8 through 4-13 are suggested here.

8   Dots, Ties, Fermatas

Dots, ties, and fermatas are all symbols that can be used to *lengthen a note* beyond its normal value. We have already discussed how the length of a pitch can be doubled merely by using the next larger note value.

At times, however, we may want to increase the value by only one-half, or one-fourth, and so on. Or we may wish to lengthen it by extending it over the bar line into the next measure; or we may simply want to *pause* on a particular note for special emphasis. Using the following notational devices, we can achieve any of these effects.

Dots

A **dot,** placed to the *right* of a note (♩.), increases the value of that note by one-half its original value. Example 4-J shows the dotted half note and the dotted quarter note in context.

4-J

Dotted half note; dotted quarter note

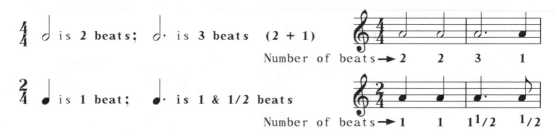

A **double dot** following a note increases the length by one-half the value of the preceding dot (or three-fourths of the note's original value).

4-K

Double dotted notes (half note and quarter note)

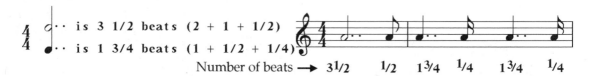

Note: Rests can also be dotted or double dotted.

WORKBOOK 4-14 through 4-17 are suggested here.

Ties

Another way to lengthen the duration of a note is to use a **tie.** This symbol is a curved line joining two notes of the *same* pitch:

It implies that the second note should not be sounded but merely held for the length of the total value of the two tied notes.

This device is particularly useful for extending a pitch's durational value over the bar line. In such a case, a dotted note would not work because it would put too many beats in one measure. A tied note might also be used instead of a double dotted note for easier reading.[3] See example 4-L.

---

[3] The tie is also useful for showing lengthened note values where the durational value does not fit the system. See Part Two, Unit II (Compound Meters).

4-L   **Tied notes**

(Easier to read)

WORKBOOK 4-18 is suggested here.)

Fermatas

One last sign used to show increased length for a particular note is the **fermata** (𝄐). Placed above a note, this symbol signifies a *pause,* not a rest. It means that the note should be held beyond its normal length, although it does not specify precisely how long it should be held.

    The length of the pause is at the discretion of the performer or the conductor. Used judiciously, such pauses can create a very effective moment in music.[4]

4-M   **Fermata**

Sum – mer's gone, Leaves have blown, Win–ter's on ITS way.

WORKBOOK 4-19 and 4-20 are suggested here.

9   Upbeat (Anacrusis)

Pieces sometimes begin on a beat other than beat 1. If beat 1 is missing at the outset, the other beat or beats are called **upbeats** (or *pickup*), the formal term for which is **anacrusis.** Upbeats are borrowed from the last measure of the piece (or the last measure of one section in longer pieces).

    The first measure to contain beat 1 is counted as *measure 1.* Beat 1 of the first measure (which is the *first accented note* of the piece) is called the *downbeat.* Obviously, if beat 1 is missing at the outset, the downbeat is being delayed, a technique that adds real rhythmic vitality to the music.

---

[4] Fermatas are often used at the ends of phrases in chorales and at the final notes of pieces.

As an example, "Auld Lang Syne" starts on an upbeat. Note the emphasis this places on beat 1 of the first full measure. To hear the difference, sing the line as written with the upbeat and then without the upbeat.

4-N (CD)   **"Auld Lang Syne" (traditional)**

Should auld ac-quain-tance   be   for - got

The national anthem of the United States begins with one upbeat (divided between two pitches).

4-O (CD)   **"The Star-Spangled Banner" (J. S. Smith)**

In "Rhinestone Cowboy," which has four beats to a measure, the melody starts on beat 2, making beats 2, 3, and 4 all upbeats, before finally landing on the downbeat of measure 1. The prolonged upbeats provide an elaborate preparation for the first strong downbeat.

4-P (CD)   **"Rhinestone Cowboy" (Glen Campbell)**

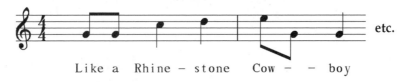

Like a   Rhine – stone   Cow – – boy

WORKBOOK 4-21 is suggested here.

10 Tempo/Metronome

Tempo is the rate of speed at which the *beat* moves. Although composers are not always specific regarding tempo (leaving the decision to the performer), tempo indicators do exist.

The commonly used indicators are Italian words that mean "fast," "slow," and so on. As we noted with dynamic marks, some composers prefer to indicate tempo with their native language. Before 1600, tempo indications were not used, since the tempo was dictated by the text in the music.

The **tempo indicators** most frequently encountered in music literature are listed here, from slowest to fastest. For a more extensive list, see Appendix C.

Italian Word	Definition
largo	very slow
lento	slow
adagio	leisurely slow
andante	a walking pace
moderato	moderate
allegretto	moderately fast
allegro	fast and lively
presto	very fast
prestissimo	very, very fast
ritardando	gradually slowing down
accelerando	gradually speeding up

Metronome

The question will probably arise, How fast is *fast*? how slow is *very slow*? and so on. What is slow for one person may not be the same as for another; and what seems a slow tempo to us one day may not seem so another day. When composers want to be certain that these relative terms are understood in a precise sense, they provide a metronome marking.

The **metronome** is a mechanical or an electric device that can be adjusted to produce the desired number of beats per minute. For example, the composer specifies that the quarter note should be played at 80 per minute by showing M.M. = 80.[5] The performer can then set the metronome at 80 and play the piece, one quarter note to each beat of the metronome.

Even without metronome indicators, skilled performers know that a quarter note in *allegro* is somewhere between 84 and 144 M.M., *andante* is 56–88 M.M., and so on.

11 Repeat Signs

A number of methods are used to indicate that the piece, or a section of the piece, should be repeated. Although it is easy to rewrite a few measures, symbols called **repeat signs** make it possible to save space when the parts to be repeated are lengthy.

---

[5] The M.M. is an abbreviation for Maelzel's Metronome. Johannes N. Maelzel is the individual who in the early 1800s made the invention popular.

Two dots to the left of a double bar line (:‖) indicate that the music is to be repeated. Example 4-Q illustrates a melody that is repeated exactly, but with a second line of text.

4-Q   **Double dots indicating a repeat from the beginning**

Note that the dots are located to the left of the solid bar-line.

When the repeat is from somewhere other than the beginning of the piece, two sets of double bars/double dots are used (as shown in measures 3 and 4 in example 4-R. This tells the performer to repeat the section *between* the signs.

4-R   **Double dots indicating the repeat of a section**

Note that the dots are to the right of the first double bar and to the left of the second.

Example 4-R would be performed as follows:
Measures: 1   2   3   4   **3**   **4**   5   6

If the entire piece (or an entire section of a piece) is to be repeated, **Da Capo,** meaning "from the beginning" and abbreviated *D.C.,* may be used. This is synonymous with the repeat sign shown in example 4-Q.

4-S   ***D.C.* indicating a repeat of the entire piece**

Da Capo al fine (D.C. al fine) directs the performer to go back to the beginning but end where the music is marked with the Italian word *fine* (which means "the end").

4-T   ***D.C. al fine***

Example 4-T would be performed as follows:
Measures: 1   2   3   4   5   6   7   8   **1**   **2**   **3**   **4**

Dal Segno (D.S.), or *Dal Segno al fine* (D.S. al fine), indicates a return to the sign 𝄋. It is used when the repetition is to start somewhere other than the beginning of the piece.

4-U   **D.S. al fine**

Example 4-U would be performed as follows:
Measures: 1   2   3   4   5   6   7   8   **3**   **4**

Frequently, a different ending is written for the repeated music. The piece or the section then has first and second endings.

4-V   **First and second endings**

Example 4-V would be performed as follows:
Measures: 1   2   3   **4a**   1   2   3   **4b**

WORKBOOK 4-22 is suggested here.

12 Legato and Staccato

Although the terms *legato* and *staccato* have some relevance to rhythm, they relate primarily to *performance style*.

Legato, which is indicated by a curved line called a *slur* (⌢), means that the notes are to be played smoothly or in a "connected manner." (*Note:* This slur is not to be confused with the curved line that is used to tie two notes so that the second is not sounded again but held for the full length of both notes within the tie.)

Staccato implies that the pitches are to be played in a short or detached manner, just the opposite of legato. *Staccato* is indicated by a dot above or below the note (♩̇ ♩).

Legato   Staccato

Summary   In this chapter, we have examined notational symbols and devices used by composers to indicate *time* and *rhythm* in music. We looked at the various note types and saw their relevance to the duration of sound. We further studied how the notes are organized into patterns of fixed temporal units, with meters signifying those temporal units. Measures and bar lines were presented as a means of denoting metrical units.

Ways in which note values might be lengthened were discussed: ties, dots, and fermatas. The upbeat was noted as a means of delaying the first accented beat in the piece, thus producing a certain sense of excitement and expectation.

The metronome was shown as a device for ensuring that the precise tempo is adhered to. Finally, various signs and symbols for designating material that is to be repeated were discussed.

It would be appropriate at this point in the course to commence the study of the seven Units on Rhythm in Part Two.

The following table summarizes facts and concepts contained in this chapter.

Note types	Whole, half, etc.; specify duration
Note values	1 whole = 2 halves, etc.; specify relative values
Rests	Whole, half, etc.; specify silence
Beats	Recurring patterns of accented and unaccented sounds
Pulse	Rhythmic division within the beats
Bar lines	A vertical line dividing the music into metrical units
Double bar	Two vertical parallel lines marking the end of the piece or of a section
Meter	The beat pattern being used
Dot	A sign placed after a note to lengthen the note's value by one-half
Double dot	A sign placed after a note to lengthen the note's value by three-fourths
Tie	A curved line joining two notes of the same pitch; indicates second note is to be held (not repeated)
Fermata	A symbol placed above a note to indicate a pause (no specific length)
Upbeat	Any beats occuring before beat 1
Tempo	The speed of the beat
Metronome	A device for accurately depicting/performing tempo
Double dots/Double bars	Symbols specifying that music is to be repeated from the beginning or from a previous set of double dots/double bars
D.C. al Fine	A designation that tells the performer to return to the beginning and play to the word *Fine* (the end)
D.S. al Fine	A designation that tells the performer to return to the *dal segno* sign and repeat to *Fine*
Legato	A term, indicated by a slur, that tells the performer to play in a smooth (connected) style
Staccato	A term, indicated by a dot above or below the note, that tells the performer to play in a crisp (detatched or disconnected) manner

Chapter Review

Terms/Concepts

1.	Duration	14.	Fermatas
2.	Unison	15.	Accents
3.	Note types	16.	Upbeat (Anacrusis)
4.	Note values	17.	Tempo
5.	Flags/Beams	18.	Tempo indicators
6.	Rests	19.	Metronome
7.	Meter	20.	Repeat signs
8.	Beat	21.	Double dots
9.	Bar lines	22.	*Da Capo*
10.	Measure	23.	*Dal Segno*
11.	Double bar lines	24.	*Fine*
12.	Dotted notes	25.	Legato
13.	Ties	26.	Staccato

Review Questions

1. What determines whether we use a *beam* or a *flag* to join two or more notes?

2. What does a *rest* call for in performance?

3. If a piece does not begin on *beat 1*, all notes before beat 1 are called what?

4. What is the difference between a *legato* and a *staccato* performance?

5. What symbol can be used to indicate that a *different ending* should be played after a piece (or a section of a piece) has been repeated?

6. Define the following terms or symbols:

    a. *Andante*_____

    b. *Allegro*_____

    c. *Moderato*_____

    d. *Ritardando*_____

    e. *Accelerando*_____

    f. *ff*_____

    g. *p*_____

Chapter Drills

(Solution to the first item in each drill is provided where appropriate.)
Answers to all Chapter Drills can be found in Appendix A.

1.   Name the type of note(s).

2.   Directly beside the note, correct any errors in stem direction or location.

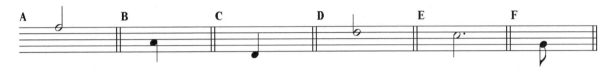

3.   Give the number of values requested that could be contained in the given note.

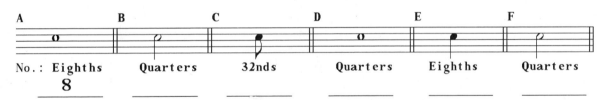

4.   Name the type of rest and draw the equivalent note value beside it.

5.   Write one note that equals the combined value of the notes given.

6. Write one note only that completes each measure in the meter given.

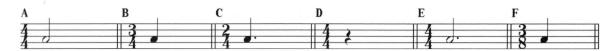

7. Write one rest only that completes the measure in the meter given.

8. Write four different measures of rhythm for each of the two meters given.

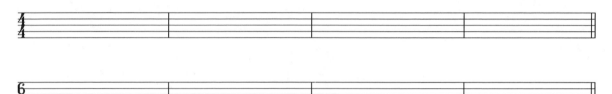

9. Write the number of beats each dotted note/rest should receive.

10. Write the total value (number of beats) of each tied note.

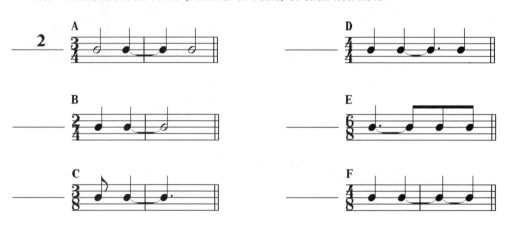

11. Place bar lines where appropriate for the meter indicated.

12. Provide the appropriate time signature for the following four measures.

13. What is meant by each of the following symbols?

a. $\frac{4}{4}$ _____   d. *D.C.* _____

b. *Fine* _____   e.  _____

c. _____

14. In each of the following examples, give the numbers for the measures in the order in which they should be played.

a.

A = _____

b.

B = _____

Organizational

Element:

Melody

This section of the text deals with techniques for the organization of sound and time into melodies. Melody has been the basis of music and has reigned supreme, so to speak, since earliest times. Although it is impossible to have melody without rhythm, rhythm has been subservient to melody for much of its history in Western music.

It is probably impossible to state what it is that makes a beautiful, memorable melody, but certain techniques of melodic composition can be observed. Each time and place seems to possess its own characteristic melodies; yet, each melody has its own distinctive musical logic. In spite of this individuality, however, certain basic principles seem to be evident.

In the following four chapters, we will examine various techniques for composing melodies.

Scales

1 Introduction

$\mathcal{C}$omposers generally select their melodic and harmonic pitch material from existing patterns or configurations called scales. The term **scale** comes from the Latin word *scala,* meaning "ladder." As a musical concept, it denotes an arrangement of pitches in consecutive ascending or descending order within the octave.

Scale is a generic term that encompasses many varieties of pitch configurations. Most scales contain from five to eight of the available twelve pitches within the octave. This chapter presents a brief summary of several scale options. Chapters 6 and 7 are devoted exclusively to a study of the major and minor scales.

2 Diatonic Scale

For whatever musical, acoustical, or psychological reasons, certain scales have had more appeal than others in a particular era or culture. The most commonly used scale in the Western world is the **diatonic scale.**[1] Even in much twentieth-century music, where we encounter a great deal of experimentation and change, the diatonic arrangement still prevails.

The diatonic scale has seven pitches and contains five whole steps and two half steps.[2] It can start on any pitch and ascend or descend to the next pitch of the same name. In other words, if the scale starts on C and ascends, it will end on the C one octave above.

---

[1] The term *diatonic* has connotations other than a body of scales. It serves also to describe a composition that restricts the pitch selection entirely to the seven that belong to its scale, to the exclusion of the other five available pitches, or at least to a limited and controlled use of the other five potential pitches.

[2] In Chapter 7, we will discuss one alteration to this scale that produces a step larger than a whole step (1½ steps).

The location of the five whole steps and two half steps will vary, depending upon the starting note. In a diatonic scale starting on C (and using only the white keys), the half steps will occur between steps 3 and 4 (E and F) and steps 7 and 1 (B and C).

5-A   **Diatonic scale starting on C**

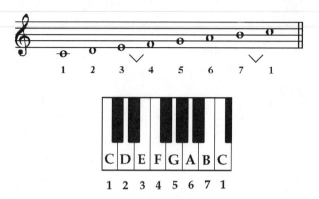

In a diatonic scale starting on A (using only white keys), the half steps will be between steps 2 and 3 and steps 5 and 6.[3]

5-B   **Diatonic scale starting on A**

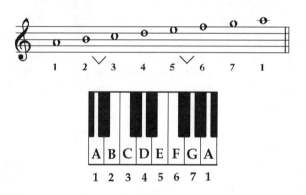

WORKBOOK 5-1 and Aural Skills 5-1 are recommended here.

3   Modes of the Diatonic Scale

Each change in location of the whole steps and half steps results in a different sound. Each scalar arrangement has a specific name; collectively, the scales are known as the church, or Medieval, **modes.** This text is limited to a detailed study

---

[3] These two arrangements of the whole steps and half steps are known as diatonic major (*Ionian*) and diatonic minor (*Aeolian*), respectively. They will be discussed in detail in the next two chapters.

of only two of these, Ionian and Aeolian, which are the equivalents of what are now referred to as the **major mode** (white keys C–C) and the **minor mode** (white keys A–A), respectively; but it is worthwhile to be aware of the others.

The major and minor modes have predominated since 1600. Since the end of the nineteenth century, however, the others have been used frequently in classical styles, jazz, and rock. Example 5-C shows seven diatonic modes.

5-C   **The seven modes of the diatonic scale**

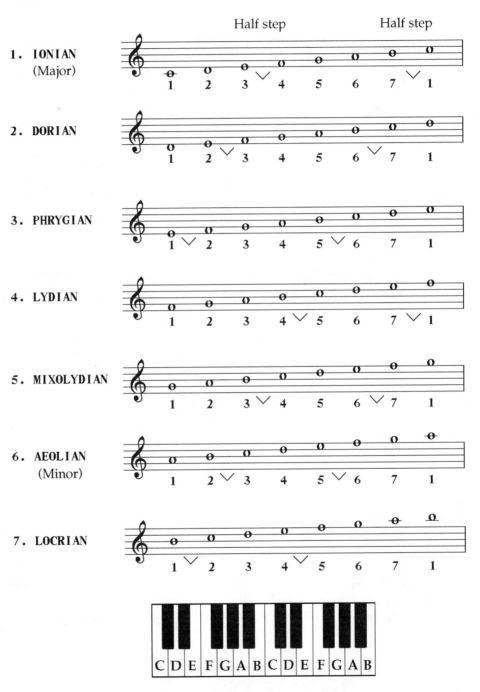

A change of mode can make a real difference in the sound and character of a piece. The following three examples (5-D through 5-F) are designed to demonstrate this point. Each is written in a different mode of the diatonic scale. On the compact disc, each piece is played first in the mode in which it is written, then in two other modes.

5-D (CD)　　　　　**"On Top of Old Smoky" (American)**

This composition is based on the major (Ionian) mode: C to C (half steps between 3 and 4 and between 7 and 1).

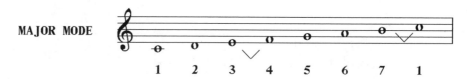

On the CD, this is played (1) in the major mode; (2) in the minor mode; and (3) in the Dorian mode.

5-E (CD)　　　　　**"Balalaika" (refrain)**

This composition is based on the minor (Aeolian) mode: A to A (half steps between 2 and 3 and 5 and 6).

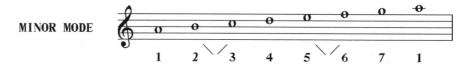

On the CD, this is played (1) in the minor mode; (2) in the major mode; and (3) in the Dorian mode.

5-F (CD)   **"Early in the Morning" (sea chanty)**

This composition is based on the Dorian mode: D to D (half steps between 2 and 3 and 6 and 7).

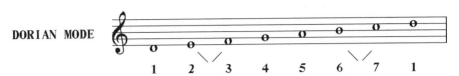

DORIAN MODE

1   2   3   4   5   6   7   1

On the CD, this is played (1) in the Dorian mode; (2) in the major mode; and (3) in the minor mode.

See Workbook, score #13, "Scarborough Fair" for another example of Dorian mode.

WORKBOOK 5-2 and Aural Skills 5-2 are recommended here.

4   Blues Scale

Although rarely used in classical music, the **blues scale** is a familiar characteristic of many styles of jazz and rock. Since this scale has origins in African music tradition and contains quarter tones, it is not possible to notate it precisely with standard notation (which is based on the whole-step/half-step system). However, we approximate its sound by lowering the 3rd, 5th, and 7th of a diatonic major scale as follows:

5-G   **Blues scale**

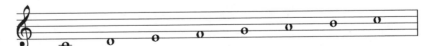

Blue-note alterations applied to diatonic C major

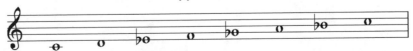

(This is only one of several versions [modes] of the blues scale, although this may be the most popular.)

In performance, however, we are actually hearing a pitch that exists somewhere between E and E-flat, and so on. These pitches can be produced on stringed, brass, and woodwind instruments but not on traditionally tuned keyboards. In fact, jazz pianists often play two pitches (for example, G-flat and G-natural) simultaneously to simulate the quarter tone between the two. Example 5-H is based on the blues scale shown in example 5-G.

5-H (CD)   **"Blues For Daddy-O" (Frank Foster)**

(Note that the alterations are not necessarily permanent throughout; for example, E♭, G♭, B♭ can alternate with E♮, G♮, B♮.)

5 Chromatic Scales

The term *chromatic* comes from the Greek word *chroma*, meaning "color." In this scale, each of the twelve pitches is used—all the *colors*, so to speak. The **chromatic scale** consists entirely of half steps.

Example 5-I shows the chromatic scale, ascending and descending. Compare the notes with the keyboard to observe that no pitch is skipped; each of the twelve is present. (Note also that sharps are generally used when pitches are ascending and flats when descending.)

5-I   **Chromatic scale**

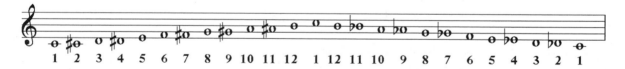

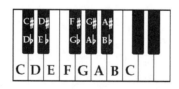

In examples 5-J through 5-L, each piece uses all twelve pitches of the chromatic scale, but each develops differently and sounds different.

5-J (CD)   **Etude, Op. 10, No. 2 (Frédéric Chopin—nineteenth century)**

The melody in the preceding example (Etude) proceeds in half steps throughout the entire piece, whereas in the next composition ("Chromatic Invention"), although all twelve pitches are used, the melody deviates occasionally from continuous half-step movement.

5-K (CD)   **"Chromatic Invention" (Béla Bartók—twentieth century)**

The complete chromatic scale is shown above the example to facilitate pitch verification.

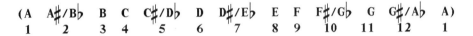

Sometimes a composition will employ the chromatic scale for only certain portions of the piece. In example 5-L, the first two measures are based on the chromatic scale, whereas the next two are not.[4]

5-L (CD)   **"Chicken Chowder Rag" (Irene Giblin)**

etc.

See Workbook, score #3, "Flight of the Bumblebee" for an example of a piece using the chromatic scale.

WORKBOOK 5-3 and Aural Skills 5-3 are recommended here.

6   Whole-Tone Scale

The **whole-tone scale** has six pitches, each a whole step apart. This scale became popular during the Impressionistic era (about 1890–1920) and has continued to be one of the many types of scales used by twentieth-century composers.

5-M   **Whole-tone scale**

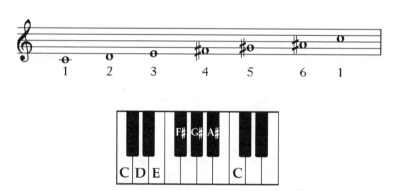

The next example (5-M) is based on a whole-tone scale that starts on D-flat.

5-M   **Whole-tone scale starting on D-flat**

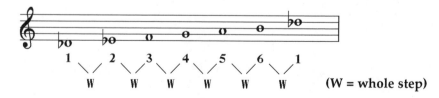

(W = whole step)

---

[4] Occasionally, a composition based on a diatonic scale (seven pitches) will use one or more of the other five pitches. Depending on the frequency of their use, a composition can be described as somewhat chromatic, very chromatic, and so on.

"Les Demons s'amusent" (Vladimir Rebikov)

WORKBOOK 5-4 and Aural Skills 5-4 are recommended here.

7 Pentatonic Scale

The **pentatonic scale** uses only five pitches. Although theoretically the five pitches can be arranged in any order, in Western music this scale generally contains two 1½-step skips. For that reason, it is sometimes referred to as a "gapped" scale.

5-O **Pentatonic scale starting on C**

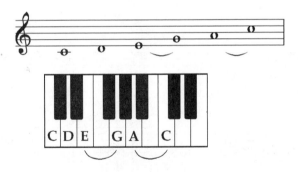

The five black keys provide a good example of the pentatonic scale. Starting on D-flat (C-sharp) or on G-flat (F-sharp) and playing all five black keys produces a popular form of the pentatonic scale.

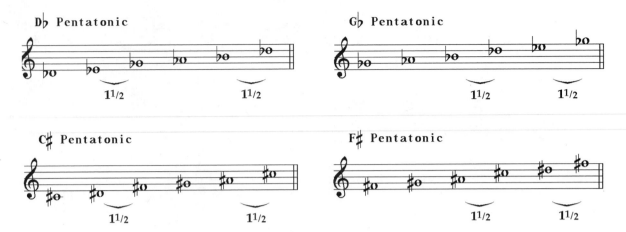

Note: Other versions of this scale exist (for example, minor pentatonic) and are used in jazz, rock, and other types of music.

As with each of the other types of scales we have discussed, the pentatonic scale has its own special sound. Examples 5-Q and 5-R are based on pentatonic scales G-flat and D-flat, respectively. (Also see "Tom Dooley" (13-A) in Chapter 13 for another example of a melody based on a pentatonic scale.)

5-Q (CD)   **"Amazing Grace" (traditional)**

This composition uses a G-flat pentatonic scale.

5-R (CD)   **"Oh Hanukkah" (Jewish folk song)**

This composition uses an E-flat pentatonic scale.

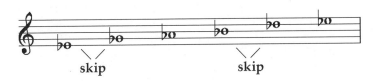

The pentatonic scale has been more popular in musical cultures of the Eastern world, but composers in the West have made frequent use of it as well. This is especially true in folk music or in pieces where the composer is attempting to evoke the sound of ethnic folk music. It is used frequently in jazz and other popular styles.

WORKBOOK 5-5 and Aural Skills 5-5 are recommended here.

8   Octatonic Scale

The **octatonic scale** is an eight-pitch scale consisting of alternating whole steps and half steps. It sometimes is referred to as the *whole-step/half-step scale* and, more commonly, as the *diminished scale*.[5] It can start either with a whole step or with a half step.

5-S   **Two forms of the octatonic scale**

Starting with a Whole Step   Starting with a Half Step

[5] The rationale for this terminology will not be addressed in this book.

This melody is based on a C octatonic scale.

W = whole step
H = half step

The octatonic scale is a twentieth-century phenomenon. Although we can find pieces written with the diatonic, chromatic, and pentatonic scales before this century, the whole-tone scale and, more especially, the octatonic scale are virtually nonexistent in previous musical periods in Western music.

WORKBOOK 5-6 and Aural Skills 5-6 are recommended here.

9 Tone Row

The **tone row,** which is not a scale (and which is frequently referred to as a *series*), was invented by the twentieth-century composer Arnold Schoenberg as an alternative to the scales we have been discussing. The *row* consists of an arbitrary, but fixed, arrangement of the twelve pitches. The arrangement normally remains binding for a whole work. Unlike the chromatic scale, in which the pitches occur in half-step order, the row can present the pitches in any order.

Variety is achieved through various techniques such as inverting the row, playing it backwards, transposing it, and so on.

Another significant difference between row and scale is that the row generally does not contain one pitch that serves as a focal point (tonal center) in the composition. In fact, this is precisely what the row is designed to obliterate. (More will be said about *tonal centers* in the next chapters.)

Composers will generally design a different row for each composition and even for each movement of a larger composition. The following examples show two possible *twelve-tone rows.* (*Note:* In this system, the starting pitch is called "0" and all other numbers indicate the half-step distance between the respective pitch and "0.")

5-U (CD)   **Row for Concerto, Op. 24 (Anton Webern)**

0 11 3 4 8 7 9 5 6 1 2 10

(*Note:* Every pitch is used—A A♯ B C C♯ D D♯ E F F♯ G G♯)

5-V (CD)   **Row from Etude from *Eight Piano Pieces* (Ernst Krenek)**

Note: Refer to other sources for more information concerning the manipulation of a tone row.

WORKBOOK 5-7 and Aural Skills 5–7 are recommended here.

10 Synthetic Scales

Obviously, one can conceive of many potential arrangements of the pitches within the octave other than those we have just discussed. From time to time, composers have developed an original scale for a particular composition. Such an atypical or original pitch arrangement is referred to as a synthetic scale.

A **synthetic scale** is simply any arrangement of any number of the twelve pitches other than the standard conventional arrangements. It can be designed using any size steps, including quarter tones and microtones, a technique used for many centuries in some Eastern cultures.

5-W (CD)   **Valsette (Zoltán Kodály)**

WORKBOOK 5-8 and 5-9 and Aural Skills 5-8 and 5-9 are recommended here.

Summary   Composers use scales (rows/series) as organizing pitch material for writing melodies and harmonies. Although the number of potential scales is virtually infinite, certain ones have been more popular than others in some periods or cultures and in some musical styles. The scale used almost to the exclusion of all others between 1600 and 1900 (and even today in most of the commonly heard music of the Western world) is the *diatonic* scale. The two modes of the diatonic scale most frequently used during this same time period are the *major* (Ionian) and the *minor* (Aeolian). (These two modes of the diatonic scale will be studied at length in the next two chapters.)

The Dorian, Phrygian, Lydian, Mixolydian, and (rarely) Locrian were used throughout the Middle Ages; Ionian (major) and Aeolian (minor) came into use in the sixteenth century and were used almost exclusively from 1600 to 1900; the twentieth century has seen the revival of the other five modes. This century has also seen the continued use of the *pentatonic* and *chromatic* scales, as well as the development of others such as the blues scale, octatonic and synthetic scales, and the *tone row*.

The following table summarizes facts and concepts contained in this chapter.

Scale	A series of pitches in consecutive ascending/descending order
Diatonic scale	A seven-pitch scale using whole steps and half steps
Modes	Different arrangements of the whole steps and half steps in the diatonic scale
Blues scale	A diatonic major scale with a flatted 3rd, 5th, and 7th
Chromatic scale	A twelve-pitch scale arranged in half-step order
Whole-tone scale	A six-pitch scale arranged in whole-step order
Pentatonic scale	A five-pitch scale usually containing two skips
Octatonic scale	An eight-pitch scale arranged in alternating whole-step and half-step order
Twelve-tone row	Twelve pitches arranged in any order
Synthetic scale	Any number of pitches, arranged in any nonconventional order

The following is an example (one version only) of each of the scales studied in this chapter. They are shown here *ascending* and *descending*.

Diatonic (Major)

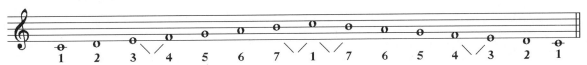

Chromatic

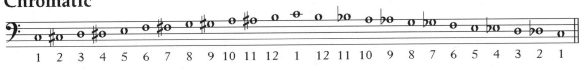

Whole-tone

Pentatonic

Octatonic

Twelve-tone

Synthetic

Blues

Chapter Review

Terms/Concepts

1.	Scale	8.	Blues scale
2.	Octave	9.	Chromatic scale
3.	Whole steps/Half steps	10.	Whole-tone scale
4.	Diatonic scale	11.	Pentatonic scale
5.	Mode	12.	Octatonic scale
6.	Major mode	13.	Tone row
7.	Minor mode	14.	Synthetic scale

Review Questions

1. What purpose do scales serve (a) for the composer and (b) for the listener?

2. Which type of scale was most popular between 1600 and 1900 and is still used in much twentieth-century music?

3. What is the difference between *mode* and *scale*?

4. Which *modes* of the *diatonic system* have been most popular since 1600?

5. Why, do you think, have composers resorted to inventing *synthetic* scales?

Aural Skills

(Aural Skills noted throughout the chapter, which require the instructor's assistance, are located in the Instructor's Manual. The following can be done by the student, in some cases working with a colleague.)

1. Working with one of your colleagues, play major scales and minor scales for each other, to determine whether you can tell the difference between the two.

2. Listen to the recording, on your CD, of the pieces from the score section of the Workbook and try to tell whether the piece is written in a major or a minor mode.

3. Choose a colleague and play the scales at the end of the Summary for each other to see if you can differentiate between them.

Chapter Drills

(Answers to all Chapter Drills can be found in Appendix A.)

1. Write each scale indicated here ascending only. Start each on C and use sharps as needed. (You may find it a help to write the scale in letter names first, then place the notes on the staff.)

a. DIATONIC SCALE (Major Mode—half steps between 3 and 4 and 7 and 1)

b. CHROMATIC SCALE

c. PENTATONIC SCALE

d. WHOLE-TONE SCALE

e. OCTATONIC SCALE (Start with either a whole step or a half step.)

f. TWELVE-TONE ROW (Do not omit or duplicate any pitch.)

g. SYNTHETIC SCALE (Use seven pitches only.)

h. WRITE ANOTHER SYNTHETIC SCALE (Start on any pitch and use eight pitches.)

2. Identify the *type* of scale in each of the following exercises. To determine which type scale is being used, do a *pitch inventory*, from A through G, writing down each pitch that appears in the scale, as shown in the first exercise.

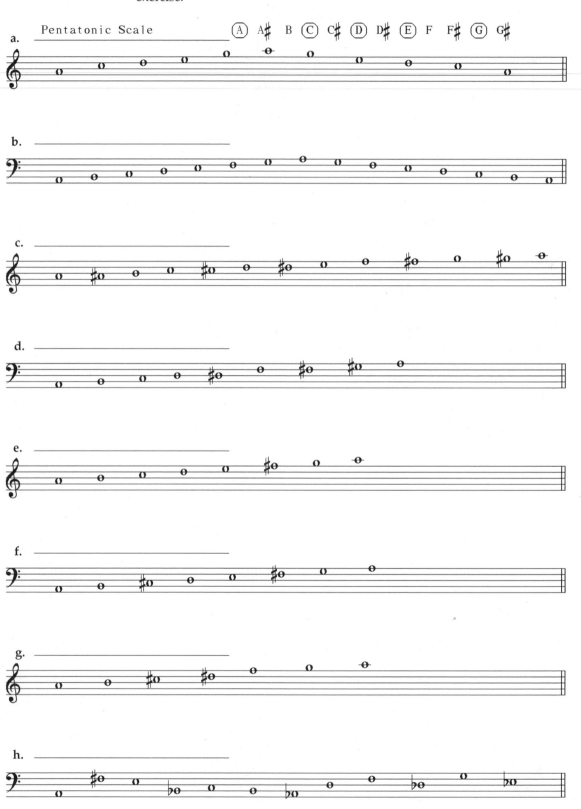

Major Scales and Key Signatures

1   Introduction

*I*n the preceding chapter, we noted that, of the many scale options, the most popular has been the seven-tone *diatonic* scale. Probably most of the music with which you are familiar is written either in the **major mode** or the minor mode of the diatonic scale. The following summary reviews what is meant by the diatonic scale.

1. A diatonic scale contains seven pitches in consecutive order and uses both whole steps and half steps.

2. The traditional diatonic scale has five whole steps and two half steps.

3. The particular location of the whole steps and half steps causes the scale to have its own character, referred to as its **mode.**

Since the sixteenth century, the most popular of the many possible modes of the diatonic scale have been major and minor, generally referred to simply as the *major and minor scales*. The major scale is dealt with in this chapter, and the minor scale in the next.

Before beginning our study of these two scales, listen to a piece written and played in major, and then listen to that same piece played in minor. Both versions can be heard on the compact disc.[1]

[1] See and listen to other pieces: (1) in major: "One More River" (Workbook: Chapter 11, Exercise 8); (2) in minor: "Shalom Chaverim" (Chapter 11, example 11-C). Also see score section of the Workbook. For pieces in major mode, see Nos. 4, 6, 7, 8, 9, 12, 14, and 15; for pieces in minor mode, see Nos. 5, 10, and 11.

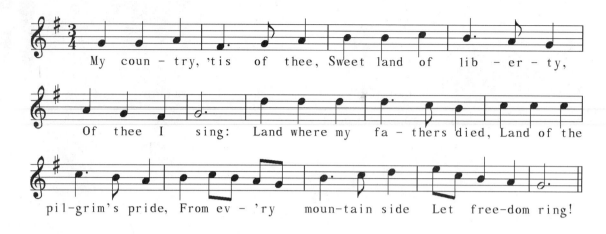

My coun – try, 'tis of thee, Sweet land of lib – er – ty,

Of thee I sing: Land where my fa – thers died, Land of the

pil–grim's pride, From ev – 'ry moun–tain side Let free–dom ring!

"America" in G minor

2 Design and Construction

A major scale has half steps between pitches 3 and 4 and between pitches 7 and 1; all
other steps are whole steps, as shown here.
("W" is used for whole step, "H" for half step.)

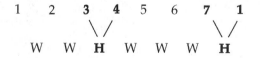

Starting a major scale on C and proceeding upward or downward one
octave to the next C, using only the white keys, produces the configuration of
C major.

C major scale shown on keyboard and on staff

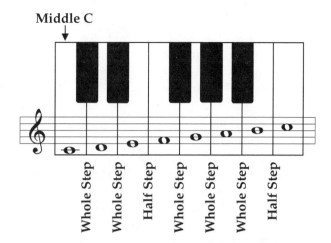

Middle C

Whole Step Whole Step Half Step Whole Step Whole Step Whole Step Half Step

      This is the only location on the keyboard where we can obtain the *major sound* using only the white keys. Although a major scale can be constructed starting on any of the twelve pitches, every location other than C–C requires the use of one or more black keys. The only thing necessary to re-create the sound of the major scale *from any starting point* is to reproduce *exactly* the pattern of whole steps and half steps. See example 6-C.

Process for determining whole-step/half-step arrangement for G major

1.   Write the letter names from G to G.

2.   Number them: 1 2 3 4 5 6 7 1.

3.   Mark the steps that must be half steps.

        G A B C D E F G
                      \ /   \ /
        1 2 **3** **4** 5 6 **7** **1**

4.   Examine the distance between each two pitches for accurate size. For example:

    1–2 (G–A) must be a whole step, and it is. (Proceed this way up to 6–7.)

    6–7 (E–F) must be a whole step, but it isn't; *therefore, the F must be raised to F-sharp.*

    7–1 (F–G) must be a half step, and *because of the F-sharp,* it now is.

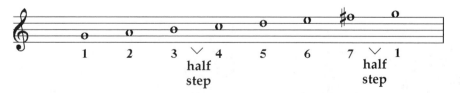

      1   2   3   4   5   6   7   1
                       half   half
                       step   step

Note: When an alteration is required to achieve the correct distance between two pitches, alter the second of the two pitches, that is, the pitch on the right.

3 Transposition

The process of *moving* the scale to a new location is known as *transposition*. We can transpose the major scale from C to any of the other eleven pitches. However, having worked through the process in example 6-C, you will have discovered how time-consuming it can be. The process can be simplified by the use of **key signatures.**

Key signatures serve as signposts to indicate precisely which combination of pitches is being used in the pattern. Each time the pattern is transposed, a new key is created and a new key signature is established. Once we discover that a major scale starting on G requires an F-sharp, we can memorize that information for future use. One sharp (F-sharp) is the *key signature* for the G major scale.

Key signatures are located to the immediate right of the clef sign on each staff. A sharp placed on line F tells us that all the F's in the piece should be played F-sharp. This precludes our having to write the required sharp as an accidental each time the pitch is used.

6-D   **G major using accidental, then key signature**

In the following example, the melody is written first in the key of C major, then in D major and E major. All three versions are recorded on the CD. Notice that the piece sounds the same, but higher in pitch, with each transposition.

6-E   **"Merrily We Roll Along" (traditional)**

Note: The pitch on which the scale begins and ends is known as the *tonic*.

WORKBOOK 6-1 and 6-2 and Aural Skills 6-1 are recommended here.

4   Key Signatures

Example 6-F shows the name of each scale that requires sharps and indicates the number and names of those sharps. Notice that as each new sharp is added, the previous ones remain. Notice also that the F-sharp and C-sharp scales are so named because these pitches are already "sharped" in the key signature.

6-F

Seven major scales with sharps

Name of Scale	G	D	A	E	B	F♯	C♯
Number of ♯'s	1	2	3	4	5	6	7
Names of ♯'s	f♯	f♯	f♯	f♯	f♯	f♯	f
		c♯	c♯	c♯	c♯	c♯	c♯
			g♯	g♯	g♯	g♯	g♯
				d♯	d♯	d♯	d♯
					a♯	a♯	a♯
						e♯	e♯
							b♯

The next example (6-G) shows all the major scales with sharps and their respective locations on both the treble and the bass staffs.

Major scales with sharps

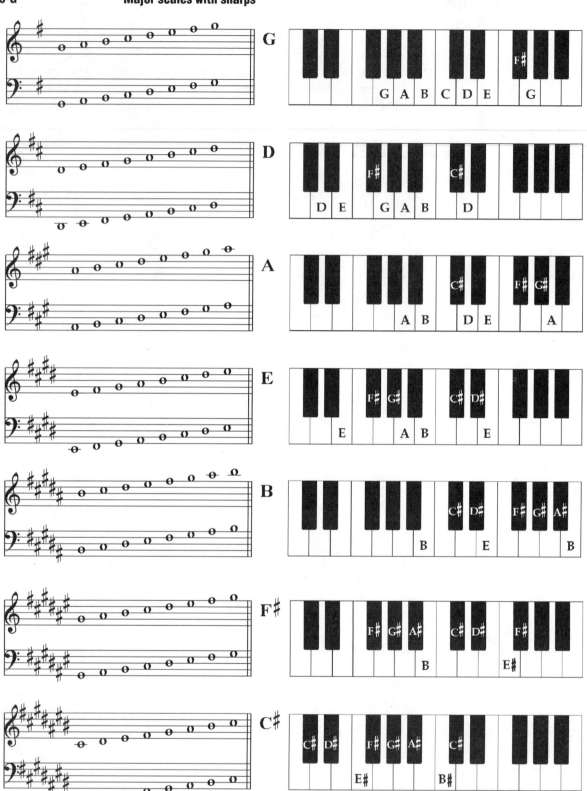

Example 6-H shows the scales that require flats to properly reproduce the whole-step/half-step pattern.

6-H **Seven major scales with flats**

Name of Scale	F	B♭	E♭	A♭	D♭	G♭	C♭
Number of ♭'s	1	2	3	4	5	6	7
Names of ♭'s	b♭	b♭	b♭	b♭	b♭	b♭	b♭
		e♭	e♭	e♭	e♭	e♭	e♭
			a♭	a♭	a♭	a♭	a♭
				d♭	d♭	d♭	d♭
					g♭	g♭	g♭
						c♭	c♭
							f♭

An idea that might help in memorizing the names of the sharps and flats is to memorize one set and say it backwards to obtain the other set.

6-I **Sharps and flats in the order of their appearance**

- ->

F	C	G	D	A	E	B
B	E	A	D	G	C	F

<- -

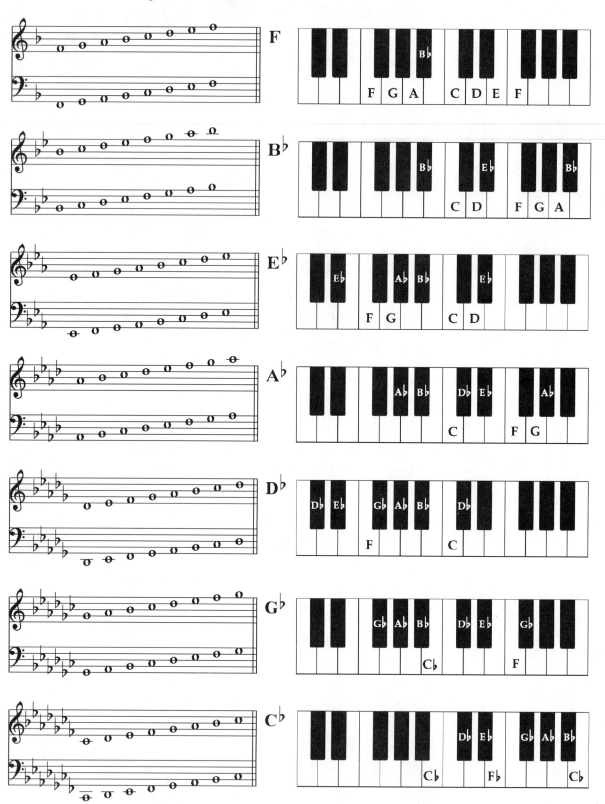

Although there are only twelve pitches, there are *fifteen major scales* in general use. This is because three scales are *enharmonics* of each other (different names for same pitches).

6-K　　　　　　**The enharmonic scales**

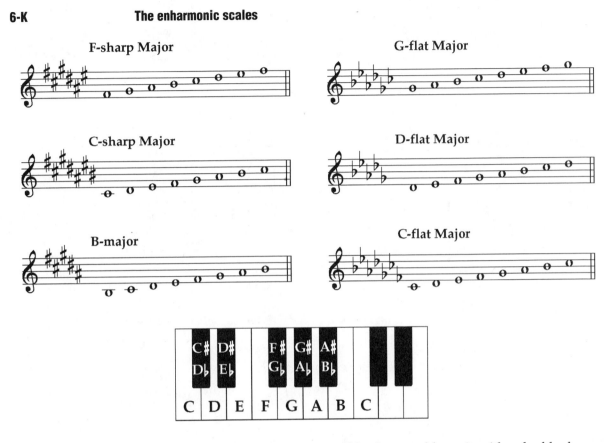

Although other scales are possible, they would require either double sharps or double flats, making them cumbersome to read. For that reason, they are excluded from the regular system. (Note that the major scales have either sharps or flats—not both.)

WORKBOOK 6-3 through 6-8 are suggested here.

5　Staff Location of Key Signatures

Key signatures are always located in the exact same place on the staff—a convention that simplifies music reading.

To be musically literate, one must be able to readily identify the key of a piece. Success with most of the material yet to be studied in this text is dependent upon a good working knowledge of key signatures. The following "memory aid" may be helpful.

The total number of sharps and flats for each letter name equals the sum of seven.[2]

6-M   **Memory aid for learning key signatures**

C	G	D	A	E	B	F♯	C♯	
0	1	2	3	4	5	6	7	Sharps
C♭	G♭	D♭	A♭	E♭	B♭	F	C	
7	6	5	4	3	2	1	0	Flats
7	7	7	7	7	7	7	7	Total of ♯s & ♭s

WORKBOOK 6-9 through 6-12 are suggested here.

6   Circle of Fifths

You may already have noted that each scale with sharps is five letter names above its preceding scale and each scale with flats is five letter names below its preceding scale.

The **Circle of Fifths** provides a helpful visual image of this concept. If the entire circle is read counterclockwise, you will notice that each key is a fifth

---

[2] A variety of practice techniques can be used: flash cards (available in Workbook), computer software, writing and rewriting the signatures, or repeating them over and over (just as you once learned your multiplication tables). Also, paging through music literature and identifying the key for each piece is good practice.

below its preceding key. (This idea will also be helpful when dealing with harmonic concepts later in the text.) Example 6-N depicts the Circle of Fifths for all fifteen major keys, including the enharmonic scales. Notice the **enharmonic scales** shown at the bottom of the circle.

6-N   **Circle of Fifths (major scales)**

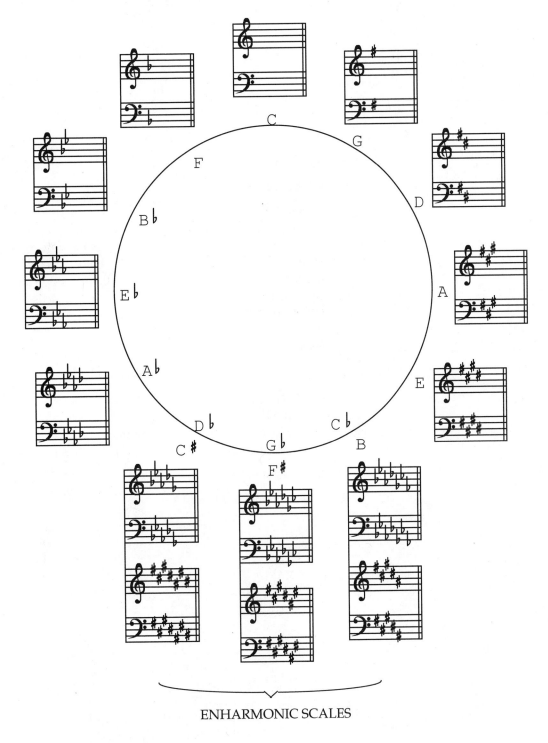

ENHARMONIC SCALES

WORKBOOK 6-13 is suggested here.

7 Scale-Degree Names

Each pitch in a scale is called a *scale degree,* and each has its own name, indicated in the following list.

6-0

Scale-degree names

Scale degree 1 = **Tonic**

Scale degree 2 = **Supertonic**

Scale degree 3 = **Mediant**

Scale degree 4 = **Subdominant**

Scale degree 5 = **Dominant**

Scale degree 6 = **Submediant**

Scale degree 7 = **Leading tone**

Scale degree 1 = **Tonic**

Each diatonic scale begins and ends on its *tonic,* or **keynote, or key tone,** which serves as the focal point of the scale and of the entire piece written with that scale. All other scale-degree names derive from their location and their significance relative to the tonic. Second in significance to the tonic is the *dominant,* the fifth pitch in the scale.[3] The rationale for each scale-degree name is as follows:

Supertonic is one step *above* the tonic.

Dominant and Subdominant are located a *5th above and a 5th below* the tonic, respectively.

Mediant and Submediant are a *3rd above and a 3rd below* the tonic, respectively; or, Mediant is midway between tonic and dominant, and Submediant is midway between tonic and subdominant.

Leading tone is one half step below the tonic.

WORKBOOK 6-14 is recommended here.

[3] The fifth degree of the scale is called *dominant* because of its *dominating* role in harmony as well as in melody. It is also the most prominent overtone (after the octave) in the harmonic series. (See Appendix F.)

8 Syllable Names

Another set of names for the seven scale degrees originated as a device for learning to sing melodies.[4] It consists of applying **syllables** (*do re mi fa sol la ti*) to the scale.

Example 6-P shows four ways of referring to the members of any scale: numbers, letters, syllables, and scale-degree names.

6-P   **Names for pitches in the diatonic major scale**

C	D	E	F	G	A	B	C
1	2	3	4	5	6	7	1
Do	Re	Mi	Fa	Sol	La	Ti	Do
TONIC	SUPER-TONIC	MEDIANT	SUB-DOMINANT	DOMINANT	SUB-MEDIANT	LEADING TONE	TONIC

WORKBOOK 6-15 and Aural Skills 6-2 are recommended here.

9 Tonality

The term **tonality** implies that a composition is written in a specific key, with a specific **tonal center,** or **key center.** It indicates precisely which seven pitches are diatonic (belonging to the set) and which five are chromatic (outside the set).

The *tonic* serves as a tonal "center of gravity" or "home base." Composers organize the pitches so that the listener can sense the tonal center. This enables the listener to follow the evolution of the composition. Movement *away from* and *back to* the tonal center can help the listener follow the composition and grasp its meaning.[5]

At times, the tonal center may deliberately be obscured to heighten tension or interest and thus make its return more desirable and satisfying. (To understand the need most of us have for hearing the tonal center, go back to examples 5-D, 5-E, and 5-F and play or sing each piece, omitting the last note.)

The concept of tonality does not exclude the use of one or more of the five *nondiatonic* (chromatic) tones. The piece in example 6-R is written in E-flat major, but the F-sharps and the A-natural (chromatic tones indicated by the accidentals) add colorful embellishment to the melody without destroying the E-flat tonality.

---

[4] This pedagogical technique was invented about A.D. 1000 by Guido d'Arezzo and is still in use today.

[5] Later in the text, we will see that this key center plays a prominent role in the harmony also.

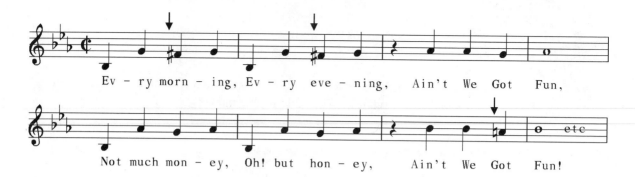

Tonal music has had a long history, beginning with our earliest musical traditions in ancient Greece. Countless compositions have been written using tonality as the organizational basis. In summary, tonality implies

1.   The use of a scale

2.   A tonal center (tonic or focal point)

3.   Loyalty to that tonal center (gravitation to the tonic)

4.   A hierarchy of roles among the other six pitches

5.   A 7 + 5 system (7 diatonic and 5 chromatic)

From the seventeenth to the twentieth century, the tonal center was reinforced not only by the melody but also, perhaps even more forcefully, by the harmony. In the early twentieth century, however, some composers devised alternative approaches to tonal composition. Such music is generally referred to as *atonal*. **Atonality** negates most, if not all, of what tonality implies. (The *tone row*, discussed in Chapter 5, is one method of composing atonal music.)

WORKBOOK 6-16 and Aural Skills 6-3 are recommended here.

Summary   In this chapter, we have seen how the diatonic major mode is constructed and how this design can be transposed to any pitch, making possible twelve different pitch locations.

We noted that key signatures can facilitate the recognition of specific *key centers* (or *tonal centers*) and pitch content. We saw how the *enharmonic scales* bring to fifteen the total number of *key signatures*.

The following summarizes the above information on major scales presented in this chapter.

One major scale has no sharps or flats.

Seven have sharps.

Seven have flats.

The *Circle of Fifths* was shown as a visual and pedagogical device for assisting with the memorization of key signatures.

Four labels for scale degrees were noted: letter names (A, B, and so on), numbers (1, 2, and so on), syllables (*do, re,* and so on), and scale-degree names (tonic, supertonic, and so on). Finally, we noted the role of tonality in musical composition and in the musical experience.

WORKBOOK 6-17 and 6-18 are recommended here.

The following table summarizes facts and concepts contained in this chapter.

Major Scale	A diatonic scale with half steps between 3 and 4 and 7 and 1
Transposition	The process of moving the design of any scale to any of the other eleven locations
Key signature	A symbol signifying specific pitches in the scale
Number of key signatures	15 in common usage
Number of major scales	15: 7 with sharps; 7 with flats; 1 with no sharps or flats
Circle of Fifths	A visual aid for learning keys and key signatures
Scale-Degree Names	
Tonic	Scale degree 1
Supertonic	Scale degree 2
Mediant	Scale degree 3
Subdominant	Scale degree 4
Dominant	Scale degree 5
Submediant	Scale degree 6
Leading tone	Scale degree 7
Syllable Names	*Do, re, mi, fa, so, la, ti*
Tonality	Implies the use of a scale; a tonal center; loyalty to that tonal center; 7 pitches belong, the other five are out of the system
Diatonic and Chromatic	*Diatonic* refers to 7 pitches that belong to the scale; *chromatic* refers to those 5 pitches that do not belong
Enharmonic keys	**C♯ / D♭ F♯ / G♭ B / C♭**

Chapter Review

Terms/Concepts

1.	Mode	11.	Key tone
2.	Major mode	12.	Tonal center
3.	Transposition	13.	Tonic
4.	Key signature	14.	Supertonic
5.	Key	15.	Mediant
6.	Circle of Fifths	16.	Subdominant
7.	Enharmonic scales	17.	Dominant
8.	Tonality/Atonality	18.	Submediant
9.	Keynote	19.	Leading tone
10.	Key center	20.	Syllable names

Review Questions

1. What is the whole-step/half-step design of a *major scale*?

2. Why do musicians memorize all fifteen key signatures?

3. What is meant by *transposition*?

4. The *Circle of Fifths* serves what purposes?

5. What does *tonality* imply?

Chapter Drills

(Answers to all Chapter Drills can be found in Appendix A.)

1. Using the following steps, write the major scales indicated.

   a. Above the staff, write the letter names for the entire octave.

   b. Number each letter (starting with 1 and proceeding through the octave).

   c. Mark the proper location of the half steps.

   d. Enter the appropriate sharp(s) or flat(s).

   e. Put the scale and the key signature on staff.

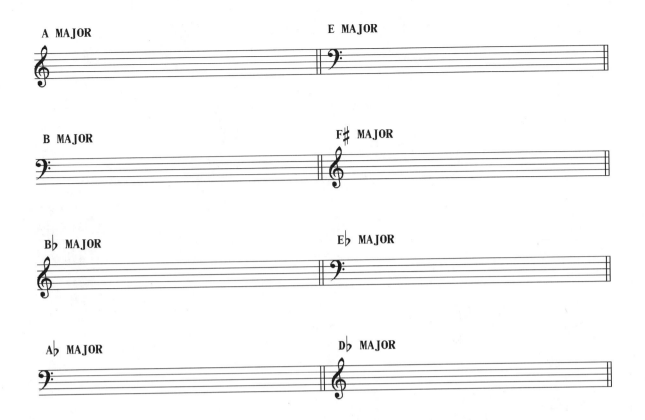

2. Give the name of the major key for each key signature given.

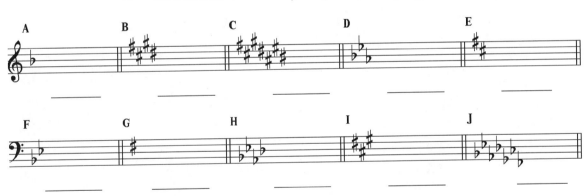

3. Practice writing the key signatures for 7 sharps and 7 flats, first in the treble clef and then in the bass clef. (Be sure to add your clef signs.)

4. Indicate the number of sharps or flats that each major key has.

a. _____ **D**   d. _____ **B♭**   g. _____ **F♯**

b. _____ **E♭**   e. _____ **B**   h. _____ **G♭**

c. _____ **D♭**   f. _____ **G**   i. _____ **F**

5. Give the name of the major key that has the number of sharps or flats indicated.

a. _____ 6 sharps   d. _____ 2 flats   g. _____ 4 sharps

b. _____ 3 flats   e. _____ 7 sharps   h. _____ 4 flats

c. _____ 0 sharps/flats   f. _____ 1 flat   i. _____ 2 sharps

6. Practice drawing the Circle of Fifths.

7. Place the appropriate key signature in the appropriate location on the staff, and enter the correct tonic (key center) for each. (Watch the clef signs.)

F MAJOR   D-FLAT MAJOR   E MAJOR   C-SHARP MAJOR

A-FLAT MAJOR   D MAJOR   C-FLAT MAJOR   F-SHARP MAJOR

8. Give the scale-degree name for each of the following pitches in the key indicated.

a. _____ A in C major   f. _____ D in G major

b. _____ F♯ in D major   g. _____ F in F major

c. _____ B in C major   h. _____ D in F major

d. _____ F in E♭ major   i. _____ C♯ in D major

e. _____ B♭ in F major   j. _____ C in B♭ major

Minor Scales and Key Signatures

1   Introduction

*O*ur study now moves to the design and construction, transpositions, and key signatures of the minor scale. In this chapter, we also will study the relationship between the modes (major and minor) and the three *forms* of the minor scale.

2   Design and Construction

In the **minor scale,** the two half steps are between steps 2 and 3 and steps 5 and 6. All others are whole steps.

7-A   **Whole-step/half-step arrangement of the minor scale**

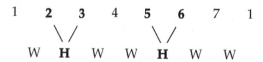

Starting a scale on A and proceeding upward or downward one octave, using only white keys, produces the a minor scale. What you are looking at here is the *natural form* of the minor. We will study the other two forms later in the chapter.

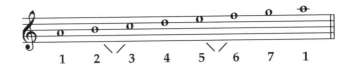

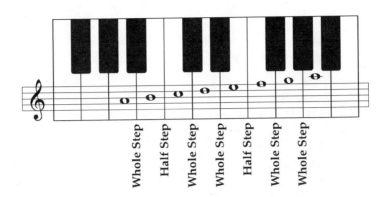

From A to A is the only location on the keyboard where the whole-step/half-step arrangement automatically yields the *minor sound* without the use of one or more of the black keys.

Note: Throughout the remainder of this text, we will use lowercase letters and numerals to refer to minor and uppercase to refer to major.

3   Transposition

The minor scale (just like the major) can be *transposed* to any of the other eleven starting pitches. To create the sound of minor, simply line up all seven letter names within the octave, beginning and ending on the same pitch, and alter pitches as necessary to achieve half steps between 2 and 3 and 5 and 6.

7-C   **Process for determining the whole-step/half-step arrangement for a minor scale starting on d**

2–3 (E–F) must be a half step, and it is.

5–6 (A–B) must be a half step, but it is not; *therefore, the B must be lowered to B-flat.*

Rather than engage in this time-consuming process to determine the whole-step/half-step location, it is much easier to simply memorize the *key signatures*. The same fifteen key signatures already studied for the major scales can be applied to minor.

4 Relative Major/Minor

Each major scale shares a key signature with a minor scale. Scales that have the same key signatures are referred to as *relatives*. Every major scale has a **relative minor,** and every minor scale has a **relative major.** For example, C major, which has no sharps or flats, is related to a minor, which likewise has no sharps or flats.

Thus, if a piece has no sharps or flats in the key signature, it can be either in C major or in a minor. Whether it is C major or a minor is determined by whichever of the two pitches is serving as the *key center*, or *tonic*. If the key center is C, the piece is in C major; if the key center is a, it is in a minor.

7-D   **C major and a minor key signatures and scales (the key signature is no sharps and no flats)**

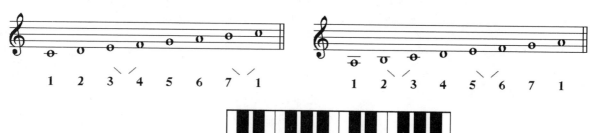

In example 7-E, two pieces are shown, each with F-sharp as the key signature. Because the tonic (focal point) of the first is G, the tonality is G major, whereas the tonic of the second is E, making the tonality e minor.

7-E (CD)   **Melodies with the same key signature, (A) the first showing G major tonality, (B) the second showing e minor tonality**

(A) G MAJOR (German folk song)

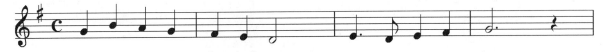

(B) e MINOR (Italian folk song)

A simple way to memorize the key signatures for the minor scales is to remember that the minor key is located *three letter names*—with a distance of exactly three half steps—below its relative major key.[1] For example, a minor is three letter names (and three half steps) below C major.

$$
\begin{array}{ccc}
A & B & C \\
1 & 2 & 3
\end{array}
$$

← — — — — — —

Reverse this process when going from the minor to the relative major; that is, go to the key that is three letter names and three half steps *above* the minor.

WOOKBOOK 7-1 through 7-4 are suggested here.

5   Key Signatures

Example 7-F shows the key signatures and scales for each of the fifteen *relative* major and minor keys.

[1] Some prefer to think of the relationship as six pitches above—for example, C *up* to A.

7-G   **Circle of Fifths: Relative major and minor**

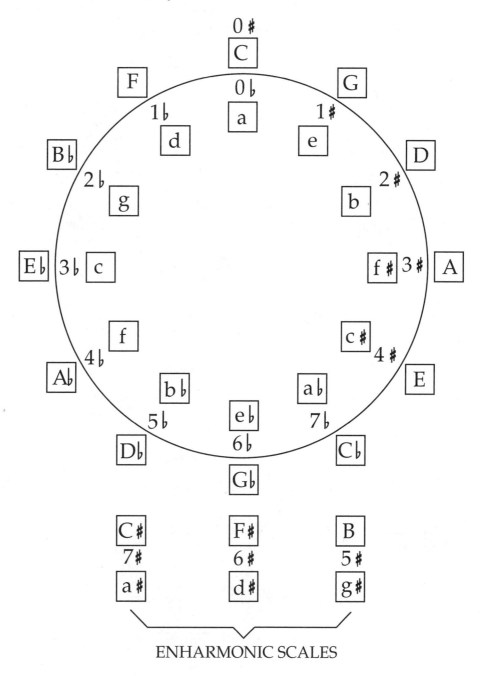

ENHARMONIC SCALES

WOOKBOOK 7-5 through 7-17 are suggested here.

The same fifteen key signatures can be used to denote any of the other five modes mentioned in Chapter 5 (Dorian, Phrygian, Lydian, Mixolydian, and Locrian). However, this text concentrates only on major (Ionian) and minor (Aeolian).

7 Parallel Major and Minor

Two modes *starting on the same pitch*—that is, two modes having the same key center or tonic—are called *parallels*. C major is the **parallel major** of c minor; c minor is the **parallel minor** of C major.

7-H **Parallel major/minor scales**

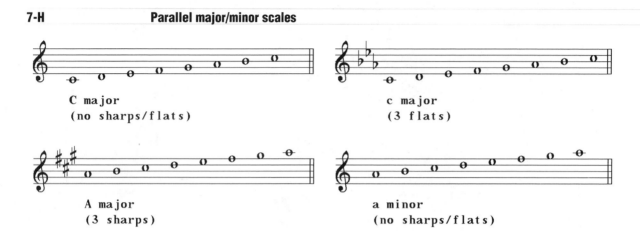

In summary (see example 7-I),

1. Scales sharing the same tonic are *parallels:*
    (same tonic; different signatures; different *modes*).

2. Scales sharing the same key signature are *relatives:*
    (same signature; different tonics; different *modes*).

7-I **Comparison of parallel major/minor and relative major/minor**

C major and c minor are *parallels:* same tonic; different key signature.

C major and a minor are *relatives:* same key signature; different tonic.

Compositions sometimes switch back and forth between parallel major and minor but keep the same tonic. This is not transposition; it is merely *changing modes*. (Refer again to "America," example 6-A.)

Example 7-J starts in c minor. It then changes to C major and continues to fluctuate between these two modes throughout. Notice that accidentals are used to show the cancellation of the three flats from the key signature when it changes to C major. Listen to the recording on the CD to hear the effect of these changes.

"Come Back to Sorrento" (Ernesto de Curtis)

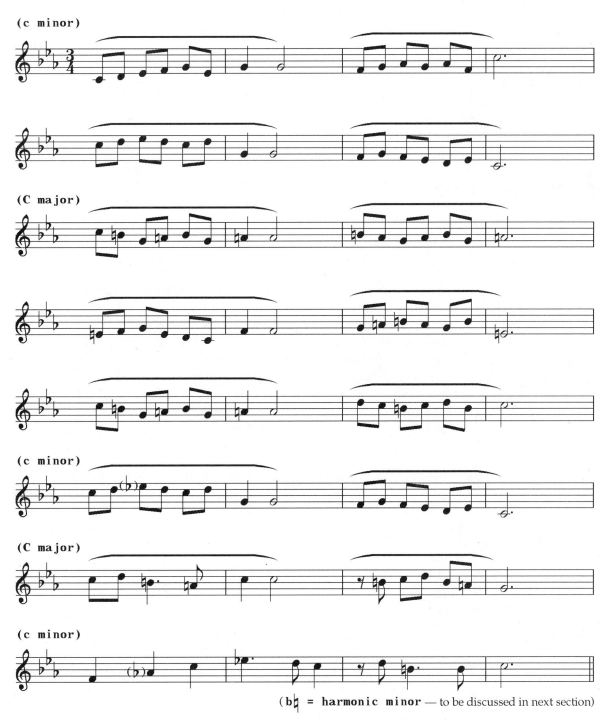

(b♮ = harmonic minor — to be discussed in next section)

WORKBOOK 7-18 through 7-20 are suggested here.

To summarize, recall that *the tonality of a piece is dependent upon its keynote (tonic) and the interrelationships among the pitches belonging to that key*. In example 7-J, although the piece vacillates between major and minor, C is the tonic throughout.

Whenever the tonic changes (for example, from C major to its relative, a minor, or to *any* other pitch), the tonality is changed. A change of tonality within a piece is called a **modulation;** a change of mode within a piece is called a **mutation.** Composers take advantage of such techniques to enhance musical interest. ("Time in a Bottle" is an example of *mutation.* The first half of the piece is in d minor and the second half in D major. "We Three Kings of Orient Are" is an example of *mutation* and *modulation.* The first sixteen measures are in e minor and the last sixteen are in G major—one sharp (F♯) in key signature. Both pieces are located in the Score section of the Workbook, Nos. 16 and 17.)

WORKBOOK 7-21 through 7-24 are suggested here.

8   Three Forms of the Minor

The minor scale we have been discussing—with half steps between 2 and 3 and between 5 and 6—is called the **natural minor** scale. For a variety of reasons—some clear and some not so clear—composers, as well as their listeners, seem to prefer a half step between 7 and 1 (*leading tone* to the tonic), which does not exist in the natural minor scale.

For that reason, musicians have altered the natural minor scale by *raising the seventh degree one half step,* creating what is called the **harmonic minor.** (Its desirability for harmonic purposes will be discussed in Chapter 9.)[2]

Example 7-K shows these two versions of minor: the a natural minor and the a harmonic minor scales. Each has a half step between 2 and 3 and 5 and 6, but the harmonic minor has another half step, this one between 7 and 1. Notice that this creates a one-and-one-half-step skip between 6 and 7.

7-K

Comparison of the natural and harmonic forms of a minor

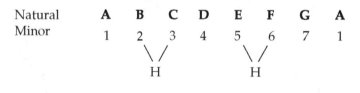

---

[2] In some cases, this alteration (raising the seventh a half step) will require the use of a double sharp (×)—for example, in the harmonic minor forms of scales: g♯, d♯, and a♯.

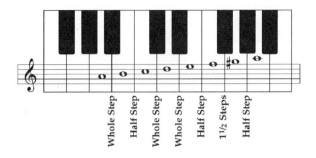

Aural Skills 7-1 is recommended here.

Although the harmonic minor satisfied a desired melodic and harmonic effect, it created a "problem" in the melody. The 1½-step skip between 6 and 7 was objectionable to some performers as well as to some listeners, and thus brought about yet another form of the minor scale, the **melodic minor.**

To obtain a half-step leading tone to the tonic by raising the seventh scale degree but avoid the large skip of 1½ steps, in melodic minor the sixth scale degree also is raised:

7-L   **Melodic minor scale**

Melodic	A	B	C	D	E	F♯	G♯	A
Minor:		\ /				\ /		
	1	2	3	4	5	6	7	1

This results in minor sound in the bottom four pitches, and major in the top four. Because the "leading tone to the tonic" is "necessary" only when 7 actually proceeds upward to the tonic (and not when moving away from the tonic), composers have resorted to raising 6 and 7 when *ascending* and lowering them to their original natural-minor form when *descending,* thus achieving the best of both worlds.

Example 7-M shows the ascending and descending versions of the melodic form of the minor scale.

7-M   **Melodic form of the a minor scale**

Example 7-N shows all three forms of the d minor scale: natural, harmonic, and melodic.

Three forms of the d minor scale

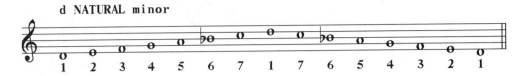

d NATURAL minor

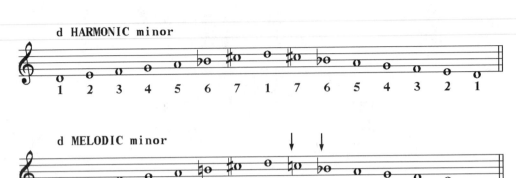

WORKBOOK 7-25 and 7-26 and Aural Skills 7-2 are recommended here.

9 Scale-Degree Names

Because the distance between 7 and 1, in the natural form of the minor scale, is a whole step (instead of a half step as in the major scale), the seventh scale degree is called **subtonic,** not *leading tone.*

7-O   **Scale-degree names for minor**

Scale degree 1 = Tonic

Scale degree 2 = Supertonic

Scale degree 3 = Mediant

Scale degree 4 = Subdominant

Scale degree 5 = Dominant

Scale degree 6 = Submediant

Scale degree 7 = **Subtonic**

Scale degree 1 = Tonic

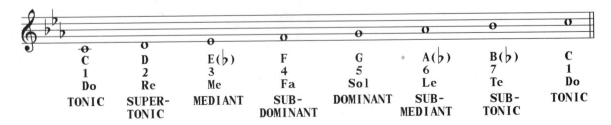

Summary   In this chapter, we studied the design of the minor scale with its half steps between 2 and 3 and between 5 and 6. We saw how this scale also can be transposed to the other eleven pitches and how the fifteen key signatures used for major scales can be applied to minor.

We studied the concept of *relative major/minor* and noted how this can facilitate the memorization of the minor key signatures.

We made the distinction between relative major/minor and *parallel major/minor*. We noted that two scales sharing the same tonic are called *parallel* major and minor, whereas two scales sharing the same key signature (but not the same tonic) are *relative* major and minor.

We pointed out that movement from the major mode to the minor without a change of tonic is known as *mutation*, whereas a change of tonic (change of tonality) is called a *modulation*.

Finally, the three forms of minor were described and their purpose explained. The next chapter deals with a review of these scales (plus others introduced in Chapter 5) in an attempt to show how they are used in making melodies.

WORKBOOK 7-27 through 7-30 are recommended here as a review of Chapters 6 and 7.

The following table summarizes facts and concepts contained in this chapter.

Minor Scale	A diatonic scale with half steps between 2 and 3 and 5 and 6
Relative major/minor	Same key signature, different key centers (tonalities): (C major/a minor)
Relative minor	Three half steps/three letter names below major: C → a
Relative major	Three half steps/three letter names above minor: a → C
Parallel major/minor	Same key center (tonality), different key signatures, different modes C major/c minor
Modulation	A change of key center (tonic) = *change of tonality* but same mode
Mutation	A change of mode (same key center)
Three Forms of Minor	Natural, harmonic, and melodic
Natural	Follows the key signature
Harmonic	Raises the 7th scale degree one half step to provide a half-step *leading tone* to the tonic
Melodic	Raises 6 and 7, ascending, to provide a *leading tone* to the tonic but without creating a one-and-one-half-step skip between 6 and 7 (as is the case in harmonic minor); lowers 6 and 7 when descending (thus, it is simply natural minor when descending)
Subtonic	The 7th scale degree in natural minor (a whole step away from tonic)

Chapter Review

Terms/Concepts

1. Minor scale
2. Relative major/minor
3. Parallel major/minor
4. Subtonic
5. Mutation

6. Modulation
7. Natural minor
8. Harmonic minor
9. Melodic minor

Aural Skills

(Aural Skills Exercises noted throughout the chapter, which require the instructor's assistance, are located in the Instructor's Manual. The following can be done by the student working with a colleague.)

1. Play major and minor scales for each other to see if you can tell the difference between the two.

2. Play the three forms of the minor for each other to see if you can tell the differences among the three.

Review Questions

1. What causes the difference in sound between a diatonic scale in the *major mode* and one in the *minor mode*?

2. What do *relative major and minor* keys have in common?

3. What do *parallel major and minor* keys have in common?

4. What do composers achieve by using the *harmonic form* of the minor scale?

5. What do composers achieve by using the *melodic form* of the minor scale?

Chapter Drills

(Answers to all Chapter Drills can be found in Appendix A.)

1.   Which minor key is indicated by the following key signatures?

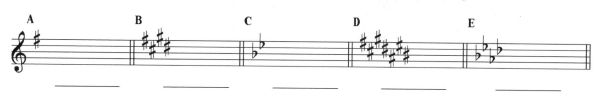

2.   Give the major and minor keys for each of the following signatures.

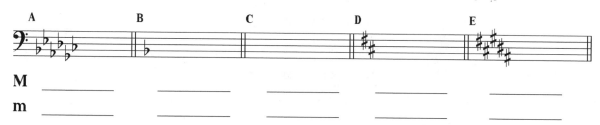

M _____   _____   _____   _____   _____

m _____   _____   _____   _____   _____

3.   First give the name of the minor key represented by the signature; then beside each give the appropriate key signature for the parallel major.

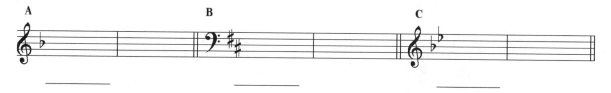

4. Based on the key signature and the key tone (tonic) provided, give the correct key and mode (M or m).

A _____ B _____ C _____ D _____ E _____ F _____

G _____ H _____ I _____ J _____ K _____ L _____

5. Give the appropriate key and key signature. (Just give the number of sharps or flats.)

   a. RELATIVE of G major _____ _____

   b. PARALLEL of A major _____ _____

   c. RELATIVE of f minor _____ _____

   d. PARALLEL of f minor _____ _____

   e. PARALLEL of G major _____ _____

6. Write the three forms of the e minor and the f minor scales (ascending and descending). Be sure to use a key signature and add accidentals where necessary. (Add clef signs, starting with treble and alternating with bass.)

e natural minor

e harmonic minor

e melodic minor

f natural minor

f harmonic minor

f melodic minor

7. Write the following scales.

g harmonic minor

f sharp natural minor

a flat harmonic minor

B major's relative minor (Melodic form)

E major's parallel minor (Harmonic form)

f minor's relative major

8. Practice drawing the Circle of Fifths for major and minor keys. (Be sure to show all the enharmonic keys.)

9. Place the appropriate key signature in the proper location on the staff, and enter the correct tonic (key center) for each.

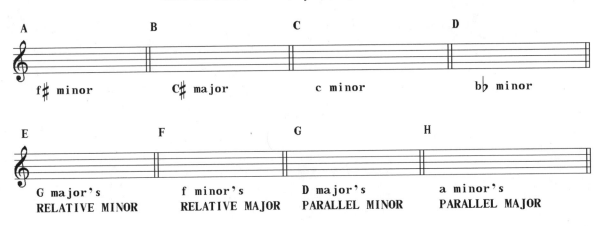

A   B   C   D

f♯ minor   C♯ major   c minor   b♭ minor

E   F   G   H

G major's
RELATIVE MINOR   f minor's
RELATIVE MAJOR   D major's
PARALLEL MINOR   a minor's
PARALLEL MAJOR

Melody

1 Introduction

This chapter focuses on several basic aspects of **melody.** It provides a synthesis of materials studied in Chapters 5 through 7, that is, the various types of scales (diatonic major and minor, chromatic, whole-tone, and pentatonic, and the tone row). It also recalls, and elaborates on, the melodic concepts and techniques introduced in Chapter 2. Here we will also concentrate on the use of these scales in the creation of melodies and on the effect each type of scale can have on a particular melody.

Although the subtleties of "good" melody are at times difficult to pinpoint, the analysis of many successful melodies makes certain noteworthy qualities and characteristics obvious. This chapter addresses some of those qualities and characteristics.

Finally, this chapter offers opportunities for the composition of original melodies and for the analysis of existing melodies.

2 Melody

In Chapter 2, we defined melody as *a series of pitches (or tones) that conveys a musical idea.* Melody results from the manipulation of sound (of varying pitches and lengths) to yield a recognizable musical shape or contour. Each melody has its own musical logic.

Melody (sometimes less formally referred to as the **tune**) has a long tradition. For much of the history of music, melody was the essential element; there was no purposeful or written harmony (which still is the case today in many non-Western cultures). Musicologists theorize that melody is probably the oldest *element* of music, having developed from speech inflection. (Speech possesses the two constituents of melody: pitch variation and rhythm.)

We stated earlier that composers generally choose their melodic pitch material from the many types of scales. We will now examine melodies composed from diatonic scales, chromatic scales, pentatonic scales, and so on. So that you might better follow this discussion and better understand the effect the different scales can have on melody, each example is based on essentially the same melodic idea but is altered in each case to include only those pitches that belong to the respective scale.

3 Diatonic Melodies

The melodies in the next two examples are based on the same *diatonic scale* and are in the same key. However, each is in a *different mode* of this scale.

8-A (CD)   **"The Diatonic Waltz in C Major" (JD)**

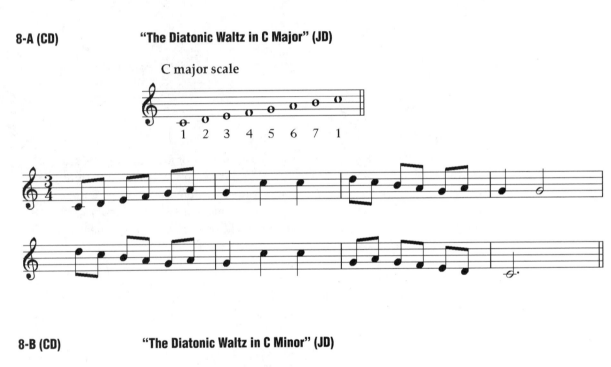

8-B (CD)   **"The Diatonic Waltz in C Minor" (JD)**

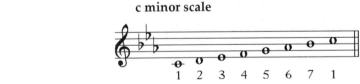

WORKBOOK 8-1 and 8-4 and Aural Skills 8-1 are recommended here.

4 Chromatic Melodies

Although a diatonic composition may make occasional and discreet use of any of the five nondiatonic (chromatic) pitches, music generally has tended to be more diatonic than chromatic.[1]

Nevertheless, melodies have been constructed from the *chromatic scale*. Example 8-C demonstrates how the "waltz" melody sounds when based on the chromatic scale, wherein all twelve pitches are presented, much of the time in half-step order.

8-C (CD)   **"The Chromatic Waltz" (J.D.)**

Chromatic scale

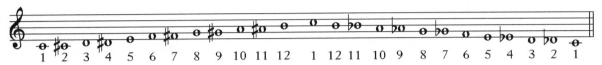

WORKBOOK 8-5 and 8-6 and Aural Skills 8-2 are recommended here.

5 Whole-Tone Melodies

A completely different musical effect will result from the use of the *whole-tone scale*, which has only six whole steps (and no half steps). Because this scale does not have a half-step leading tone to the tonic, it can create a sense of tonal ambiguity.

In Western music, the whole-tone scale became popular with the Impressionist composers in the late nineteenth century and continues to be used by contemporary composers.

In example 8-D, the same "waltz" shown in examples 8-A through 8-E is altered to include only the six pitches of a whole-tone scale, starting on C.

[1]See Chapter 6 (section 9) on *tonality*, and example 6-Q, "Ain't We Got Fun" by Richard Whiting.

8-D (CD)   "The Whole-Tone Waltz" (J.D.)

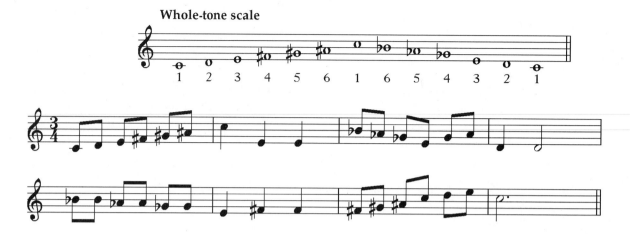

WORKBOOK 8-7 and 8-8 and Aural Skills 8-3 are recommended here.

6   Pentatonic Melodies

The *pentatonic scale,* with only five pitches and with the conventional arrangement of two skips (each 1½ steps), is another pitch source for many melodies, especially folk-type melodies. In spite of its pitch limitation, it is an extremely versatile scale. Any one of the five pitches seems to serve equally well as a tonal center, thus making it possible to begin, pause, or end on any one of the five.

The next example shows the "waltz" composed from a pentatonic scale, beginning on C.

8-E (CD)   "The Pentatonic Waltz" (J.D.)

WORKBOOK 8-9 and 8-10 and Aural Skills 8-4 are recommended here.

7 Tone-Row or "Twelve-Tone" Melodies

The *tone row* (or *series,* as it is frequently called) is not a scale. In scales, all respective pitches appear in successive order, whereas in a tone row they can appear in any order. The tone row is similar to the chromatic scale in that it can contain all twelve pitches, but the twelve pitches will not occur in the continuous and consecutive *half-step order* characteristic of the chromatic scale.

In many cases, the row serves to obscure a tonal center, making all twelve pitches sound equal, and thus providing an interesting alternative to the scales we have been discussing.

Music composed with a twelve-tone row (series) is frequently referred to as "twelve-tone music." This type of composition is a twentieth-century phenomenon, and it is used by many contemporary composers.

In example 8-F, the "waltz" is altered again, this time to include all twelve pitches, now arranged in an arbitrary order chosen by the composer.

8-F (CD)   **"The Tone-Row Waltz" (J.D.)**

Twelve-tone row

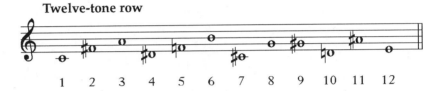

WORKBOOK 8-11 and 8-12 and Aural Skills 8-5 are recommended here.

To compose a good melody, one must do more than select the pitch materials from among the many scales just discussed. In Chapter 2, we talked about various organizational techniques that can be applied to melodic composition. A review of that material here would be helpful before proceeding.

The remainder of this chapter is devoted to an examination of ways in which pitches can be arranged to create a melody, to give it its shape, its logic, its musical meaning.

8   Motivic Melodies

Melodies often derive from, or are based on, a small group of notes called a **motive.** A motive is a short melodic/rhythmic idea that is susceptible to change through creative manipulation. The motive can either be repeated exactly or be varied in some way.

Variation of a motive is known as *imitation.* Although the imitative options are virtually infinite, the following are those types that are most commonly used.

1. **Sequence:** Presents the motive on a higher or lower pitch.

2. **Inversion:** Presents the motive in the opposite direction (for example, ascending instead of descending).

3. **Register:** Moves the motive to a different octave.

4. **Rhythm, timbre, dynamics:** Presents the motive with any alteration of these.

5. **Transposition:** Presents the motive in a new key (a new tonality).

This type of melodic construction is attractive because the motive provides a *unity* within the melody, making it more readily perceivable to the listener. (In some compositions, not only the melody but entire sections of the piece are based on a single motive and evolve from *motivic manipulation.*)

The melody in example 8-G evolves from a simple three-note rhythmic/melodic motive. In this eight-measure melody, the motive is heard six times. In the three instances where it is varied, it still retains enough of its original identity to be recognizable.

8-G (CD)   **Motivic melody (based on first measure of "Joy to the World")**

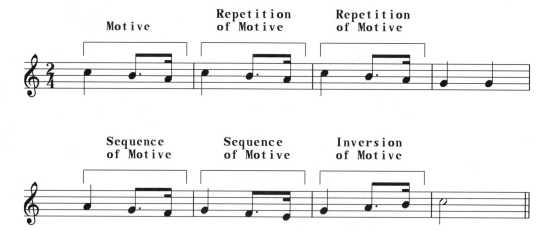

1. *Motive* is presented in measure 1.

2. *Exact repetition* of motive is presented in measure 2.

3. *Exact repetition* of motive is presented in measure 3 (before the melody comes to a slight pause in measure 4 and then continues to evolve in measure 5).

4. *Sequence* of motive is presented in measure 5 (now on a lower pitch).

5. *Sequence* of motive is presented in measure 6 (on yet another lower pitch).

6. *Inversion* of motive is presented in measure 7 (turned in the opposite direction) before the melody ends in measure 8.

8-H is another example of a **motivic melody.** Here again the motive is presented in measure 1 and is then sequenced on higher pitches in measure 2 and in measure 3, where it is slightly modified. (You might even hear measures 5, 6, and 7 as somewhat reminiscent of the motive.)

Measures 9 through 11 return to the motive, so that we have heard the motive, either identically or in some imitative fashion, in at least six of the sixteen measures.

8-H (CD)   **Motivic melody: "American Patrol" (F. W. Meacham)**

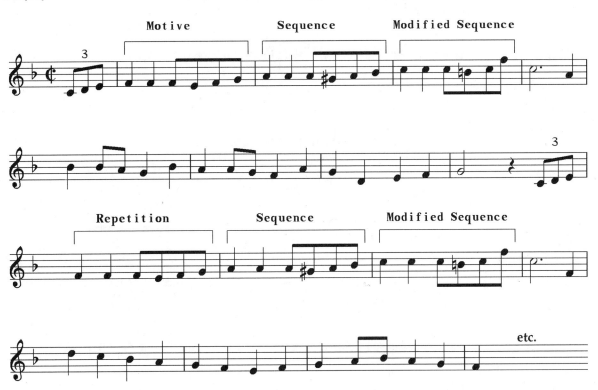

Sometimes composers will base an entire composition (or a large portion of a composition) on a single motive. Beethoven's Fifth Symphony is a good example. The main theme of the first movement of this symphony is based on a four-note motive, which is then sequenced. Much of the entire movement derives from this motive. (Listen to a recording of this work and try to count the number of times you hear the motive, which is shown in example 8-I.)

8-I (CD)   **Motive from Beethoven's Fifth Symphony, first movement**

9 Through-Composed Melodies

In example 8-J, the melody begins with the same three-note group as in example 8-G, but this time these three notes do not serve as a motive from which the melody derives. Now the melody is **through-composed.**

A through-composed melody simply evolves on its own, without the reiteration of a basic rhythmic/melodic idea. (You may now recognize this melody as "Joy to the World.")

8-J (CD)   **Through-composed melody: "Joy to the World" (George Frideric Handel)**

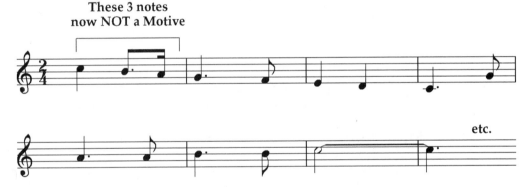

The national anthem of the United States is another example of a through-composed melody.

8-K (CD)   **Through-composed melody: "The Star-Spangled Banner" (J. S. Smith)**

WORKBOOK 8-13 and Aural Skills 8-5 are recommended here.

10 Melodic Variation

In Chapter 13, we will discuss the significance of *unity and variety* as a basic principle of form in music. The **repetition** of a melodic idea is a well-known technique for achieving unity and variety.

However, the constant repetition of the same material, heard in the exact same way, can be monotonous. For that reason, composers usually *vary* their musical material in a number of ways, some of which have already been noted (motivic variation). There are numerous other ways in which melodic material can be manipulated to achieve both unity and variety in the music. The following sections explore some of these possibilities.

Melodic Variation through Transposition

As noted in Chapters 6 and 7, *transposition* is simply changing the tonal center by moving it to a higher or lower key. (Transposition is different from *sequence*, wherein the material is presented on higher or lower pitches while remaining in the same key, with the tonal center unchanged.)

Transposition provides an opportunity to hear the musical material again, but the new key will make it sound fresh while still familiar. In example 8-L, the same melody is presented in four different keys.

8-L (CD)   **C major melody transposed to D major, E major, and F major**

WORKBOOK 8-14 is suggested here.

Melodic Variation through Embellishment

Another variation technique is **embellishment,** in which decorative pitches are added to the original melody pitches, as shown in example 8-M. This is the same melody as the one used to demonstrate transposition in example 8-L, but now pitches are added above and below the principal pitches.

8-M (CD)   **Melody embellished or simplified**

This example contains *triplets;* see Rhythm Unit IV.

Original Melody

Melody with EMBELLISHMENT

The opposite of embellishment is also possible. We can remove some pitches from a melody line, leaving only a bare reminder of the original. A good example of this technique can be seen by reversing the two lines in example 8-M; in other words, think of the embellished version as being the original.

Both of these variation techniques are used in all styles of music and are particularly characteristic of jazz improvisation.

Melodic Variation through Change in Rhythm or Meter

In the next two examples, the melody is varied, first by changing the rhythm (8-N), and second by changing the meter (8-O). (Changing the meter, of course, effects a change in rhythm as well.)

8-N (CD)   **Melody with rhythmic change**

Original Melody

Melody with New RHYTHM

Melody with meter change

Original Melody

Melody with New METER (and new rhythm)

Melodic Variation through Change of Register

Changing the *register* of the melody means changing its "location" from one level of pitch to another. This is another method of manipulation to achieve variety while maintaining unity. Example 8-P shows the melody written one octave higher than the original and then one octave lower. This can freshen the sound and heighten melodic interest and recall.

Melody with register change

Original melody

Melody in New REGISTER (1 octave higher than original)

Melody in New REGISTER (1 octave lower than original)

Melodic Variation through Change of Mode

In Chapter 7, we discussed change of mode. We can change from one mode to any of the other six modes of the diatonic scale, but changing from major to minor (and vice versa) is by far the most common.

Example 8-Q shows "Greensleeves" as originally written in the minor mode (melodic form), and then in the parallel major mode. Both arrangements can be heard on the CD. (Refer to examples 8-A and 8-B and to example 6-A for other examples of mode change in a melody.)

8-Q (CD)   **"Greensleeves" (Old English Melody)**

Melody in **e minor**

Melody changed to **E major**

Melodic Variation through Other Manipulative Techniques

It is possible also to change the *timbre* of a melody, or the *harmony* accompanying it. Likewise, *dynamic* or *tempo* changes can vary the sound of the melodic idea while keeping it sufficiently intact that the listener can recognize and recall it.

Remember that music is a *temporal* art and, as such, it must be retained in the mind if the work is to be fully grasped and the aesthetic experience fully achieved. Rehearing the musical material in some varied form aids the memory in recalling that material.

Although there are numerous ways in which a melody might be varied, those listed in this chapter are the most commonly used types.

WORKBOOK 8-15 and 8-16 are suggested here.

Summary   In this chapter, we have examined some ways in which melodies are composed, starting with a selection of pitch materials, such as a scale, and proceeding to the organization of those pitches into patterns. We have also seen how the challenge to provide both unity and variety (and thus to maintain interest while aiding the listener in recalling the musical material) can be met by the composer's use of various *imitative* and *variation techniques*.

The following table summarizes facts and concepts contained in this chapter.

Melody	A series of pitches arranged to convey a musical idea or thought (frequently derived from preexisting pitch patterns called *scales*)
Diatonic melody	A melody based on any mode and on any tonality (key) of the diatonic scale
Chromatic melody	A melody based on the half-step arrangement of the chromatic scale
Whole-tone melody	A melody based on the whole-step arrangement of the whole-tone scale
Pentatonic melody	A melody based on the five-tone pentatonic scale
Tone-row melody	A melody based on a composer's arbitrary arrangement of the twelve pitches within the octave
Motivic melodies	Melodies that derive from a basic rhythmic/melodic unit of notes known as a *motive*
Through-composed melodies	Melodies that simply evolve without the reiteration of a basic motive
Melodic variation	The achievement of *unity and variety* in a melody by the use of numerous types of *varied* repetitions
Types of variation	Sequence, transposition, embellishment (or the opposite), rhythm or meter changes, register, mode, tempo, or dynamic changes, and so on

Chapter Review

Terms/Concepts

1. Motive
2. Motivic melody
3. Tune
4. Through-composed
5. Repetition

6. Sequence
7. Inversion
8. Transposition
9. Embellishment

Review Questions

1. What is the difference between a *motivic* melody and one that is *through-composed*?

2. Why do composers *repeat* musical ideas? Why do they *vary* them?

3. List at least ten ways that *melodic material* can be varied.

4. What is the difference between *sequence* and *transposition?*

5. What is one of the first choices a composer makes when writing a melody?

Aural Skills

In all your music listening, try to determine the type of scale and mode being used; try to determine whether the melody is motivic or through-composed. If it is motivic, see if you can hear sequences, inversions, embellishments, and the like.

Chapter Drills

1. Directions for melodic analysis: Using the information provided in this chapter, in Chapter 2, and in the following summary, analyze each of the melodies in this section of Drills.

    a. Determine key, scale, mode.
    (This is achieved by doing a *pitch inventory* as shown in Melody A.)

    b. Decide if it is conjunct or disjunct.
    (Comment on the *degrees* of conjunct or disjunct.)

    c. Decide if it is motivic or through-composed.
    (If *motivic*, bracket and describe the type of variation, if any.)

    d. Describe the contour.
    (Note *highest and lowest pitches* and overall *range*.)

PITCH INVENTORY (always start with letter A):

(A)	A♯/(B♭)	B	(C)	C♯/D♭	(D)	D♯/E♭	(E)	(F)	F♯/G♭	(G)	G♯/A♭
1	2	3	4	5	6	7	8	9	10	11	12

MELODY A = F major (F G A B♭ C D E F

MELODY B =

C

MELODY C = _____

D

MELODY D = _____

E

MELODY E = _____

F

MELODY F = _____

2. Write your own original melodies and either play these yourself for the class or ask a colleague to play them. (Be sure to choose your clef sign and indicate your key signature and the type of scale you are using.)

3. Using only the black keys, compose your own melodies. Any pitch of the five will generally serve as a beginning pitch, a "pause" pitch, or the final pitch.

PRELUDE TO SECTION D

Organizational

Elements:

Harmony

and

Texture

*J*n the next four chapters, we will deal with the elements of harmony and texture in music.

About A.D. 900, musicians began to experiment with adding voices at pitches above or below the original melody. The added pitches were sung along with the original melody, and for some time, the additional voices sang in the same rhythm as the original melody. Eventually, however, these added voices acquired an independence, making it possible for the listener to hear two or more separate melodies going on at the same time. Often these simultaneously performed melodies created rich harmonies and textures.

About 1600, musicians began to harmonize their music with complete chords. Certain successions of chords were chosen because of their ability to clearly define the tonality of the composition.

Once harmony had become a significant organizational element in music, it began to influence melody. Between 1600 and 1900, melodies frequently derived directly from the chord progressions, with or without decorative pitches. (This is still the case in much contemporary music in the *popular* genres.)

Intervals

1   Introduction

*A*n **interval** is *the distance between any two pitches*—for example, from C to D, from A to F-sharp, and so on. Intervals are the basis of the harmonic element in music. They also play a significant role in melody. When we describe melodies as either *conjunct* or *disjunct*, we are characterizing the *intervallic structure* of the melodic content, that is, the distance from one pitch to the next successive pitch.

In the following study of intervals, we will differentiate between those heard as *melodic* and those heard as *harmonic* intervals, between their sizes (*number* and *quality*), and between *simple* and *compound* intervals.

2   Melodic and Harmonic Intervals

Pitches arranged horizontally on the staff, so as to be heard *successively*, are **melodic intervals.** When vertically aligned, so that both pitches are heard *simultaneously*, they are **harmonic intervals.**[1]

9-A   **Melodic intervals and harmonic intervals**

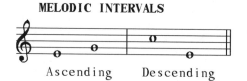

ASCENDING   DESCENDING

[1] When three or more pitches are sounded simultaneously, the sonority is called a *chord*, which is the topic of Chapter 10.

3 Interval Number

Intervals are measured in two ways: by their number size and by their quality. The **number** of an interval (whether melodic or harmonic) is determined by the distance from one pitch to the other on the staff.

From one line to the very next space (above or below) is a *number 2 interval*. From a line to the next line (above or below), with a space intervening, is a *number 3 interval*. Intervals are labeled simply 2, 3, and so on, and are referred to simply as a 2nd, a 3rd, and so on.

In example 9-B, note that to determine the *number size* of the interval, we count every line or space encompassed by the two notes: the line or space on which the first note is located, the lines and spaces between the two, and the line or space on which the second note is located.

9-B   **Interval "number size"**

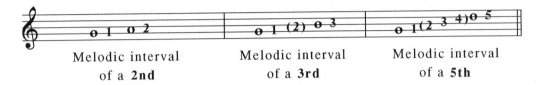

| Melodic interval
of a **2nd** | Melodic interval
of a **3rd** | Melodic interval
of a **5th** |

Interval numbers can also be determined by counting the letter names encompassed in the interval. From one letter name to the adjacent letter name (C–D) is a 2nd; with one intervening letter (C–E), it is a 3rd; and so on. (Always count the first, the last, and any intervening letters.)

When the same pitch is sounded twice in succession (for example, middle C to middle C), the melodic interval is called a **unison** or *prime*. Likewise, when two or more instruments or voices sound the same pitch at the same time, they are performing "in unison."

The distance from any pitch to the next pitch *of the same letter name* (above or below) is an **octave**.

9-C   **Melodic and harmonic unison (prime) and octave**

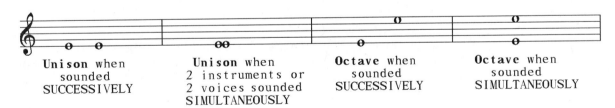

Unison when
sounded
SUCCESSIVELY

Unison when
2 instruments or
2 voices sounded
SIMULTANEOUSLY

Octave when
sounded
SUCCESSIVELY

Octave when
sounded
SIMULTANEOUSLY

Example 9-D provides a visual summary of the information pertaining to the *number size* of intervals.

9-D **Interval number size: from unison to octave**

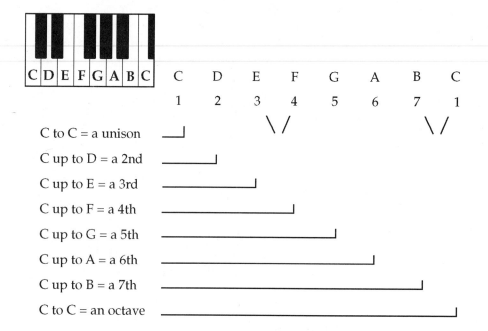

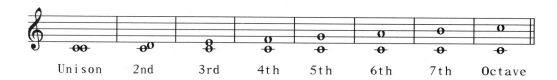

| Unison | 2nd | 3rd | 4th | 5th | 6th | 7th | Octave |

WORKBOOK 9-1 through 9-4 and Aural Skills 9-1 are recommended here.

4   Interval Quality

A second way to measure intervals is by their quality. **Quality** is determined by a precise measure of distance between two pitches, that is, by the actual number of *steps* involved.

Number Size = Number of *letter names* involved.

Quality   = Actual number of *steps* involved.

Although accidentals do not alter the interval number (for example, C to E will be a 3rd whether it includes sharps, flats, double sharps, or double flats), they do alter the interval's quality. Example 9-E shows fifteen versions of C–E, and in each case, regardless of the accidentals, the interval is a 3rd.

9-E **Interval C–E**

(All fifteen intervals will sound different, but each is a **3rd**.)

Notice that the interval can be changed at either end or at both ends. Obviously, each of the fifteen versions of C–E in the preceding example will sound different. This difference is described as the interval's quality and is designated by the following modifiers:

Major *(abbrev. M)*

Minor *(abbrev. m)*

Diminished *(abbrev. d)*

Augmented *(abbrev. A)*

To determine *quality,* use **major** as your norm.

A half step larger than major is **augmented.**

A half step smaller than major is **minor.**

A whole step smaller than major is **diminished.**

9-F **Various qualities of the interval of a 2nd: C–D**

C to D (a *whole step*) is a M 2nd.

C to D-flat (a *half step*) is a m 2nd.

C to D-sharp (*one and a half steps*) is an A 2nd.

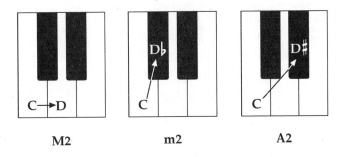

M2   m2   A2

Various qualities of the interval of a 3rd: C–E

C to E (*two whole steps*) is a M 3rd.

C to E-flat (*one and a half steps*) is a m 3rd.

C-sharp to E-flat (*only one whole step*) is a d 3rd.

C to E-sharp (*two and a half steps*) is an A 3rd

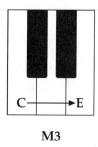 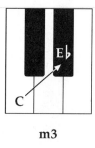  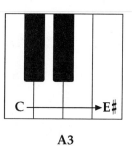

M3   **m3**   **d3**   **A3**

Instead of *major* and *minor*, the qualifier "perfect" is used for *unisons, octaves, 4ths*, and *5ths*. It is important to note that perfect intervals behave differently from other intervals in that there is no minor quality.

A half step larger than perfect is augmented.

A half step smaller than perfect is diminished.

The perfect, augmented, and diminished unison, 4th, 5th, and octave

UNISONS:

PU   AU   AU

4ths: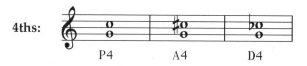

P4   A4   D4

5ths: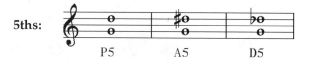

P5   A5   D5

OCTAVES: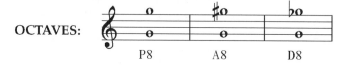

P8   A8   D8

5 Major and Perfect Intervals

The diatonic major scale contains four major and four perfect intervals (when each is measured from the tonic). Example 9-I shows the number of steps included in each major and each perfect interval of the octave C to C.

9-I **Interval sizes (numbers and qualities)**

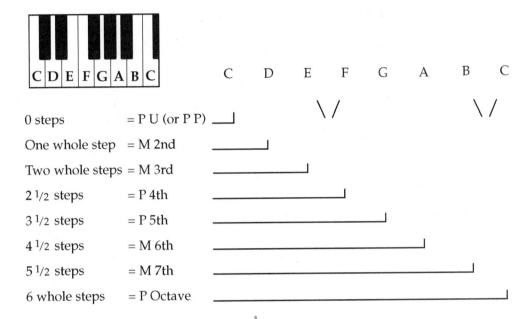

0 steps	= P U (or P P)	
One whole step	= M 2nd	
Two whole steps	= M 3rd	
2 1/2 steps	= P 4th	
3 1/2 steps	= P 5th	
4 1/2 steps	= M 6th	
5 1/2 steps	= M 7th	
6 whole steps	= P Octave	

Since it can be quite time-consuming to count steps beyond the simple 2nd or 3rd, the following method for determining interval size is recommended.

STEP 1. Relate each interval to a major scale.

STEP 2. If the higher pitch in the interval appears in the *major* scale of the lower pitch, the interval is *major* (or *perfect*).

STEP 3. Then proceed to use *major* (or *perfect*) as your norm.

For example, apply this method to the interval E to G-sharp:

1. In the key of E major there is a G-sharp.

2. Conclusion: The interval is a M 3rd.

For the interval E to C:

1. In the key of E major there is a C-sharp.

2. Conclusion: The interval is a m 6th.

Note: This is another instance where knowing your key signatures spontaneously is an asset.

WORKBOOK 9-5 through 9-11 and Aural Skills 9-2 are recommended here.

6   Interval Inversion

Interval inversion literally means turning the interval upside down (the higher tone now becomes the lower tone and the lower tone becomes the higher tone).

When we invert an interval, its *number size changes:* A 2nd becomes a 7th; a 3rd becomes a 6th; and so on. Note that any interval plus its inversion always totals 9.

9-J   **Interval inversion changes the interval *size*.**

A 2nd becomes a 7th (=9).

A 3rd becomes a 6th (= 9).

A 4th becomes a 5th (= 9).

A 5th becomes a 4th (= 9).

A 6th becomes a 3rd (= 9).

A 7th becomes a 2nd (= 9).

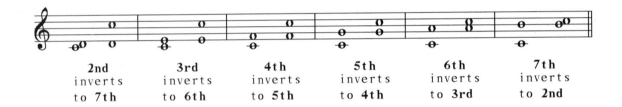

| 2nd inverts to 7th | 3rd inverts to 6th | 4th inverts to 5th | 5th inverts to 4th | 6th inverts to 3rd | 7th inverts to 2nd |

WORKBOOK 9-12 is suggested here.

When an interval of a 2nd, a 3rd, a 6th, or a 7th is inverted, its *quality changes* as well as its number size. When a unison, an octave, a 4th, or a 5th is inverted, its *quality does not change* (one reason these intervals are referred to as "perfect").

Interval inversion changes interval *quality* (in major, minor, diminished, and augmented intervals but not in perfect intervals).

A major interval when inverted becomes minor.

A minor interval when inverted becomes major.

An augmented interval when inverted becomes diminished.

A diminished interval when inverted becomes augmented.

A perfect interval when inverted remains perfect.

M ⟶ m

m ⟶ M

d ⟶ A

A ⟶ d

P ⟶ P

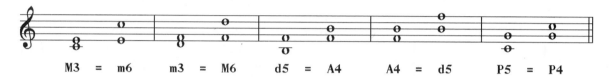

WORKBOOK 9-13 is suggested here.

7   Simple and Compound Intervals

Intervals *within an octave* are **simple intervals.** Intervals *larger than an octave* are called **compound intervals.** We can refer to compound intervals by their exact sizes—for example, 9ths, 10ths, 11ths, 12ths, 13ths—or as *compound* 2nds, 3rds, 4ths, and so on.

Quality does not change because an interval is compound. The simple interval C to D is a major 2nd; the compound interval C to D is a major 9th (or a compound major 2nd).

Simple and compound intervals

M 9th = a compound M 2nd

M 10th = a compound M 3rd

WORKBOOK 9-14 through 9-16 are suggested here.

8   Consonant and Dissonant Intervals

Certain intervals represent the element of repose, whereas others convey the element of tension. The former are referred to as **consonant intervals,** the latter as **dissonant intervals.**

Consonant intervals	Dissonant intervals
Unisons	2nds
3rds	7ths
Perfect 4ths*	
Perfect 5ths	
6ths	
Perfect Octaves	

* Note: Some have regarded the 4th as dissonant also.

Although *consonance* and *dissonance* are relatively subjective phenomena, the resolution of dissonance to consonance has been an acceptable method for creating tension and repose in musical composition for many centuries.

Tension is more evident when intervals are heard simultaneously (harmonic) than when heard consecutively (melodic). Listen to the first few notes of the familiar tune "Chopsticks," which starts on the dissonant interval of a 2nd and then, after six repetitions, resolves to a consonant 3rd.

"Chopsticks" (traditional)

Summary   Intervals are basic to harmony and to melody. Two pitches sounded simultaneously constitute a *harmonic* interval; sounded successively, a *melodic* interval. Intervals are characterized by their size, that is, by their *number* and their *quality*. They are qualified as *major, perfect, minor, diminished,* or *augmented.* They can be inverted, in which case they change their number and—with the exception of the perfect intervals—their quality.

Intervals larger than the octave are called *compound* intervals. Compound intervals may be reduced to simple intervals for discussion and analysis. Certain intervals are *dissonant* and others *consonant,* thus providing a tension/release experience for the listener.

The following table summarizes the highlights of this chapter:

Melodic interval	Two pitches heard successively
Harmonic interval	Two pitches heard simultaneously
Interval number	The number of letter names encompassed in an interval
Interval quality	The actual number of steps encompassed in an interval
Interval inversion (number change)	Number size changes in all inversions
Interval inversion (quality change)	Quality changes in M, m, d, and A, but not in perfect
Simple interval	Any interval within the octave
Compound interval	Any interval larger than an octave
Consonant intervals	Intervals that sound stable (unisons, 3rds, 5ths, 6ths, octaves)
Dissonant intervals	Intervals that sound unstable (2nds, 4ths, 7ths)

WORKBOOK 9-17 through 9-19 are suggested here.

Chapter Review

Terms/Concepts

1. Interval
2. Melodic/Harmonic intervals
3. Interval size
4. Interval number
5. Interval quality
6. Unison
7. Octave
8. Major
9. Perfect
10. Diminished
11. Augmented
12. Interval inversion
13. Simple intervals
14. Compound intervals
15. Consonant intervals
16. Dissonant intervals

Review Questions

1. What is the difference between a *melodic interval* and a *harmonic interval*?

2. What is the difference between *number size* and *quality* in intervals?

3. What are the terms we use to designate *quality* in intervals?

4. Which intervals change their number size when *inverted*?

5. Which intervals change their quality when *inverted;* which do not?

6. What is the difference between a *simple interval* and a *compound interval?*

7. Which intervals are *consonant;* which *dissonant?*

Aural Skills

Aural Skills Exercises noted throughout the chapter, which require the instructor's assistance, are located in the Instructor's Manual. The following can be done by the student working alone or with a colleague.

1. Practice singing major 2nds/minor 2nds; major 3rds/minor 3rds; and so on.

2. Working with a colleague, play simple intervals for each other to identify.

3. When attempting to develop a facility for recognizing the various sizes of intervals, it is sometimes helpful to use familiar melodies that contain the specific interval, as a reminder of the sound. The following tunes are suggested, although you may find others more familiar to you.

m 2 (Ascending)

(A) PINK PANTHER (Henry Mancini)

(B) TIME IN A BOTTLE (Jim Croce)

M 2 (Ascending)

(A) HAIL TO THE CHIEF (James Sanderson)

(B) AMERICA (Patriotic)

m 3 (Ascending)

(A) HELLO DOLLY (Jerry Herman)

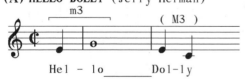

(B) LULLABY   Johannes Brahms)

M 3 (Ascending)

(A) KUM BA YAH (African American)

(B) WHAT NOW MY LOVE (G. Becaud)

P4 (Ascending)

(A) BRIDAL MARCH (Richard Wagner)

Here comes the Bride!

(B) STAR WARS (John Williams)

P5 (Ascending)

(A) TWINKLE, TWINKLE (Traditional)

Twink-le, twink-le lit-tle star

(B) THEME: SUMMER OF '42 (M. Legrand)

The sum – mer smiles

m6 (Ascending)

(A) SIDE BY SIDE – CHORUS (H. Woods)

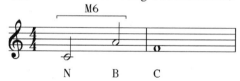

Through all kinds of weath-er

M6 (Ascending)

(A) NBC Broadcasting (Commercial)

N   B   C

(B) JINGLE BELLS (Traditional)

Dash-ing through the snow

m7 (Ascending)

(A) WEST SIDE STORY (Leonard Bernstein)

There's a   place for us

(B) SHE'S OUT OF MY LIFE (Tom Bahler)

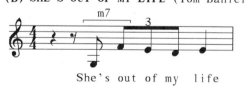

She's out of my life

P8

(A) LET IT SNOW, LET IT SNOW (J. Styne)

Oh the weath-er out-side is fright-ful

(B) OVER THE RAINBOW (Burton Lane)

Some-where ov-er the rain-bow

m2 (Descending)

(A) APRIL SHOWERS (Louis Silvers)

m2

Though A-pril show – ers

(B) AS LONG AS HE NEEDS ME (Lionel Bart)

m2

As long as he needs me

M2 (Descending)

(A) THE WAY WE WERE (Marvin Hamlisch)

M2   3

Mem –'ries   light the corners

(B) AUTUMN IN NEW YORK (Vernon Duke)

M2

Au- tumn in New York

m3 (Descending)

(A) AMERICA THE BEAUTIFUL (Samuel Ward)

m3

Oh beau-ti-ful for spac-ious skies

(B) I JUST CALLED TO SAY I LOVE YOU (Stevie Wonder)

m3

I just called __ to say

M3 (Descending)

(A) SUMMERTIME (George Gershwin)

M3

Sum-mer – time _____

(B) MERRILY WE ROLL ALONG

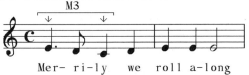

M3   ↓   ↓

Mer– ri-ly   we roll a-long

P4 (Descending)

(A) BORN FREE (John Barry)

P4   — 3—

Born free,_____ as free as the
(wind blows)

(B) HALLELUJAH CHORUS (G. F. Handel)

P4

Hal – le – lu – jah!

P5 (Descending)

(A) FEELINGS (Moris Albert)

P5

Feel-ings (nothing more
than feelings)

(B) IT DON'T MEAN A THING (Duke Ellington)

P5

It don't mean a thing
(If it ain't got that swing)

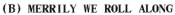

m6 (Descending)

(A) ARTHUR'S THEME (Burt Bacharach et al.)

Once in your life, you'll find her

(B) LOVE STORY-Theme (Francis Lai)

Where do I be-gin to tell the
(story of how great a love can be

M6 (Descending)

(A) SWEET CAROLINE (Neil Diamond)

Sweet Car - o-line_____

(B) NOBODY KNOWS THE TROUBLE I'VE SEEN (Spiritual)

Oh no-bo - dy knows the

m7 (Descending)

(A) AN AMERICAN IN PARIS (George Gerswhin)

M7 (Descending)

(A) BRIAN'S SONG (Michel Legrand)

P8 (Descending

(A) NADIA'S THEME (DeVorzon/Botkin)

(B) LOVE IS SWEEPING THE COUNTRY (George Gershwin)

Love is sweep - ing the

A4 (TT)

(A) MARIA (from *West Side Story* – Leonard Bernstein)

Chapter Drills

(Answers can be found in Appendix A.)

1. Indicate whether the interval is melodic (M) or harmonic (H).

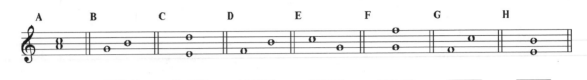

2. Give the size of each interval.

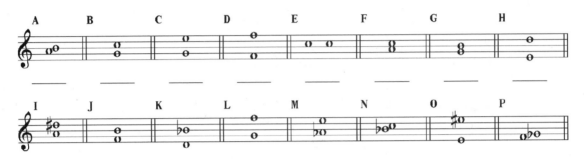

3. Write a second note above the given note (using an accidental if necessary) to create the size and quality indicated.

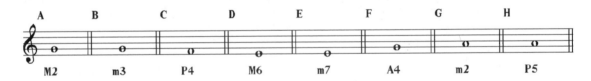

4. Alter the second pitch, with an accidental as needed, to write the quality of the interval requested. Write answers above the staff in letter names.

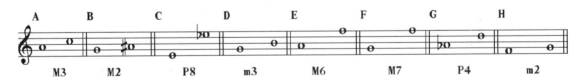

5. Identify the size and quality of each interval; then, in the empty measure beside it, invert each and identify the size and quality of the inversion.

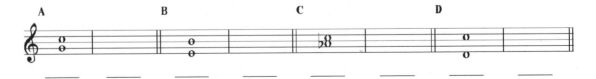

6. Reduce the compound intervals to simple intervals and identify their size and quality.

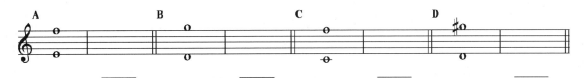

7. In the following melody, indicate the size of each melodic interval.

Between Beats	Size	Quality	Between Beats	Size	Quality
1 & 2	____	____	15 & 16	____	____
2 & 3	____	____	16 & 17	____	____
3 & 4	____	____	17 & 18	____	____
4 & 5	____	____	18 & 19	____	____
5 & 6	____	____	19 & 20	____	____
6 & 7	____	____	20 & 21	____	____
7 & 8	____	____	21 & 22	____	____
8 & 9	____	____	22 & 23	____	____
9 & 10	____	____	23 & 24	____	____
10 & 11	____	____	24 & 25	____	____
11 & 12	____	____	25 & 26	____	____
12 & 13	____	____	26 & 27	____	____
13 & 14	____	____	27 & 28	____	____
14 & 15	____	____	28 & 29	____	____

Chapter 10

Chords

1 Introduction

*T*his chapter focuses on chords: their construction, content, quality, and inversions. It also looks at the various labels and symbols used to differentiate between chords, their qualities, and their inversions.

2 Difference between Interval, Chord, and Triad

Recall that two pitches sounding simultaneously produce a harmonic *interval*. Three or more pitches sounding simultaneously constitute a **chord**. The term **triad** is reserved for chords with only three pitches.

Interval: two pitches sounded simultaneously

Triad: three pitches sounded simultaneously

Chord: three or more pitches sounded simultaneously

10-A   **Interval, triad, and chord**

INTERVAL   TRIAD   CHORD
                (or CHORD)

148

3 Tertian, Secundal, Quartal, and Quintal Chords

Although chords can be built by stacking intervals of any size, those built in thirds are by far the most common. These are known as *tertian chords.*

Chords built in seconds are called *secundal chords.*[1] Those built in intervals of 4ths are *quartal;* in 5ths, *quintal.*

Secundal chords: built in 2nds

Tertian chords: built in 3rds

Quartal chords: built in 4ths

Quintal chords: built in 5ths

10-B   **Different types of chords**

4 Tertian Harmony

Harmony based on chords built in thirds is known as **tertian harmony.** This type of harmony was standard from 1600 to 1900, and although it is not the exclusive harmony of the twentieth century, it is still the most commonly used. It is most readily evident in the popular styles—for example, jazz, popular songs, rock, folk, country, and musical theater.

In this text, we will concentrate on tertian chords and tertian harmony. Therefore, throughout the remainder of this text, the word *chord* implies one built in thirds.

5 Components of a Chord

To write or play a chord, simply use *every other* letter name, stacking them one above the other. The following example shows a chord built from every member of the musical alphabet. Notice we are starting from a bottom pitch and building upward, in thirds.

---

[1] Stacked seconds are generally referred to as *tone clusters* rather than chords.

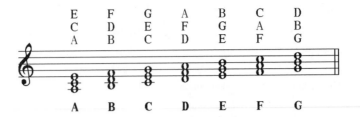

Each chord has three components:

1.   **Root:** the bottom pitch of the chord

2.   **Third:** the first pitch above the root

3.   **Fifth:** the second pitch above the root

Note: A chord whose root is a sharp or a flat is treated the same as one with its root on a white key; that is, every third letter name is used.

WORKBOOK 10-1 through 10-3 are suggested here.

6   Chord Qualities

Like intervals, chords will vary in the *quality* of their sound, depending upon the size of the respective intervals. The terms used to designate the quality of a chord are the same as those used to designate the quality of an interval: *major, minor, diminished,* and *augmented.* As with intervals, we can use uppercase or lowercase abbreviations to refer to the quality of the chord.

M = major

m = minor

A = augmented

d = diminished

        In each case, it is the quality of the 3rd above the root and the quality of the 5th above the root that determine the overall quality of the chord.

Major chord = a M 3rd + a P 5th

Minor chord = a m 3rd + a P 5th

Diminished chord = a m 3rd + a d 5th

Augmented chord = a M 3rd + an A 5th

Another way to think of it is this:

M = M3 on bottom + m3 on top

m = m3 on bottom + M3 on top

d = m3 on bottom + m3 on top

A = M3 on bottom + M3 on top

10-D   **Four chords built on root A (M, m, d, A)**

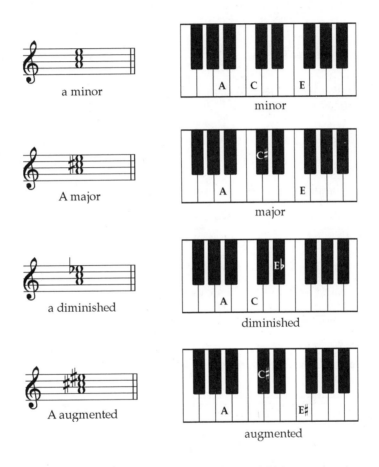

WORKBOOK 10-4 through 10-8 and Aural Skills 10-1 are recommended here.

7   Chord Names and Chord Symbols

All chords are named by their *roots*. They can be referred to in several ways:

1.   By letter name (of the root)

2.   By scale-degree name (of the root)

3.   By roman numeral (of the root)

Letter Names

A chord built from C (C-E-G) is called the C chord; from D (D-F-A), the D chord; and so on.

10-E   **Letter names for chords**

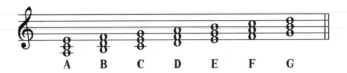

Scale-Degree Names

Chords also are referred to by their scale-degree names: *tonic, supertonic,* and so on.

Tonic chord: built on scale degree 1

Supertonic: built on scale degree 2

Mediant: built on scale degree 3

Subdominant: built on scale degree 4

Dominant: built on scale degree 5

Submediant: built on scale degree 6

Leading tone: built on scale degree 7

(Subtonic: built on 7, a whole step from 1)

10-F   **Degree names for chords (shown in C major)**

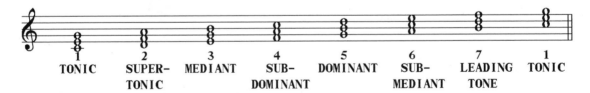

WORKBOOK 10-9 through 10-11 and Aural Skills 10-2 are recommended here.

Roman Numerals

We can refer to chords *within a specific scale* by their scale-degree number. In this case, roman numerals are used, as opposed to arabic numbers. Roman numeral labels are used primarily for the analysis of music literature written between 1600 and 1900. They have the advantage of showing how a particular chord is functioning within a specific tonality. Again, uppercase and lowercase denote quality.

Uppercase for major (I)

Lowercase for minor (i)

Lowercase and a small o for diminished (i⁰)

Uppercase and a + sign to indicate augmented (I+)

(The quality of individual chords is exactly the same in every major scale: The tonic is major, the supertonic is minor, and so on.)

10-G

Roman numerals showing chord qualities in major

(Chord qualities are exactly the same in every natural minor scale: The tonic is minor, the supertonic is diminished, and so on.)

10-H

Roman numerals showing chord qualities in minor

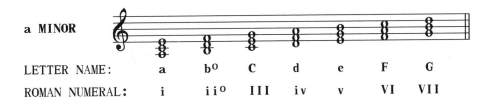

The following is a summary of the chord qualities in diatonic major and minor scales.

In a *major key:*   I, IV, and V are major.
ii, iii, and vi are minor.
vii⁰ is diminished.

In *natural minor:*   i, iv, and v are minor.
III, VI, and VII are major.
ii⁰ is diminished.

Recall that in the *harmonic form* of the minor scale, the seventh degree of the scale is raised a half step; thus, the quality of any chord containing that pitch (the raised 7th) will be altered. The chords affected by harmonic minor are those built on scale degrees 3, 5, and 7.

(a minor — harmonic form)

III becomes III⁺　　　v becomes V　　　VII becomes viiº

Note: VII in natural minor is called the subtonic chord; altered, as in harmonic minor, it is called a leading-tone chord—just as in major.

WORKBOOK 10-12 through 10-18 and Aural Skills 10-3 are recommended here.

Popular-Music Symbols

Generally, in the various styles of popular music (popular songs, jazz, rock, folk, and the like), the harmony will be indicated by the letter name of the chord placed above the staff containing the melody notes.

　　"Pop symbols" (as they are frequently referred to) show the root of the chord as well as its quality. They also indicate whether the chord should be a simple triad or a chord with added thirds, as shown in example 10-J.

10-J　　　　**"Pop" symbols showing variations of the C chord**

C = C major triad

Cm = C minor triad

C+ = C augmented triad

C⁰ = C diminished triad

C7 = C major triad with an added minor 7th

CM7 = C major triad with an added major 7th

C9 = C major triad with an added minor 7th and a 9th

(See Appendix E.)

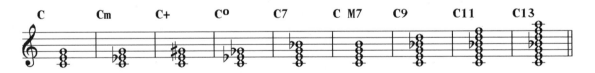

(See example 11-M for a jazz tune using "pop" symbols.)[2]

WORKBOOK 10-19 and 10-20 are suggested here.

---

[2] In popular music, the symbol "7" always means a minor 7th. If the composer wants a major 7th, it must be indicated "M7." This is not the case with classical symbols, where "7" will always mean a diatonic "7" unless otherwise indicated.

8 Inversions

Chords are not always written and played with the root as the lowest-sounding pitch. They also can appear with the 3rd or the 5th on the bottom. These rearrangements, called **inversions,** are used to create interesting bass lines or simply to provide harmonic/melodic variety in the music. We refer to a chord's position as follows:

Root position: The root is the *lowest-sounding* pitch.

1st inversion: The 3rd is the *lowest-sounding* pitch.

2nd inversion: The 5th is the *lowest-sounding* pitch.

9 Inversion Symbols

The inversions have symbols that today are used primarily for the purpose of harmonic analysis.[3] The symbols used to designate the *position* of a chord are shown in example 10-K.

10-K

Inversion symbols

Root position = roman numeral (I)

1st inversion = roman numeral plus $_6$ (I_6)

2nd inversion = roman numeral plus $_6^4$ (I_6^4)

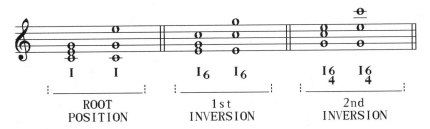

(Notice that no specific arrangement of the pitches above the lowest-sounding note is required. The position of the chord is determined solely by the lowest-sounding pitch. For a more complete explanation of suffix symbols, see more advanced theory texts.)

---

[3] Inversion symbols had their origin in the Baroque era (1600–1750), when they functioned as a type of shorthand for the keyboardist. The keyboard performer *improvised* an accompaniment for the other instruments or voices merely from the bass line of notes and the inversion symbols provided.

This is analogous to what happens in most styles of jazz, where, along with the melody, only the "pop" symbols are provided, to specify the harmony. The melody in this style is frequently referred to as the "head." The keyboard player provides the harmonic background as specified by the chord symbols while the other instruments improvise along with this chord accompaniment. This type of performance in the trade is known as "blowing over the (chord) changes."

A brief explanation of the inversion symbols is warranted here. The 6 used to indicate first inversion is an abbreviation of the original shorthand. It is really $\frac{6}{3}$ and it means that six pitches and three pitches above the bass note you will find the other two chord members. The symbol for the second inversion ($\frac{6}{4}$) means that the fourth and sixth pitches above the bass are the other members of this particular chord.

A chord's quality is not affected by inversion. If a chord is major in root position, it will be major in any inversion.

10 Chords with Added 7th

We can continue stacking thirds above the root. The next third (beyond the 3rd and the 5th) is the **7th** above the root. A 7th can be added to any chord, as shown in the next example.

10- L

7ths added to every chord in the C major scale

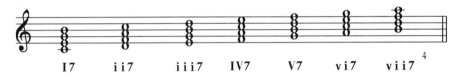

I7   ii7   iii7   IV7   V7   vi7   vii7 [4]

The next thirds above the 7th are the 9ths, 11ths, and 13ths, with the 13th being the limit. After that, any additional third will be merely a repetition of a pitch already added. By the time we reach the 13th, every member of the respective diatonic scale is present in the chord.

10-M

The 13th and all pitches of the diatonic scale

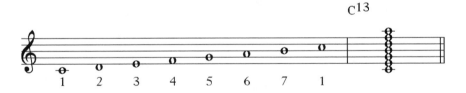

C13

1   2   3   4   5   6   7   1

WORKBOOK 10-21 through 10-29 are suggested here.

[4] The vii chord is a diminished triad. When the diatonic 7th is added, the chord is called "half-diminished" and the symbol is [0] with a slash through it.

Very often this chord is heard with a nondiatonic 7th added, and it is then called "fully diminished," meaning that both the triad and the 7th are diminished. The symbol in this case is [0] (without the slash).

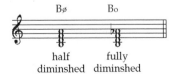

B∅   B○
half   fully
diminished dimished

Summary   In this chapter, we have looked at how chords are built by stacking intervals. We have mentioned the various types of chords but described in detail the most commonly used type: those built in thirds.

We also studied how chords can be inverted, the symbols used to denote specific chords and their inversions, and the rationales behind those symbols.

The following table summarizes the factual information contained in this chapter.

Interval	Two pitches sounding simultaneously.
Triad	Three pitches sounding simultaneously.
Chord	Three or more pitches sounding simultaneously.
Secundal chord	Built in intervals of 2nds.
Tertian chord	Built in intervals of 3rds.
Quartal chord	Built in intervals of 4ths.
Quintal chord	Built in intervals of 5ths.
Root	Pitch on which the chord is built.
Third	First pitch above the root.
Fifth	Second pitch above the root.
Seventh	Third pitch above the root.
Major triad	Major 3rd plus a perfect 5th.
Minor triad	Minor 3rd plus a perfect 5th.
Diminished triad	Minor 3rd plus a diminished 5th.
Augmented triad	Major 3rd plus an augmented 5th.
Major keys	I, IV, V are major; ii, iii, vi are minor; vii^0 is diminished.
Minor keys	i, iv, v are minor; II, VI, VII are major; ii^0 is diminished.
Chord names	Letter names (C, D, etc.).
	Scale-degree names (tonic, etc.).
Chord symbols	Roman numerals (I or i, etc.).
	"Pop" symbols (C7, etc.).
Inversion symbols	Subscript $_6$ means first inversion.
	Subscript $_6^4$ means second inversion.

Chapter Review

Terms/Concepts

1. Chord
2. Triad
3. Tertian harmony
4. Root/Third/Fifth
5. Inversions
6. 7th chords

Review Questions

1. What is the difference between *interval*, *chord*, and *triad*?

2. Explain the difference between the following types of chords: *secundal*, *tertian*, *quartal*, *quintal*.

3. What are the three components of a triad?

4. What intervals are required to produce the following chords: *major, minor, diminished, augmented*?

5. Give three ways that we can label chords.

6. Which chords are affected by *harmonic minor*, and what is the effect in each case?

7. What numbers are used to designate *1st* and *2nd inversion* chords?

Aural Skills

Aural Skills Exercises referred to throughout this chapter, which require the instructor's assistance, are located in the Instructor's Manual. The following can be done by the student working with a colleague.

1. Have a colleague play chords for you to identify the quality. It is helpful to do them in this order:

   a. Major and minor

   b. Major and augmented

   c. Minor and diminished

   d. Diminished and augmented

   e. A mixture: major, minor, diminished, augmented

Chapter Drills

1. Spell tertian chords using the following roots:

   a. F _____   e. A _____

   b. B _____   f. C _____

   c. D _____   g. G _____

   d. E-flat _____   h. F-sharp _____

2. Using the note provided as the root, write the chords in the quality indicated.

3. Identify the chords by letter name and give the quality.

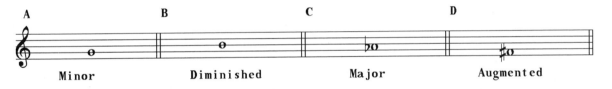

4. Using the note provided as the 3rd of the chord, write the complete chord in the quality indicated.

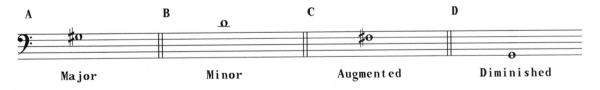

5. Using the given note as the 5th, write the complete chord in the quality requested.

6. Write the major chords in the two keys indicated.

7. Write the chord indicated by the roman numeral in the mode and key specified.

8. Give the roman numeral for each chord in the specified key; give the scale-degree name for each chord. (Indicate key first.)

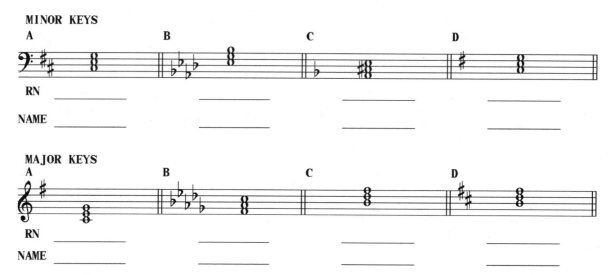

9. Write the chords specified by the "pop" music symbols.

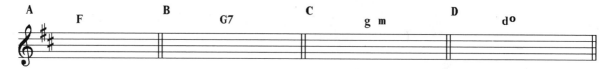

10. Write the chords and inversions in the key specified, in the position indicated.

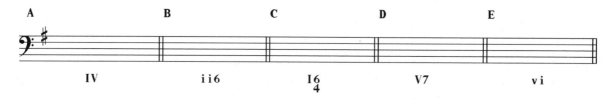

Harmony

11

1   Introduction

*I*n a narrow sense, a chord is harmony. Chords add *depth* to music, a dimension that is not present with just melody and rhythm.[1] However, harmony generally implies more than this single unit of sound (chord). In its broader sense, **harmony** implies a succession of chords and their interrelationships.

A succession of chords can add a rhythmic dimension to music and thus, along with melody and rhythm, can aid in propelling the music through time. Harmony then functions in two ways: one vertical, the other horizontal. Whereas the *vertical aspect* (depth) is provided by harmony alone, the *horizontal aspect* (motion) of music is provided by melody, rhythm, and harmony.

In this chapter, we will examine some underlying concepts of harmony (harmonic rhythm, nonchord tones, and chord progressions), some fundamental techniques for harmonizing a melody, and some basic techniques for analyzing the harmony in a composition.

2   Harmonic Rhythm

Motion in music is sensed through rhythm, which can emanate from a variety of sources. It can be provided by rhythm instruments, such as drums, as well as by the melodic and harmonic rhythm. The succession of chords, or *chord changes*, can serve as a rhythmic pulse in music.

---

[1] In this respect, harmony in music is analogous to perspective in painting.

Harmonic rhythm refers to the *rate of chord change* (the rate of the harmonic change) in a piece. Harmonic rhythm can aid in establishing the overall structure of music and can cause a variety of musical effects.

In each of the six measures shown in example 11-A, the melody, meter, and rhythm remain exactly the same, but each measure has a different harmonic rhythm.

(In harmonic analysis, note values commensurate with the rate of chord change are used to show harmonic rhythm.)

11-A   **Six harmonic rhythms**

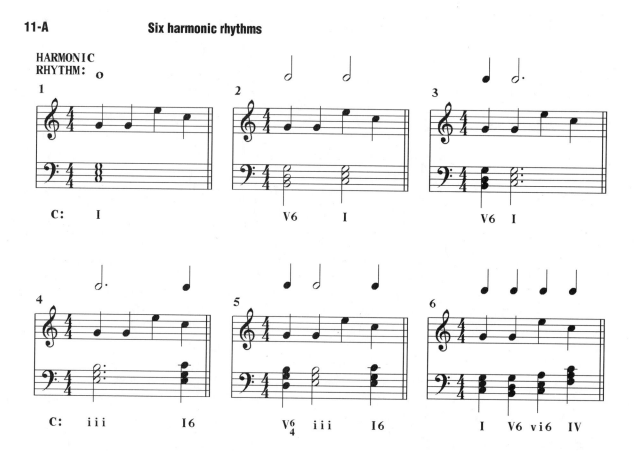

Because there is a limit to the amount of musical information a listener can absorb within a specific time frame, frequent chord changes tend to dictate a relatively slow tempo.

In example 11-B, with only two exceptions, there is a chord change on each beat of each measure, typical of hymn-style composition.

11-B (CD)   **Doxology (Bourgeois)**

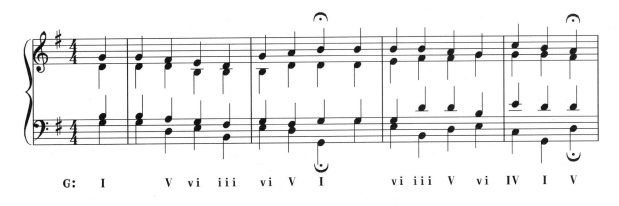

G: I   V vi iii vi V I   vi iii V vi IV I V

vi V I V I6 IV V vi V I vi V ii I6 V I

Example 11-C shows an approach opposite to that of example 11-B. In this example, one chord serves to harmonize the entire piece, resulting in a *static harmony*. Infrequent chord changes are typical in some popular styles, especially folk songs, where the primary emphasis is on melody and text.

11-C (CD)   **"Shalom Chaverim" (Israeli song)**

Sha - lom cha-ve-rim, sha - lom cha-ve-rim, sha - lom,   sha -

lom, Le hit-ra - ot, le hit-ra - ot, sha - lom, sha - lom.

11 Harmony **163**

See Workbook, Scores #9, "Marriage of Figaro"; #10, "One Grain of Sand"; #15, "The Water Is Wide."

WORKBOOK 11-1 through 11-3 and Aural Skills 11-1 are recommended here.

3   Nonchord Tones

In example 11-B, each note belongs to a specific chord. In most music, however, there are notes that are not part of the chord with which they are heard. This can be seen in example 11-C, where the chord E-G-B harmonizes the entire piece but pitches other than those three appear in the melody: F-sharp, A, and D.

Pitches that are heard along with a chord but that are not part of that chord are called **nonchord tones** (abbreviated NCT) or nonharmonic tones (NHT).

NCTs can be diatonic (belonging to the key) or chromatic. They can add harmonic color and melodic interest to the music. (As noted earlier, harmonizing each melody note could necessitate performing the piece in a slower tempo than perhaps desired.) The commonly used types of NCTs are

Passing tone

Upper and lower neighboring tones

Changing tone

Anticipation

Suspension

Appoggiatura

Escape tone

Pedal point

Each NCT is classified on the basis of the way in which it is approached and left. Although there is not complete consensus among musicians on terminology and definitions, the following distinctions are widely used.

Passing Tone

Passing tones (PT) are nonchord tones that are approached and left in stepwise motion, continuing *in the same direction*. Passing tones may appear on a strong (APT) or a weak beat.

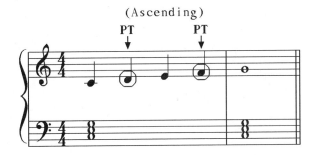

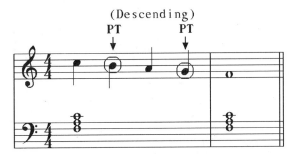

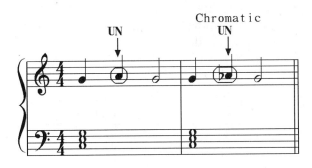

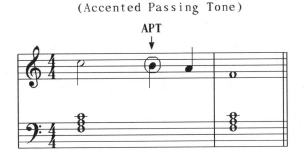

Neighboring Tone

There are two versions of the **neighboring tone** (NT). The *upper neighbor* (UN) is an ascending step to a NCT, followed by a return to the chord tone. The *lower neighbor* (LN) is a descending step to a NCT, followed by a return to the chord tone.

11-E   **Neighboring tones**

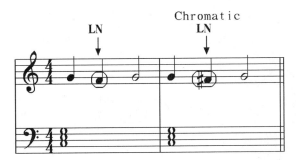

Changing Tone

Changing tones (CT), sometimes called *neighbor group,* are a sort of combination of upper neighbor and lower neighbor tones, but the return to the chord tone does not occur until both nonchord tones have been heard.

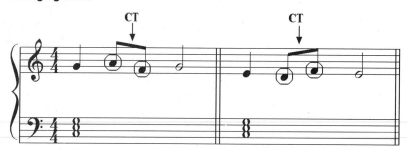

Anticipation

Anticipation (ANT) is a pitch that precedes the chord to which it belongs. It is not a member of the chord with which it is heard, and it *anticipates* the succeeding harmony.

11-G   Anticipations*

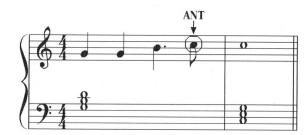
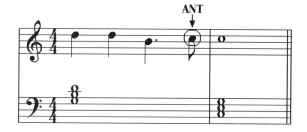

Suspension

Suspensions are the opposite of anticipations. In a **suspension** (SUS), a pitch from the preceding chord is held over (frequently a tied note) into the new harmony and then resolved stepwise to a pitch in the new chord.[2]

11-H   Suspensions*

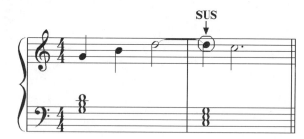
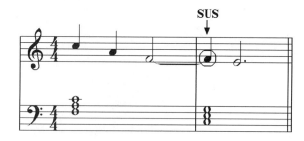

* The chords shown here in the bass clef are not meant to show the best possible voice leading but to simply exhibit the concept.

[2] The term *retardation* is frequently used to refer to suspensions that resolve stepwise upward, instead of the more normal, descending resolution.

Appoggiatura

The **appoggiatura** (APP) is a NCT that is entered by a skip and then resolved stepwise, in the opposite direction of the skip, to a chord tone. The appoggiatura is generally on a strong beat.

11-I   **Appoggiatura**

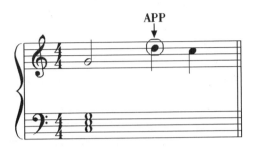

Escape Tone

The **escape tone** (ESC) is the opposite of an appoggiatura. This NCT is approached stepwise and is *left* by a leap, in the opposite direction.

11-J   **Escape tone**

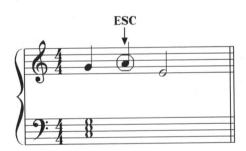

Pedal Point

The **pedal point** (PED) is a NCT that is sustained throughout one (and frequently more than one) chord change. It derives its name from organ music in which one pitch is sustained on a foot pedal while the harmony above changes.

Although the pedal point is frequently the lowest-sounding pitch, it is likewise often heard in the higher or middle voices.

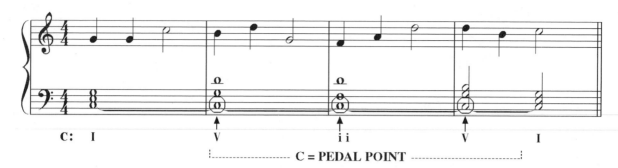

WORKBOOK 11-4 through 11-6 and Aural Skills 11- 2 are recommended here.

4   Chord Progressions

Besides determining the harmonic rhythm in a composition and deciding which pitches will be part of a chord and which will be nonchord tones, the composer also chooses specific chords: tonic, dominant, and so on.

In any diatonic key, each pitch will be a member of three separate chords. Each pitch will be the root of one chord, the 3rd of another, and the 5th of yet another, thus providing three harmonic options to the composer.

The *tonic, dominant,* and *subdominant* chords best define tonality. Among the three of them, all pitches of the respective diatonic scale are present, so it is possible to use these chords exclusively to harmonize a tune.

11-L   **Chords I, IV, V, V7 harmonizing pitches in C major**

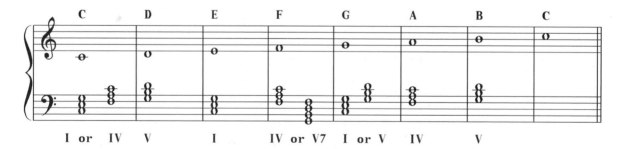

Although these three chords suffice to harmonize any diatonic scale degree and serve to define the specific tonality, harmony can be made more interesting by replacing them with the *supertonic, mediant, submediant,* and *leading tone* (or *subtonic*) chords.

In Chapter 14, on Form, we will see that the tonic, dominant, and subdominant chords also serve to define the musical sentence structure and the overall form of a composition.

WORKBOOK 11-7 is suggested here.

5   Harmonizing a Melody

When harmonizing a composition, proceed as follows:

1.   Determine the *key* and the *mode.*

2.   Decide the appropriate *harmonic rhythm.*

3.   Decide the type of *chord progressions.*

4.   Determine the *form* and location of *cadences* (to be discussed in Chapter 14).

WORKBOOK 11-8 through 11-12 are suggested here.

6   Analytical Techniques

A complete analysis of a musical composition, done before the piece is practiced (and memorized) for performance, generally will shorten practice time and enhance the actual performance of the work. Thoroughly understanding all musical elements in a composition makes it possible to play the piece with a sensitivity to its musical meaning, and to communicate the musical information in a musically meaningful manner to the listener.

The following steps can serve as a guide for analyzing the harmonic content of a composition.

1.   *Determine the key and the mode.* (In more advanced theory courses, you will encounter pieces that change keys and modes.)

2.   *Analyze each chord* in the respective key and indicate its position: root or inversion. (Analysis can indicate how a specific chord is functioning and help the performer shape the musical line. In more advanced theory courses, you will also encounter nondiatonic chords.)

3.   *Account for all the nonchord tones.*

4.   *Note the harmonic rhythm.*

WORKBOOK 11-13 through 11-15 are suggested here.

7   Lead Sheet Reading Techniques

Jazz scores (as well as most popular-music styles) provide letter-name symbols to specify the harmony. Frequently, the arrangement of the chord in performance (referred to as "voicings") is left to the discretion of the performer (although "C/G" would tell the performer to play the C major chord in its third inversion, that is, with G in the bass).

The chord symbols are located above the measures to which they refer, as shown in the next example.

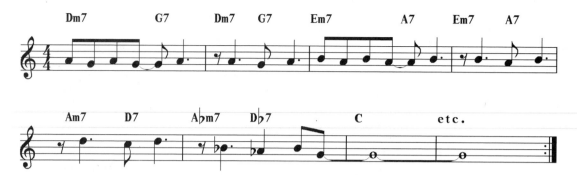

The chords called for in example 11-M are as follows:

See Workbook, Score #1, "Autumn Leaves."

WORKBOOK 11-16 is suggested here.

Summary   This chapter dealt with a basic study of the musical element *harmony*. We noted that chords function in certain ways to define the tonality of the piece. Diatonic chords (chords that belong to the key, as opposed to those that do not) emphasize the respective tonality, with tonic, dominant, and subdominant chords being the strongest indicators.

We looked at how the harmonic rhythm, which results from the rate of chord changes, can assist in propelling the music through time as well as enhancing or confirming the overall style of the music.

We further noted how pitches other than members of a specific chord (NCTs) can be used to embellish melody or harmony. Finally, we examined the "lead sheet" approach to indicating the harmony, which is used in various popular styles of music.

NCTs	Approached by	Left by
Passing tone (PT)	Step	Step in same direction
Neighboring tone (NT)	Step	Step in opposite direction
Changing tone (CT)	Step	Skip in opposite direction; step in opposite direction
Anticipation (ANT)	Step (or leap)	Same tone (or leap)
Suspension (SUS)	Same tone	Step down
Appoggiatura (APP)	Leap	Step
Escape tone (ESC)	Step	Leap
Pedal point (PED)	Same tone	Any tone

Chapter Review

Terms/Concepts

1.	Harmony	7.	Anticipation
2.	Harmonic rhythm	8.	Suspension
3.	Nonchord tones	9.	Appoggiatura
4.	Passing tone	10.	Escape tone
5.	Neighboring tone	11.	Pedal point
6.	Changing tone		

Review Questions

1. How does a rapid rate of chord change (*harmonic rhythm*) generally affect the tempo?

2. What purposes do *nonchord tones* serve?

3. The type of *chord progression* we use can serve what purpose, relative to *tonality*?

4. What is the difference between the manner in which harmony is notated in traditional classical music and in the "lead sheet" approach in jazz?

5. What steps should be followed in doing a harmonic analysis of a piece?

6. What steps should you follow if you want to harmonize a melody?

7. Name a style of music that generally has a slow harmonic rhythm.

8. Name a style of music that generally has a fast harmonic rhythm.

Aural Skills

Aural Skills Exercises noted throughout the chapter, which require the instructor's assistance, are located in the Instructor's Manual. The following exercises can be done by the student working alone or with a colleague.

1. As you listen to music now, do the following:

    a. Concentrate on the harmonic changes (harmonic rhythm) to note whether the changes are frequent or infrequent.

    b. Try to begin to hear nonchord tones (passing tones, neighboring tones, and so on).

Chapter Drills

1. The following pieces are provided for harmonic analysis. Use the following procedure for each.

a. Determine the key and mode.

b. Analyze the chords (show roman numeral and any inversion).

c. Circle and label all NCTs.

d. Indicate the harmonic rhythm.

(A)

HARMONIC
RHYTHM:

POLLY WOLLY DOODLE (American)

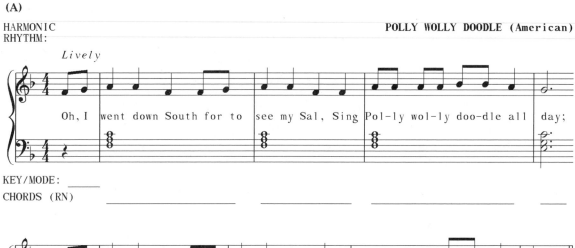

KEY/MODE: _____

CHORDS (RN) _____ _____ _____ _____

(B)

JACOB'S LADDER (Traditional)

HARMONIC
RHYTHM

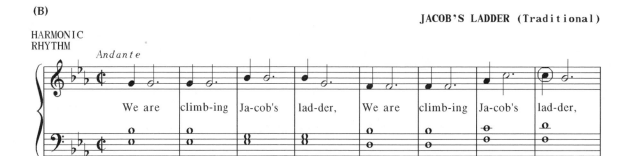

KEY/MODE: _____

CHORDS (RN) _____ _____ _____ _____

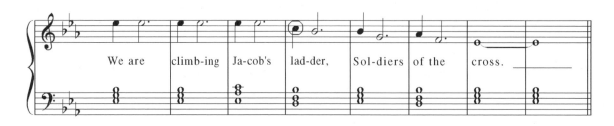

The following is a composition for complete harmonic analysis.
(The nonchord tones here are circled.)

(C)

Texture

12 ●

1   Introduction

*M*elody and harmony combine to create an element in music called **texture.** Texture results from the interweaving of musical sounds, analogous to woven threads in fabric. It refers to the *density* of the music, and, thus, the number and the type of sounds heard simultaneously affect the texture in varying degrees.[1]

We use relative terms such as *heavy, thick, dense,* and *light, thin, transparent* to describe various textures. Example 12-A shows an accumulation of layers of sound. With each additional layer, the texture becomes "thicker," or denser.

12-A (CD)

Symphony No. 5, in C minor, 1st movement, measures 1–8 (Ludwig van Beethoven)

(a)   Four-note melodic *motive* is presented, unaccompanied by other sounds.

(b)   Motive is imitated sequentially, still unaccompanied.

(c)   Motive is repeated, but this time another pitch is added on the 4th note.

(d)   Motive is played while the two previous pitches are tied, producing three layers of sound.

(e)   A fourth layer is added.

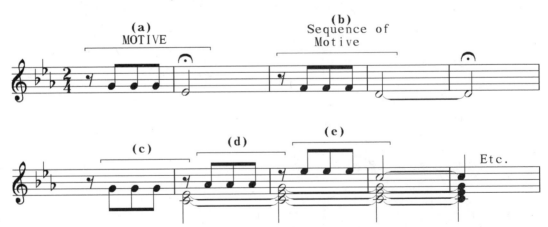

[1] Texture can also be affected by timbre (because of overtones) and by rhythm.

174

The common types of texture are

1. Monophony (monophonic texture)

2. Homophony (homophonic texture)

3. Polyphony/Counterpoint (polyphonic/contrapuntal texture)

2 Monophony

Monophony is the simplest type of texture. It is a *single line of music, unaccompanied by other musical sounds.* (The first two statements of the motive in example 12-A are monophonic.) Even when an entire group sings in unison—that is, sings the same successive pitches at the same time—the resulting texture is monophonic.

12-B (CD)   **Monophony: "America" (Henry Carey)**

3 Homophony

Homophony refers to a type of texture in which *one line of melody is the most notable and other lines support or accompany it.* It can be simply a melody with chord accompaniment, as shown in example 12-C.

12-C (CD)   **Homophony (melody accompanied by chords): "America"**

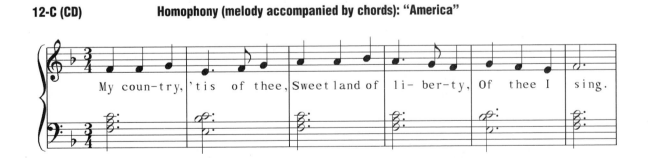

Sometimes the harmony plays a more integral role, as, for example, in four-part "block" harmony, where all chord parts (or voices) move in the same rhythm, as shown in example 12-D.

12-D (CD)   **Homophony (four-part harmony): "America"**

4 Polyphony

Polyphony implies a texture consisting of *two or more independent melodies heard simultaneously,* resulting in layers of equally important melodies.

Polyphony can be achieved either by combining two or more different melodies or by simply combining two performances of the same melody but at different time intervals. The latter is generally referred to as a *canon* or "round." In the round, each person (or group) sings the same melody but with time lags between entries.

A familiar example is the following tune, in which the first voice starts the piece and the second and third voices enter when the first arrives at the second and the third measures, respectively. The texture becomes denser as each voice is added and less dense as each voice drops out at the end.

12-E   **Polyphony: "Row, Row, Row Your Boat" (a round)**

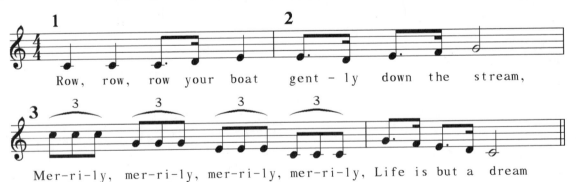

However, in most polyphonic music the melodies are not identical. Example 12-F shows three distinctly different melodies occurring simultaneously. Performing any one of these three without the others results in a **monophonic** texture; performing them simultaneously creates a **polyphonic** texture.

12-F (CD)   **Polyphonic texture (J.D.)**

Another example of polyphony is shown in example 12-G, where we have combined the melodies of two familiar tunes.

12-G (CD)   **"Joy to the World" and "Jingle Bells" (carols)**

5   Counterpoint

Counterpoint is practically synonymous with polyphony. Each implies a texture in which two or more separate but equally important melodies are being performed simultaneously.[2]

Musicians frequently reserve the term *polyphony* for vocal music (and more specifically, to that body of vocal literature from the period 900 to 1600). On the other hand, the term *counterpoint* frequently refers to a systematic study of the techniques of combining melodies. Some also prefer this term (*counterpoint*) when speaking of instrumental music. See examples 12-H and 12-I.

12-H   **Sixteenth-century polyphony: "Benedictus" (Orlando di Lasso, 1532–1594)**

The entire piece is included in the Workbook, Score #2, and on the CD.

Translation: Blessed is he who cometh in the name of the Lord.

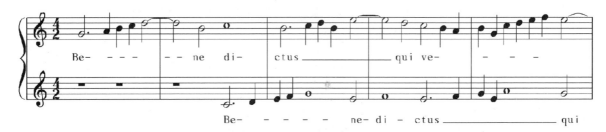

---

[2] Since polyphony and counterpoint both consist of two or more melodies heard simultaneously, the element of harmony (in the sense of two or more pitches being heard simultaneously) is present. However, the term *harmony* is generally understood in a much broader context, implying the "total harmonization" of a composition.

Although harmony clearly has a horizontal aspect, the concept denotes an emphasis on a vertical structure of music, in contrast to counterpoint or polyphony, in which the *emphasis* is essentially horizontal (linear).

Four-part ("block") harmony, such as that shown in example 12D, might possibly be thought of as *polyphonic* as well as *homophonic,* since it can be performed with separate voices singing each of the four pitches of each chord. Generally speaking, however, *polyphony* generally implies more rhythmic independence among the various voice parts.

Eighteenth-century counterpoint: Invention No. 8 (Johann Sebastian Bach, 1685–1750)

The entire piece is included in the Workbook, Score #2, and on the CD.

See Workbook, Scores #4, 5, 6, 11, 12, and 14 for examples of texture.

Summary Texture, as an organizational element of music, results from an interaction between melody (or melodies) and harmony. *Monophonic* texture, consisting of a single, unaccompanied line of music, is the least complex of all possible textures. For much of the history of music (and still in many non-Western cultures today) texture was monophonic. *Homophonic* textures are those in which the melody is supported by a chordal accompaniment, vertically aligned to the melody and moving in basically the same rhythm. *Polyphonic* or *contrapuntal* textures result when two or more equally important melodies are heard simultaneously. (Review footnote 2.)

Musical textures, whether polyphonic/contrapuntal or homophonic, can vary in density, depending upon the number of voices (layers of melody, harmony, and so on). Likewise, but perhaps in a more subtle way, rhythm and timbre can affect texture. The following table summarizes the texture types.

Monophony	Single-line melody, unaccompanied
Homophony	Melody accompanied by chords; vertical emphasis
Polyphony	Melody accompanied by melody; horizontal emphasis
Counterpoint	Melody accompanied by melody; horizontal emphasis

WORKBOOK 12-1 and 12-2 and Aural Skills 12-1 are recommended here.

Chapter Review

Terms/Concepts

1.	Texture	6.	Monophonic
2.	Monophony	7.	Polyphonic
3.	Polyphony	8.	Contrapuntal
4.	Counterpoint	9.	Homophonic
5.	Homophony		

Review Questions

1. Which two types of texture are, in fact, synonymous?

2. What is the subtle distinction between these two synonymous styles of texture?

Aural Skills

Aural Skills Exercises noted throughout the chapter, which require the instructor's assistance, are located in the Instructor's Manual. The following can be done by the student.

1. Listen to all types of music to determine whether each has a thin texture (as will be the case with much folk music, country music, popular songs) or a thick texture (as in much rock, jazz, and the like).

Chapter Drills

1. In the following five arrangements of the first four measures of "Joy to the World," determine the following:

    a. Which type of texture is used?

        Example A: _____

        Example B: _____

        Example C: _____

        Example D: _____

        Example E: _____

b. Starting with the "thinnest," list the five examples in order of density.

(1) _____ (2) _____ (3) _____ (4) _____ (5) _____

EXAMPLE A

EXAMPLE B

EXAMPLE C

EXAMPLE D

EXAMPLE E

Organizational

Element:

Form

Form has always been a basic element of music, just as it is of all the arts. Since music is a temporal art and all information must be stored in the memory until the work is completed, the challenge to the composer is significant.

Some musical forms are extremely complex, but even the most sophisticated structures result from combining the simple, basic formal concepts. It is these fundamental forms that are addressed in the next two chapters.

The very principles of form—wholeness, unity, coherence, logic—all relate to the principles of aesthetics. An understanding of form is important for all participants in a musical performance: the composer, the performer, and the listener.

Principles of Form

13

1. Unity and Variety
2. Contrast and Balance

1 Unity and Variety

*R*ecall from Chapter 2 that *form* refers to the design and structure of music. A basic principle of form in all art is **unity and variety.** Logic and coherence are essential to any type of meaningful communication, and implicit in logic and coherence is a sense of *unity.*

Too many disparate ideas introduced into a story, a painting, a musical composition, or any artwork can confuse the observer. It is natural for human beings to search for patterns and meaning, and being confronted with a multiplicity of ideas can thwart that search, frustrate the understanding, and preclude the desired result: the aesthetic experience.

Just as in a good story, the author presents one theme (or a few related themes) and then develops it, so in good music, the composer should "stick to the topic."

The composer, however, faces a challenge different from that facing other artists. Music is a *temporal* art. It enters the mind through the sense of hearing, *over a period of time.* To experience the musical work in its entirety, and thus to understand the total musical message, the listener must store the information in the memory and then recall it as the work unfolds and concludes.

Composers use *repetition* to facilitate the listener's memorization and recall. However, although the repetition of a musical idea can assist memory and recall, too much exact repetition can be monotonous. No matter how interesting the musical idea, and no matter how interestingly that idea might be presented by the performer, continuous and exact repetition can induce boredom.

To engage the listener's memory, but without tiring it, the composer repeats a musical idea with some variation. This is analogous to what happens when a writer or a speaker says "in other words" and then rephrases the idea. In some ways this rephrasing makes what has been said even clearer, but, more important, it assists in the memorization and recall of the material.

Example 13-A demonstrates this principle. In this simple folk song, the main idea is stated in the first two measures and repeated, with a slight variation, in measures 3–4 and 5–6 (see arrows). Measures 7–8 retain a rhythm very similar to the first six but alter the pitches slightly to bring the piece to a close. The tune is memorable because of the repetition; it is interesting because of the variation.[1]

　　　　　　　　"Tom Dooley" (American folk song)

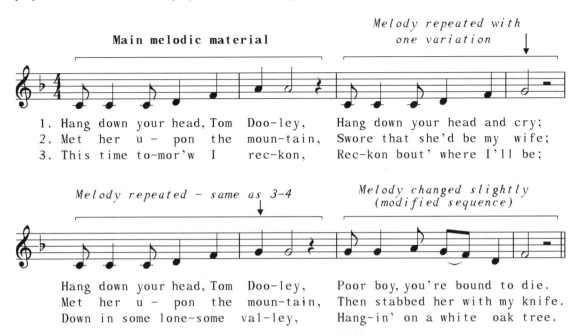

Main melodic material

Melody repeated with one variation

1. Hang down your head, Tom Doo-ley,　Hang down your head and cry;
2. Met her u - pon the moun-tain,　Swore that she'd be my wife;
3. This time to-mor'w I rec-kon,　Rec-kon bout' where I'll be;

Melody repeated – same as 3-4

Melody changed slightly (modified sequence)

Hang down your head, Tom Doo-ley,　Poor boy, you're bound to die.
Met her u - pon the moun-tain,　Then stabbed her with my knife.
Down in some lone-some val-ley,　Hang-in' on a white oak tree.

In Chapters 2 and 8, we discussed rhythmic/melodic motive. It is the principle of unity and variety that is being employed when a motive is imitated with some type of variation (sequence, inversion, and so on).

Unity, then, is the restatement of the musical idea; *variety* is simply a fresh way of restating it. Both are essential in music.

2　Contrast and Balance

Another important principle of form is **contrast and balance.** In a very short piece, such as example 13-A, no contrast material is necessary. The piece is over before we tire of hearing the main idea. In longer musical compositions, however, the introduction of contrasting material can add new interest. This *contrast* generally will serve to enhance the original idea.

In musical analysis, the main melodic idea is often referred to as the *A* theme, the contrasting idea as the *B* theme.[2] The *B* theme should complement *A*, and the two must be kept in *balance* with each other. If *B* is too different from *A*, the listener may hear it as an entirely new piece.

---

[1] Example 13-A also offers an example of *strophic form* in music, that is, two or more verses of text that use the same melodic material.

[2] Some refer to the *A* melody as the *A* theme, the *A* section, or theme 1; to the *B* melody as the *B* theme, the *B* section, or theme 2.

In the next example, "America the Beautiful," the main musical idea is stated in the first four measures. It is repeated immediately, but this time it is varied by having a different ending. The piece continues with four measures of contrasting material (*B* theme), after which the *A* theme is again heard, *and varied once again*—this time appearing at a higher pitch level.

In this short piece, the main musical idea (*A*) is heard three times (unity), but each time it is heard in a slightly different way (variety). The *B* section provides contrast. It is well balanced with *A* and serves to make the return of *A* even more satisfying.

13-B (CD)   **"America the Beautiful" (Samuel A. Ward)**

(A) Melody

O beau- ti- ful for spa-cious skies, For am-ber waves of grain,

(A) Melody varied: different ending (UNITY)

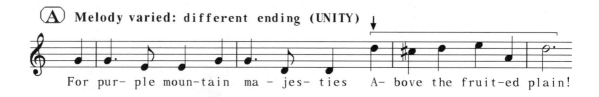

For pur- ple moun-tain ma – jes– ties A- bove the fruit-ed plain!

(B) Melody (CONTRAST)

A - mer- i - ca! A - mer – i - ca! God shed His grace on thee,

(A) Melody varied: higher pitch; different ending (UNITY)

And crown thy good with bro-ther-hood From sea to shin-ing sea!

Summary   Music is a temporal art, unfolding for the listener over a period of time. The ear receives the musical information and the mind stores it until the entire composition has evolved. Only at this point is it possible to experience the work of art as a whole.

By observing the principle of *unity and variety,* the composer assists the listener in remembering and recalling the musical information. The *contrasting* material, *balanced* with the main idea, serves to make the restatement of the original material more interesting and the whole work more memorable.

Only when one remembers and grasps the musical work in its totality can the full aesthetic experience be achieved.

Form

14

1 Introduction

*F*orm refers to the structure of a musical composition. It embodies all the other elements of music (melody, rhythm, harmony, and so on) and is, itself, determined by them. Every composition, regardless of length, has a structure that results from the interaction of all its elements and from the relationship of all its parts. In this respect, *form* is equivalent to *organization*.

It is the logical interactions and the logical relationships that enable the musical work to unfold in a coherent manner for the listener. Form enables the listener to recognize a beginning, a middle, and an end and to comprehend the musical work of art in its entirety.

Some forms are simple and easily grasped; others are more complex. In most cases, however, complex forms (called *compound forms* and sometimes referred to as *extended forms*) are merely combinations of simpler forms.[1] The simple forms, traditionally used in the music of the Western world, are the focus of this chapter. These are

The phrase

The period

The double period

Two-part song form (binary)

Three-part song form (ternary)

Rounded binary form

[1] Compound forms, such as sonata-allegro, rondo, and variation, are beyond the scope of this text.

2 Phrase

A musical **phrase** is comparable to a clause in a linguistic sentence. It is the smallest musical form.[2] Although phrase lengths vary, the standard or classic phrase is four measures. Three four-measure musical phrases are shown in the next three examples.

14-A (CD)   **"Aura Lee" (George Poulton)**

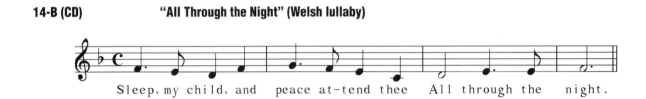

As the black-bird in the spring 'Neath the wil-low   tree.

14-B (CD)   **"All Through the Night" (Welsh lullaby)**

Sleep, my child, and   peace at-tend thee   All through the   night.

14-C (CD)   **"Drink to Me Only with Thine Eyes" (Old English Air)**

Drink to me   on-ly   with thine eyes and   I   will pledge with mine.

Although the four-measure phrase is standard, longer or shorter phrases are not uncommon. The following examples show phrases with three, five, and six measures, respectively.

Note: The curved line over the notes in examples 14-D, 14-E, and 14-F are called *slurs*. Slurs indicate that the pitches included under the slur are *to be played as a unit, that is, as a connected group.* Where there is no text to designate specific groupings, the slur serves to tell the performer how to articulate the music.

Note: Examples 14-D and 14-E each start with an upbeat; the first measure begins with the first full measure, that is, the first measure that contains beat 1, the downbeat.

14-D (CD)   **Three-measure musical phrase, by Béla Bartók**

---

[2] Some refer to the motive as the shortest musical form. Here we are considering it as a structural component of a phrase (a type of building block used to create phrases, periods, and so on).

14-E (CD)   **Five-measure phrase, by Johannes Brahms**

14-F (CD)   **Six-measure phrase: "America" (Henry Carey)**

3 Period

A **period** is a pair of consecutive and interdependent phrases, joined together to make a musical sentence. The second phrase ends with more finality than the first, bringing the musical idea to conclusion. (Occasionally, three and even four phrases are combined to create a longer and more complex musical sentence.)

The composer organizes the pitches within each phrase in such a way as to enable the listener to sense the "punctuation." At the end of the first phrase, we feel a slight pause, similar to a comma; at the end of the second phrase, we hear a final closure, like a period at the end of a sentence. (These musical punctuations are called *cadences,* a concept that will be addressed shortly.)

The first phrase is sometimes referred to as the *antecedent* phrase and the second as the *consequent* phrase.

Antecedent Phrase   Consequent Phrase

Notice that in example 14-G, the second phrase is simply a repetition of the first but with a different ending, giving a sense of completion.

14-G (CD)   **Two-phrase musical period: "Ode to Joy" from Symphony No. 9 (Ludwig van Beethoven)**

Antecedent Phrase   Consequent Phrase

In a three-phrase period, the listener feels the equivalent of a comma after each of the first two phrases, and then a period at the end of the third phrase.

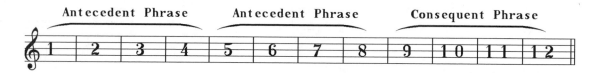

14-H is an example of a three-phrase period in which phrase 2 is a slightly varied repetition of the first phrase, but phrase 3 is different and serves to bring the musical sentence to a close.

14-H (CD)   **Three-phrase musical period: "I Want to Hold Your Hand"**
(Words & Music by John Lennon and Paul McCartney)

PHRASE 1

PHRASE 2

PHRASE 3

Parallel and Contrasting Periods

There are two types of musical periods: the *parallel* period and the *contrasting* period.

Parallel Period   If the second phrase repeats the first phrase exactly (or with some slight variation, or with a different ending), it is a **parallel period.** The theme from Beethoven's "Ode to Joy," shown in example 14-G, is a good example of a parallel period. Two other examples of parallel periods are shown in 14-I and 14-J.

14-I (CD)   **Parallel period: "Oh! Susanna" (Stephen Foster)**

This is only the first period of this song.

PHRASE 1

I _____ come from Al – la- ba – ma with my ban-jo on my knee, I'm

PHRASE 2

goin' to Loui-si- an – a   My _____ true love for to   see.

14-J (CD)   **Parallel period: "He's Got the Whole World in His Hands" (spiritual)**

PHRASE 1

He's got the whole world   in His hands, He's got the whole world in His hands

PHRASE 2

He's got the whole world   in His hands, He's got the whole world in His   hands.

Contrasting period   If phrases 1 and 2 are different, they constitute a **contrasting period,** as shown in the next two examples.

14-K (CD)   **Contrasting period: "When the Saints Go Marching In" (traditional)**

PHRASE 1

Oh, when the saints _____ go marching in, _____Oh, when the saints go marching

PHRASE 2

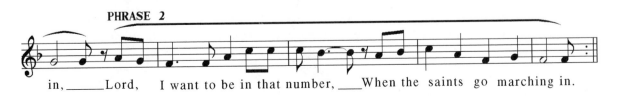

in, _____Lord,   I want to be in that number, ___When the saints go marching in.

PHRASE 1

Are   you   sleep-ing,   Are   you   sleep-ing,   Broth-er   John,   Broth-er   John?

PHRASE 2

Morning bells are ringing,   Morning bells are ringing,   Ding, Ding, Dong,   Ding, Ding, Dong.

Entire compositions consist of an accumulation of musical sentences. The principles of form discussed in Chapter 13 are significant here. The composer combines musical sentences in such a way as to make the overall composition cohesive, coherent, and comprehensible to the listener.

At this point, we will interrupt our study of form to discuss ways in which the composer can designate phrase endings (the musical punctuations we mentioned a little earlier), known as *cadences*.

4 Cadences

A **cadence** is a pause or the "close" of a musical sentence. We have been comparing the written or spoken sentence (which uses words to communicate meaning) with what happens in music. In music, we combine tones into phrases and phrases into periods to communicate musical ideas. The composer (like the writer) must specify where the pauses are and where the end is. The cadence is to music what the comma and the period are to the written or spoken word.

Composers have made use of various techniques to alert the listener to pauses and closures. Certain rhythmic, melodic, and harmonic organizations are conventional signposts for specifying the formal structure of a musical composition. We will examine a few of these conventions in the next section.

Closure can be weak (usually at the end of the first phrase of a musical period) or strong (as is often the case at the end of the period). Frequently, strongest closure is reserved for the end of an entire piece or the end of a major section of the piece. The three most commonly used cadences—the half cadence (semicadence), the authentic cadence, and the plagal cadence—are shown in example 14-M.

14-M   **Three types of cadences (shown in C major and c minor)**

1. Half (semi): Relatively weak; uses dominant harmony

C: V   c: V

2. Authentic: Strong; uses dominant proceeding to tonic harmony

C : V   I   c: V   i

3. Plagal: Strong; uses subdominant proceeding to tonic harmony

C: IV   I   c: iv   i

   The **half cadence** (semicadence) generally is used to indicate the pause at the end of the first phrase in a two-phrase period (and at the end of phrases 1 and 2 in a three-phrase period). It is occasionally used at the end of a period if the composer's goal is to propel the listener into the next period with a certain sense of expectation.

   The **authentic** and **plagal** cadences are strong and more final closures. (Some feel the authentic is even stronger than the plagal.) These two types are generally reserved for marking the end of a musical period. They convey a feeling of finality that cannot be expressed by the half cadence.

   Even in authentic and plagal cadences, some arrangements of the pitches (*voicings*) can express closure much more convincingly than others.

   The strongest closures are indicated by the *perfect* authentic cadence and the *perfect* plagal cadence. The weaker versions of these are called *imperfect* authentic and *imperfect* plagal cadences. The following summarizes this information.

Perfect Authentic Cadence [abbrev. PAC] = V to I

Perfect Plagal Cadence [abbrev. PPC] = IV to I

   (a) Both chords must be in root position.

   (b) The tonic must be on the top and bottom in the I chord.

Imperfect Authentic [IAC] or Imperfect Plagal Cadence [IPC]

   (a) Either (a) or (b) above is not adhered to.

Other types of cadences exist (as well as other techniques for defining closure), but they are beyond the scope of this text. With this information about cadences, we can now resume our study of form.

WORKBOOK 14-1 and 14-2 are suggested here.

5   Double Period

To compose a piece longer than a single period, we can combine two periods, thus creating a **double period**. In the double period, strong closure is reserved for the end of the final phrase.

Parallel Double Period   If the second period is the same as the first (or with some slight variation), it is a **parallel double period**.

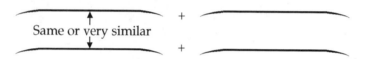

Contrasting Double Period   If period 1 and period 2 are different, they constitute a **contrasting double period**.

"Flow Gently, Sweet Afton" (example 14-N) is an example of a parallel double period; "When Johnny Comes Marching Home Again" (example 14-O) is a contrasting double period. Below each piece, a diagram is provided that shows the division of the piece into phrases and periods.

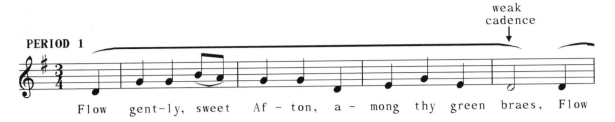

PERIOD 1

Flow gent-ly, sweet Af - ton, a - mong thy green braes, Flow

weak cadence

gent - ly, I'll sing thee a song in thy praise; My

weak cadence

PERIOD 2

Ma - ry's a - sleep by thy mur - mur - ing stream, Flow

weak cadence

gent - ly, sweet Af - ton, dis - turb not her dream.

STRONG CADENCE

ANALYSIS:

Period 1
⌒‾‾‾‾‾‾‾ + ‾‾‾‾‾‾‾⌒ = Contrasting Period

Period 2
⌒‾‾‾‾‾‾‾ + ‾‾‾‾‾‾‾⌒ = Contrasting Period

= PARALLEL DOUBLE PERIOD

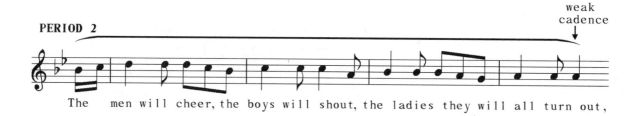

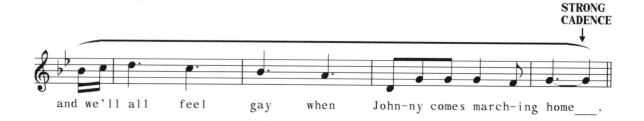

WORKBOOK 14-3 and 14-4 are suggested here.

6   Two-Part Song Form (Binary)

The **two-part song form** (also referred to as **binary** form) consists of two contrasting but related sections. Usually, each of the two sections contains a different melody, each complementing the other. Distinct closure (clear and strong cadence) at the end of each section is essential to the form.[3]

The two-part song form is one of the most commonly used musical forms. Because the two sections contain contrasting melodies, they are often referred to as the *A* and *B* sections, and the form is often called, simply, the *AB* form.[4]

Each section (*A* and *B*) can be a simple phrase (as in the case of the "blues") or a complete period or double period. The question then arises, How can we distinguish between a contrasting double period and a two-part song form? The distinction is based essentially on two things:

1.   The type of material used in each section

2.   The type of cadence that is heard at the end of the first section

In a two-part song form, the second section usually will possess a more marked individuality than will the second period in a contrasting double period. Likewise, the cadence at the end of period 1 in binary form generally will convey a sense of closure and completeness, thus making each of the two sections capable of standing alone. The following diagrams demonstrate these distinguishing features.

---

[3] Binary form frequently involves a key change between the two parts, but there are sufficient examples without a key change to justify excluding this aspect as essential to the form.

[4] In songs with a text, the *B* section is often repeated with the same text. This section is then referred to as the *chorus* or the *refrain*. See Workbook, Score #16, "Time in a Bottle."

TWO-PART SONG FORM (BINARY)

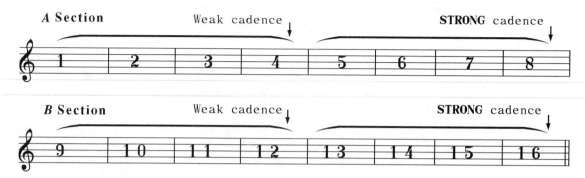

CONTRASTING DOUBLE PERIOD

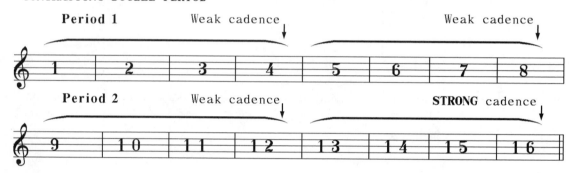

"Yankee Doodle," shown in example 14-Q, is in binary form. Note how each section (*A* and *B*) concludes with a strong cadence. Although each section could stand alone, complete in itself, in fact, each serves to provide contrast for the other.

Binary form: "Yankee Doodle" (American)

A Section

Weak cadence ↓

Fath'r and I went down to camp a- long with Cap-tain Good-in, And

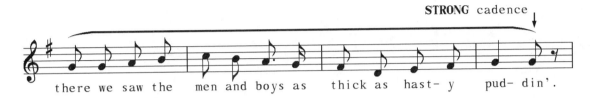

STRONG cadence ↓

there we saw the men and boys as thick as hast- y pud- din'.

B Section

Weak cadence ↓

Yan- kee Doo-dle, keep it up, Yan- kee Doo- dle Dan - dy,

STRONG cadence ↓

Mind the mu – sic and the step, and with the girls be han- dy.

WORKBOOK 14-5 is suggested here.

7 Three-Part Song Form (Ternary)

A **three-part song form,** often called **ternary** form, can be labeled *ABA.* Many consider this to be the most satisfying of all forms. Since music unfolds in time and calls on the memory to store information until the work is completed, composers have devised various techniques to aid recall.

One of the most common of such devices is restatement of a musical idea. A distinctive feature of ternary form is *statement, digression, restatement.* In ternary form, the first musical statement (*A*) is followed by a contrasting statement (*B*), and then *A* is restated.

Section A	Section B	Section A
Statement	Digression	Restatement

This can be an extremely satisfying solution to the challenge of achieving both unity and variety in musical form.

Usually, each section concludes with a strong cadence. (Occasionally, however, the strongest closure is reserved until the final cadence of the composition.) See example 14-R for an example of ternary form.

14-R (CD)   **Ternary form: Ecossaise (Ludwig van Beethoven)**

The two- and three-part song forms (*AB* and *ABA*) constitute the two most commonly used forms for popular songs, folk songs, patriotic songs, and hymns, as well as much classical literature. They also are the basis of the extended, or compound, forms that were mentioned earlier in this chapter but that are beyond the scope of this text.

WORKBOOK 14-6 is suggested here.

8 Rounded Binary Form

The last form that we will examine here is **rounded binary form.** It is a sort of combination of binary and ternary. It is binary because it is in two sections. The A section is followed by the B section, but the difference between this and the regular binary form is that here, when the A melody returns, it returns *within the B section.*

In this form, A is often heard twice before B begins, and B and A frequently repeat as a self-contained second section. The overall result is diagrammed below, and an example is shown in example 14-S.

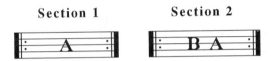

Note: It is not essential that the A section repeat.

14-S (CD)   **Rounded binary form: "Ode to Joy" (Beethoven)**

A Section

B Section

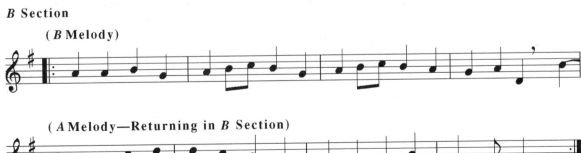

WORKBOOK 14-7 through 14-10 and Aural Skills 14-1 are suggested here.

Summary In this chapter, we have studied the basic simple forms used by composers for many centuries. We have noted how shorter forms (*phrases* and *periods*) can be combined to create larger forms, such as *double periods, two- and three-part song forms,* and *rounded binary form.* We have seen how *cadences* (various types) define form for the listener, making it possible to grasp the music's content and meaning.

Arnold Schoenberg once commented that "without organization, music would be an amorphous mass, as unintelligible as an essay without punctuation, or as a conversation which leaps from one subject to another." The techniques presented in the chapter are some of the ways in which composers provide organization that is recognizable to the listener.

The following table provides a summary of the cadences studied in this chapter.

Half	Dominant harmony (V)
Perfect authentic (PAC)	Dominant (V) to tonic (I) (Condition: Both chords in root position; tonic highest note of tonic chord)
Imperfect authentic (IAC)	Dominant (V) to tonic (I) (Any above condition absent)
Perfect plagal (PPC)	Subdominant (IV) to tonic (Conditions same as PAC)
Imperfect plagal (IPC)	Subdominant (IV) to tonic (Any above condition absent)

The following table provides a summary of the forms studied in this chapter.

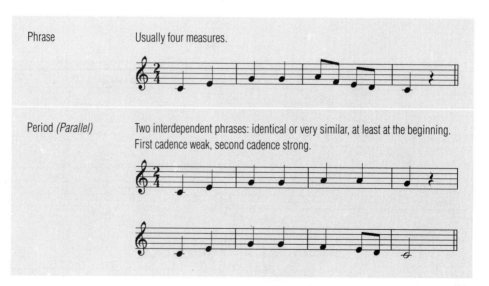

Phrase	Usually four measures.
Period *(Parallel)*	Two interdependent phrases: identical or very similar, at least at the beginning. First cadence weak, second cadence strong.

Period *(Contrasting)*   Two interdependent phrases: different but complementary. First cadence weak, second cadence strong.

Double period
(Parallel)   Two interdependent periods: each the same or very similar, at least at the beginning. Final cadence strong, all other cadences weak.

Double Period
(Contrasting)   Two interdependent periods: different but complementary. Final cadence strong, all others weak.

Two-Part Song Form
(Binary) (AB)

Two distinct, but complementary, sections or parts: each ending with strong cadence, each capable of standing alone.

Three-Part Song Form
(Ternary) (ABA)

Three distinct sections: *AB* followed by a restatement of *A;* each section usually ending with a strong cadence.

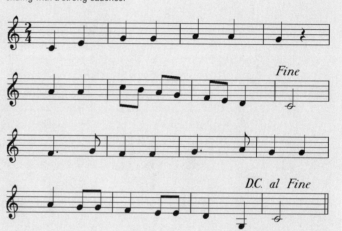

Rounded Binary

Two distinct sections: each usually ending with a strong cadence; differs from two-part (binary) form in that "*A*" returns but now as a part of the "*B*" section.

Chapter Review

Terms/Concepts

1. Phrase
2. Period
3. Parallel period
4. Contrasting period
5. Double period
6. Parallel double period
7. Contrasting double period

8. Two-part song form (Binary)
9. Three-part song form (Ternary)
10. Rounded binary form
11. Cadence
12. Half cadence
13. Authentic cadence
14. Plagal cadence

Review Questions

1. How can a composer indicate *closure*, and why is this information helpful to the listener?

2. What is the difference between a *contrasting double period* and *binary form*?

3. What is the difference between *binary form, ternary form,* and *rounded binary form*?

Aural Skills

1. As you listen to various types of music, see if you can discern the structure of the music. Note where the cadences are. Does the melody (melodies) repeat? Is the repetition exact, or varied in some way? Is there a contrasting melody? and so on.

Chapter Drills

1. Analyze the following musical examples for the form. Diagram your phrase, period, and overall formal analysis as shown in this chapter.

EXAMPLE A: _____

EXAMPLE B: _____

EXAMPLE C: _____

EXAMPLE D: _____

EXAMPLE E: _____

Organizational

Element:

Timbre

*E*arlier we remarked that composers have complete freedom to choose whichever sounds they wish. But composers have always been somewhat restricted by the available musical instruments. Likewise, they have been limited by the confines of human hearing: pitch range and audible/endurable volume.

With the exception of the piano (ca. 1750) and saxophones (nineteenth century), very few instruments have been successfully added since the eighteenth century. Because of the enormous developments in technology, however, the twentieth century has seen the birth of a myriad of musical instruments and new techniques and devices for creating, controlling, manipulating, and storing sound.

Vast changes in timbre have been made possible by innovations in technology such as the phonograph and the computer. In electronic music, we can see one of the directions music will probably take in the future. All these musical ventures call for new symbols, new theories, and revised aesthetics.

The following chapter details some of the basic concepts of timbre as it relates to acoustical and to electronic instruments.

Timbre: Acoustic and Electronic

15

1 Introduction

*T*imbre (along with pitch, intensity, and duration) is a fundamental *property of sound.* Therefore, before we begin our study of timbre as an *organizing element* in music composition, we will talk briefly about the nature of sound itself and its four basic properties.

This will be followed by an examination of some ways in which timbre can be manipulated in the organization of sound into music. We also will compare two broad types of timbre: acoustic and electronic.

More detailed information on the topics contained in this chapter can be found in Appendix F (harmonic series), in Appendix G (sections of acoustical instruments), and in Appendix H (electronic equipment for sound producing, sound processing, sound controlling, and sound storage used in the composition of electronic music).

2 Properties of Sound

In Chapter 1, we defined **sound** as *the sensation received by the ear and perceived by the mind when air has been set in motion by a vibrating object.* Each of the properties of sound affects the other three. Each property can be prescribed by the composer and then interpreted and controlled (within certain limitations) by the performer.

Pitch

A vibrating object sets air in motion, somewhat analogous to waves that result when an object hits a body of water. We actually refer to these movements of the air as **sound waves.**

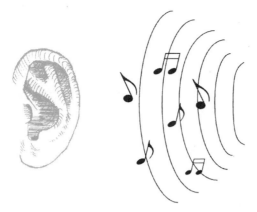

The number of sound waves reaching our ear in each second is referred to as the **frequency** of the sound. The frequency (number of **vibrations** per second) determines **pitch.** The higher the number of vibrations, the higher the pitch; the lower the number of vibrations, the lower the pitch.

15-B   Frequency

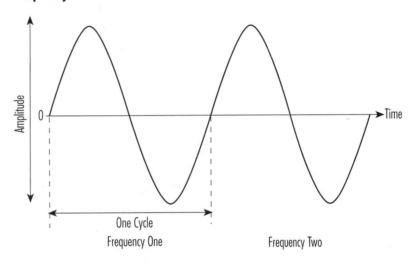

The frequency of vibrations is dependent upon the *size* of the vibrating object. Larger objects vibrate more slowly than smaller objects, thus producing fewer vibrations per second and, consequently, relatively lower pitches. Likewise, smaller objects vibrate faster and produce relatively higher pitches.

Note: The range of frequencies that a human being can actually hear is between 20 and 20,000 vibrations per second. Any pitches resulting from vibrations above or below this range generally cannot be heard by human beings.[1]

---

[1] This is the minimum and maximum frequency range for human beings. Audibility within this range varies with individuals. Frequencies above the human audible range are called *ultrasonic;* frequencies below this range are called *subsonic.*

Intensity

Intensity refers to the subjective impression of the loudness or softness of a sound that *results from the amount of energy causing the vibrations.* The *dynamics* of a sound (sometimes referred to as its *volume*) can also be demonstrated by the sound wave (where it is referred to as *amplitude*).

The unit of measure used for loudness is the **decibel.** The normal decibel range for human beings (from the softest sound we can hear until we arrive at the threshold of pain) is designated as *0 to 126 decibels.*

Duration

The **duration** of a sound is the length of time the frequencies continue. It is *a composite (with respect to time) from its onset (attack) until it subsides and is no longer audible.* Obviously, the duration of a sound is affected by many things, such as the type of attack, the amount of energy involved, and the type of vibrating object.

15-C

Duration and amplitude

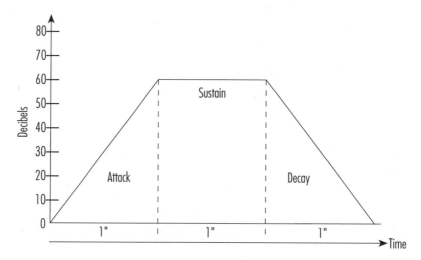

Timbre

In Chapter 2, we defined **timbre** as *the unique quality of a sound* (sometimes referred to as tone color or tone quality). We pointed out that each musical instrument and each person's voice has its own unique timbre. This uniqueness results from two primary components: the overall *spectrum* of the sound, and the *envelope* of the sound.

Spectrum When an object vibrates (a guitar string, for example), it vibrates not only as a whole but also in its various parts: in halves, thirds, quarters, and so on. Example 15-D shows a graphic of a vibrating string.

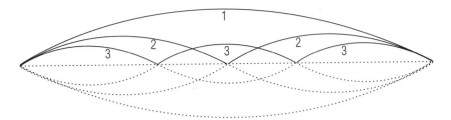

The string vibrating as a whole produces a frequency known as a **fundamental.** This is the most audible frequency, and it determines the perceived pitch. The fundamental and the other vibrating segments are called **partials.** Each partial has its own individual frequency (and amplitude), referred to as the fundamental's **overtones** and **harmonics.**

The fundamental and the overtones and harmonics collectively constitute the total harmonic content of the sound, or the **spectrum.** The spectrum of the sound assists us in differentiating between various timbres: a familiar voice, a specific instrument, and so on.[2]

Envelope   The timbre of any sound is dependent not only upon its spectrum but also upon its overall **envelope.** Every sound has an **attack** (onset of the sound), **internal dynamics** (time during which the sound is fully audible), and **decay** (cessation of the sound). These features (which vary with each sound source) are known as the sound's *envelope.*[3]

15-E   **Envelope of a sound**

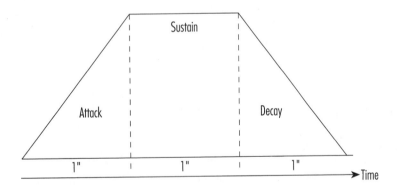

[2] Another factor determining timbre is the sound's *formant*—that is, those particular frequencies in a particular sound that resonate more notably than the other component frequencies.

[3] In addition to the overall envelope, each partial has its own *individual envelope,* which contributes to the timbral character of the sound.

Different instruments have different envelopes; that is, they have different types of attack, internal dynamics, and decay.[4]

3 Acoustic Timbre

Since ancient times, composers have chosen their timbres from human voices and from categories of instruments known as *idiophones, aerophones, membranophones,* and *chordophones.*

Idiophones: Instruments that are struck, scraped, shaken, or plucked (sticks, rattles, triangles, gongs, bells, cymbals, maracas, guiro, jew's harp, and so on)

Aerophones: Wind instruments or instruments that are blown into (flutes, horns, and so on)

Membranophones: Stretched skin instruments that are beaten (all types of drums)

Chordophones: Stringed instruments that are plucked or bowed (kitharas, lutes, harps, violins, guitars, and so on)

Instruments in these categories have been refined and perfected over thousands of years. They exist today in the *families* of conventional instruments, known as **percussion, woodwinds, brass, and strings.**

Sound produced by instruments from the categories just listed is known as *acoustic sound,* that is, sound that is not altered in any way by electronic devices. Until the twentieth century, these have been the standard timbres available to composers. (See Appendix G.)

With the development of electronics in the twentieth century, many new timbres have been discovered and are used to create new sounds in music.

4 Electronic Timbre

Electronic music is a notable innovation of the twentieth century, and timbre is a notable characteristic of electronic music.[5] Through electronically produced and electronically altered sounds (as well as through computer-generated and digitally controlled sound), we now can

1. Expand dynamic and pitch range beyond that of conventional instruments

2. Divide the octave into much smaller units *(microtones)* than the traditional twelve equal half steps of Western music

---

[4] Do not confuse this with ADSR, which is a symbolic terminology for *attack, decay, sustain, release,* associated with the manipulation of the synthesizer keyboard.

[5] Some distinguish between *musique concrète* (naturally acoustic sounds that are electronically altered in some way) and *electronic music* (sounds that are electronically produced).

3. Increase the speed (tempo) beyond what is humanly playable

4. Control the two primary components of timbre—*spectrum* and *envelope*—so as to create brand new timbres

Before the 1950s, music instruments were bowed, blown into, plucked, or struck. The development of a whole new family of electronic instruments has added new ways of producing sound: We plug into an electric current, turn knobs, and use oscillators, tape recorders, computers, signal processors, and so on.[6]

Timbres in the twentieth century have been spectacularly altered. Before the electronic era, only certain pitch ranges, spectra, and envelopes were possible. This was due to the limitations of the design of musical instruments, which, in turn, was dictated by the physical limitations of human beings (number of fingers, length of the arms, maximum potential velocity of human performance, and so on).

More than ever before, the electronic musician is in control of each of the properties of sound. All these controls are made more accessible and manageable with the synthesizer, the computer, and MIDI (an acronym for Musical Instrument Digital Interface). MIDI enables us to link various electronic components, thus enhancing the versatility of computers.

Electronics has had an impact on acoustic music as well. Most of the music we hear today is transmitted through electronic recording devices and through sound waves that reach our ears as the result of amplifiers and transducers such as earphones and loudspeakers.

Summary   In this chapter, we talked about the physical aspect of sound as exhibited through its fundamental properties (*pitch, intensity, duration,* and *timbre*). We saw that timbre results from two interacting components: the sound's *spectrum* (its complete harmonic content) and the sound's *envelope* (its complete time content). We also distinguished between two broad types of timbre: *acoustic* and *electronic*.

[6] Composers now have access to several algorithmic computer programs, sequencer programs, and notation programs. Some recent algorithmic programs on the market include *Serious Composer*, by Wayne Kirby; *M*, by Dr. T and Voyetra; and *MAX*, by Opcode.

Some sequencer programs include *Performer*, by Mark of the Unicorn; *Sequencer Plus*, by Voyetra; and *Cakewalk*, by Cakewalk.

Notation programs include *Finale*, by Wenger; *Music Printer Plus*, by Temporal Acuity Products; and *Personal Composer*, by Jim Miller.

The following table summarizes the main facts of this chapter.

Properties of Sound	
Pitch	Determined by *frequency* of vibrations; perceived as relative *highness or lowness* of sound.
Intensity	Determined by the amount of energy causing the vibrations; perceived as the relative *loudness or softness* of sound.
Duration	Determined by type of attack, energy, type of vibrating object; perceived as relative *length*.
Timbre	Determined by spectrum and envelope; perceived as unique *tone color or quality*.

Components of Timbre	
Spectrum	The total *harmonic content:* dependent upon all vibrating segments.
Envelope	The *audible content:* attack, continuum (internal dynamics), decay.

Types of Timbre	
Acoustic	Any sound unaltered by any electrical or electronic devices/controls.
Electronic	Any sound produced or altered by any *electric or electronic* means.

Chapter Review

Terms/Concepts

1. Sound
2. Pitch
3. Frequency
4. Sound waves
5. Vibrations
6. Intensity
7. Decibel
8. Duration
9. Timbre
10. Spectrum
11. Fundamental
12. Partials
13. Overtones
14. Harmonics
15. Envelope
16. Attack
17. Internal dynamics
18. Decay
19. Idiophones
20. Aerophones
21. Chordophones
22. Membranophones
23. Strings
24. Woodwinds
25. Brass
26. Percussion

Review Questions

1. What are the four fundamental *properties of sound*?

2. What is meant by each of the four properties?

3. What determines each of these properties?

4. Explain what is meant by each of the *two components* of timbre?

5. Name four categories of acoustic instruments.

6. What are the conventional *families* of acoustic instruments?

7. What is the difference between *acoustic* and *electronic sound*?

Aural Skills

When listening to music, try to differentiate between various timbres:

1. *Families* of instruments: strings, woodwinds, percussion, brass

2. Various instruments within each of these families of instruments

3. Acoustic timbres and electronically altered or electronically produced timbres

Part Two

RHYTHM

PRELUDE TO SECTION G

Organizational

Element:

Rhythm

In Chapter 1, we noted that music's two basic components are *sound* and *time*. Rhythm has to do with the time component of music—the durational property of sound—and is an essential element of music. Just as melody provides the rise and fall of pitches, rhythm serves to propel those pitches forward in time.

Rhythm is a natural phenomenon in our physical lives as well as in nature (heartbeat, pulse, inhaling/exhaling, sleeping/waking, living/dying, day/night, the seasons, and so on). Rhythm is also an important facet of language. Words and sentences have rhythm, with certain accents and inflections. Often we can recognize music as a particular style or as coming from a specific culture or era precisely because of the rhythm—for example, certain ethnic folk music, Medieval liturgical chants, Renaissance polyphonic chansons or motets, jazz, rock, and the ametric music of twentieth-century art music.

In the seven units of Part Two, we will study many of the basic concepts, techniques, and practices common to rhythm in Western music.

Before proceeding to these units, you might find it helpful to review rhythmic notation in Chapter 4.

Rhythm Unit

1.	Rhythm	5.	Rhythmic Patterns
2.	Beat	6.	Counting Method
3.	Meter	7.	Simple Meter
4.	Meter Signature	8.	Common Time and Cut Time

For this Unit, review in Chapter 4:

1.	Note values	5.	Meter
2.	Beams and flags	6.	Accents
3.	Dotted notes	7.	Bar lines
4.	Measures	8.	Double bar lines

1 Rhythm

*R*hythm has to do with the *temporal* (time) aspect of music—the *durational* aspect of sound. It is a general term that connotes the movement of music in time. Our sense of rhythm results from patterns or arrangements of sounds (regular and irregular, accented and unaccented, long and short) usually presented over a fundamental temporal unit called the beat.

2 Beat

The **beat** is the underlying and regularly recurring pulse of a composition. The beat assists us in sensing musical time. It is the beat we are feeling when we tap our foot or clap to music. Beats can be felt as *up-and-down* motion (depicted by the conductor's hand movements) and are actually referred to as *upbeats* and *downbeats*. (See Appendix D for conducting patterns.)

Rhythms are superimposed on the musical beat. To some degree, the beat regulates the rhythm, but it does not control it completely. The beat can be quite simple, whereas the rhythm might be very complex.

3   Meter

Beats are generally arranged in groups of twos, threes, or fours, with a regularly recurring accent on beat 1.

Twos: ONE two, ONE two, ONE two, ONE two

Threes: ONE two three, ONE two three, ONE two three, ONE two three

Fours: ONE two three four, ONE two three four, ONE two three four

These groupings constitute what is known as the **meter** of the composition. Meter is the basic scheme of durational values and accents that remain constant throughout the composition. The patterns of regularly recurring beats are analogous to (and have their origin in) poetic meters, which consist of regularly recurring accented and unaccented syllables.[1] Note, for instance, in example RHY-A that the accent falls on every *third* syllable and we feel a pattern of triple meter.

RHY-A   ***Some**body **cer**tainly **fum**bled the **ball**.*

4   Meter Signature

In Chapter 4, we pointed out that a **meter signature** (also called a *time signature*) is a symbol placed at the beginning of a composition to indicate the type of groupings (meter) and the unit of the beat. A meter signature consists of two numbers, one above the other (for example, $\frac{2}{4}$) and provides the following information.

The upper number indicates the number of beats per measure.

The lower number indicates a note value that gets one beat.

---

[1] It is from poetry (verse) that meter/rhythm is first established. Music was essentially vocal for much of its history. Musicians *sang* poetry, and the meter/rhythm was contained in the words. When music became an abstract art—that is, when it became separated from words—it was natural to simply adapt the poetic meters to instrumental performance.

RHY-B   **Four meters, each showing two beats per measure**

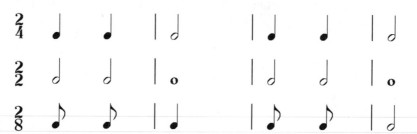

Meter, then, establishes a temporal measurement in music. It facilitates, *but does not dictate,* the establishment of rhythmic patterns. In turn, the rhythmic patterns can reinforce the meter, even though they may at times vary (sometimes considerably) from measure to measure. In example RHY-C, each four measures uses the same meter, but each has a different rhythm.[2]

RHY-C   **Four different rhythms within $\frac{4}{4}$ meter**

(C-1) "Are You Sleeping"

Are   you sleep-ing,   Are   you sleep- ing, Bro-ther John, Bro-ther John

(C-2) "Jingle Bells"

Jin- gle Bells,   Jin- gle   Bells,   Jin- gle all   the   way

(C-3) "Merrily We Roll Along"

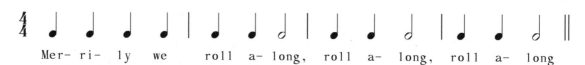

Mer- ri- ly   we   roll a- long, roll a- long, roll a- long

(C-4) "Love Somebody"

Love some- bo- dy, yes   I   do,   Love some- bo- dy, won- der who

---

[2] For an extensive study of these concepts, see *The Time of Music,* by Jonathan D. Kramer (New York: Schirmer Books, 1988).

It should be noted that although rhythm, beats, and meter are dependent upon one another, they are conceptually distinct.[3]

Aural Skills I-1 is recommended here.

5   Rhythmic Patterns

Metered rhythm can have repetitious patterns, fluctuating patterns, or recurring patterns (the last being a compromise between the first two). Example RHY-D shows a *repetitious* pattern. Note that once the pattern is established in measure 1, it never deviates. It is repeated identically in each succeeding measure.

RHY-D   **Repetitious rhythmic pattern**

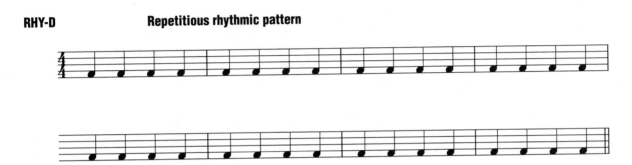

Example RHY-E shows *fluctuating* patterns. Here a pattern never repeats. The rhythm is different in each measure.

RHY-E   **Fluctuating rhythmic patterns**

Generally, rhythms are a combination of repetition and variation. Repetition helps to unify the music, and some variation serves to make it more interesting. Example RHY-F shows a *recurring* rhythmic pattern that is heard four times and that alternates with three different rhythms.

---

[3] The rhythms here are simple, but the student is reminded that there is a virtually infinite number of possible rhythms, some quite complex, that can result from divisions and subdivisions of the beat.

Aural Skills I-2 is recommended here.

6   Counting Method

To ensure an accurate performance of a rhythm, as indicated by the meter and rhythmic notation, we can count the beats as shown in example RHY-G.

RHY-G   **Counting method for $\frac{2}{4}$ $\frac{3}{4}$ $\frac{4}{4}$**

Recall from Chapter 4 that the accent falls on beat 1 in $\frac{2}{4}$ and $\frac{3}{4}$. In $\frac{4}{4}$, there is a primary accent on beat 1 and a secondary accent on beat 3. To assist you in your performance, the accents here have been marked.

Aural Skills I-3 is recommended here.

For each of the following rhythms,

1.   Write the counting under the notes.

2.   Count aloud and clap (emphasize the accented beats).

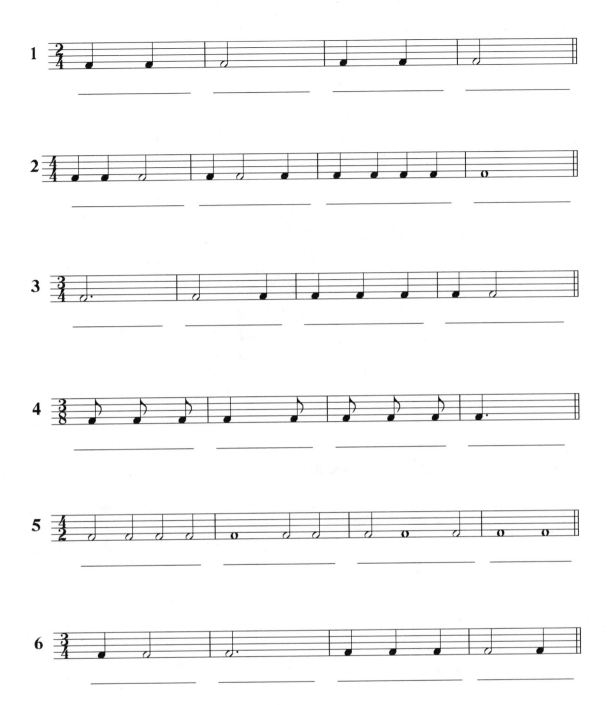

7   Simple Meter

The meters we have been working with are **simple meters,** that is, meters in which the beats divide evenly into halves. (In *compound meters,* which we will study in Unit II, the basic beat divides into thirds.)

The simple meters are shown in RHY-H, along with the note value of the basic beat and the note value that represents half that of the basic beat.

SIMPLE *DUPLE METERS*	SIMPLE *TRIPLE METERS*	SIMPLE *QUADRUPLE METERS*
$\frac{2}{2}$ = 2 / 𝅗𝅥 = 4 / ♩	$\frac{3}{2}$ = 3 / 𝅗𝅥 = 6 / ♩	$\frac{4}{2}$ = 4 / 𝅗𝅥 = 8 / ♩
$\frac{2}{4}$ = 2 / ♩ = 4 / ♪	$\frac{3}{4}$ = 3 / ♩ = 6 / ♪	$\frac{4}{4}$ = 4 / ♩ = 8 / ♪
$\frac{2}{8}$ = 2 / ♪ = 4 / ♬	$\frac{3}{8}$ = 3 / ♪ = 6 / ♬	$\frac{4}{8}$ = 4 / ♪ = 8 / ♬
$\frac{2}{16}$ = 2 / ♬ = 4 / ♬♬	$\frac{3}{16}$ = 3 / ♬ = 6 / ♬♬	$\frac{4}{16}$ = 4 / ♬ = 8 / ♬♬

Counting is uncomplicated when there is no division of the beat, as is the case with all the examples in RHY-G. However, when a beat is divided in half, or when one beat is lengthened by a **dot** (which increases its value by one-half), another counting device can be used to ensure accuracy of performance. In this case, simply count o*ne and, two and, three and,* and so on, as shown in examples RHY-I and RHY-J.

RHY-I   **Counting simple division of the beat**

RHY-J   **Counting exercises for divided beats in** $\frac{2}{4}$ $\frac{3}{4}$ $\frac{4}{4}$

Count aloud and clap each.

Exercises

For each of the following rhythms,

1. Write the counting under the notes.

2. Count aloud and clap each (emphasize the accented beat).

Exercises 6–8 are well-known tunes that are given here to facilitate your sense of divided beats in three different simple meters.

6 "The Farmer in the Dell" (traditional)

The farm – er in the dell, The farm – er in the dell,

Heigh ho the der – ry oh, The farm – er in the dell.

7 "America" (Henry Carey)

My coun-try, 'tis of thee, Sweet land of lib-er-ty, Of thee I sing;

Land where my fa – thers died, Land of the pil – grim's pride,

From ev – 'ry moun – tain side Let free – dom ring!

8 "Are You Sleeping" (English)

Are you sleep-ing, Are you sleep-ing, Broth-er John, Broth-er John?

Morning bells are ring-ing, Morning bells are ringing, Ding, ding, dong; Ding, ding, dong.

8 Common Time and Cut Time

A large C, meaning **common time,** is frequently used instead of the $\frac{4}{4}$ meter sign. A large C with a vertical line through it, which means **cut time** (*alla breve*), is often used instead of $\frac{2}{2}$. Cut time generally indicates a fast tempo.

Common time and cut time
Count aloud and clap.

"Alouette" (French Canadian)

"Merrily We Roll Along"

Unit Review

Review Questions

1. What is the difference between

   a. Beat and meter?

   b. Repetitious, fluctuating, and recurring rhythms?

   c. Simple and compound meters?

   d. Common time and cut time?

Aural Skills

Aural Skills Exercises noted throughout the unit, which require the instructor's assistance, are located in the Instructor's Manual. The following can be done by the student working alone or with a colleague.

1. Try to write (in musical notation) the rhythm of any simple familiar pieces. Caution: Some popular songs and rock compositions have complex rhythms. Use folk songs or other simple pieces.

2. Listen to as much music as possible to determine whether the rhythmic patterns are repetitious, fluctuating, or recurring.

Rhythm Exercises

The exercises on the following pages serve to reinforce the rhythmic concepts studied in Unit I. For each rhythmic exercise, proceed as follows:

1. Observe the meter.

2. Determine if any beats are divided.

3. Write the counting (and mark the accents if helpful).

4. Count aloud and clap the rhythm.

5. Start at a tempo slow enough to ensure accuracy; then try doing the exercise at a faster tempo.

6. If a metronome is available, use it to help maintain a steady beat and tempo.

7. Decide whether the rhythmic patterns are repetitious, fluctuating, or recurring.

1

2

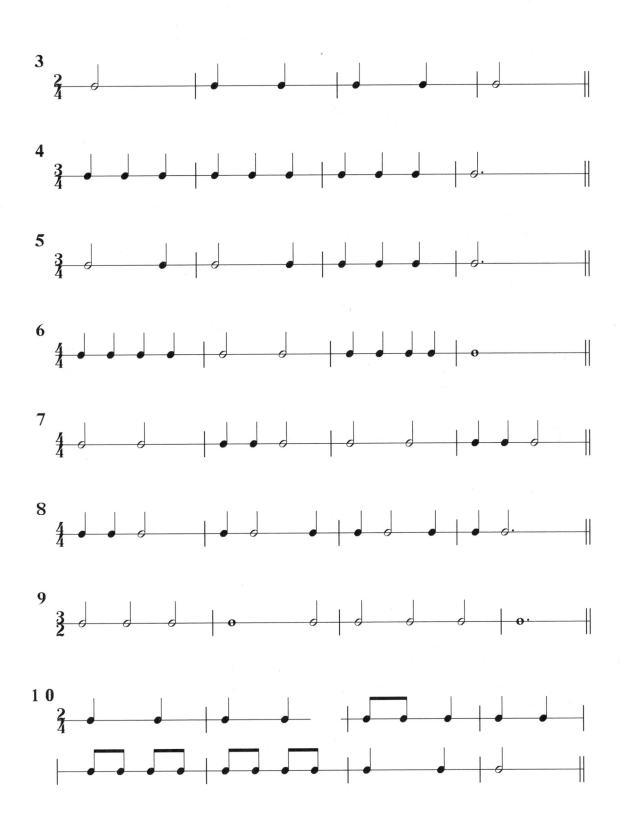

1 1

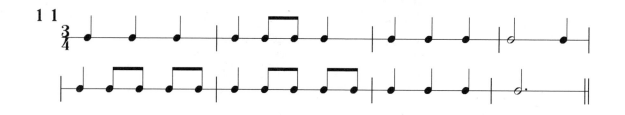

1 2

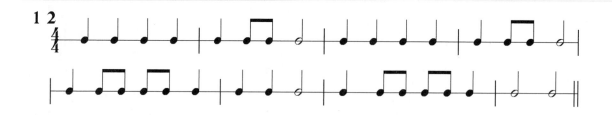

1 3

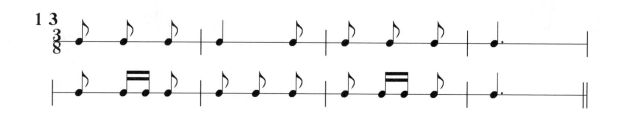

1 4

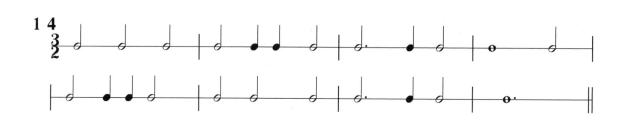

1 5

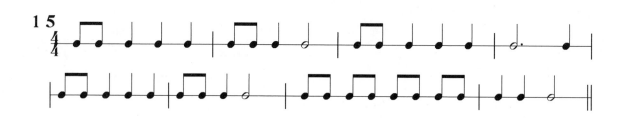

1 6

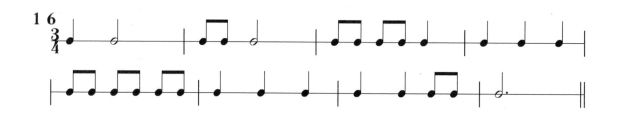

2 3

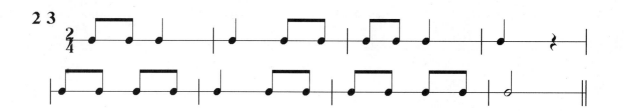

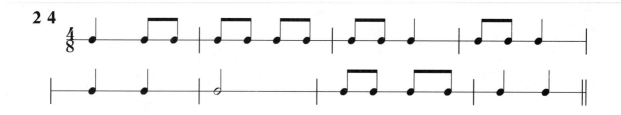

2 4

2 5

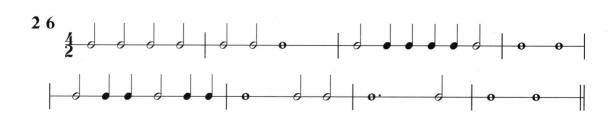

2 6

2 7

234   *Rhythm Unit I*

Direction: Use two hands for the following (RH = top notes; LH = bottom notes).

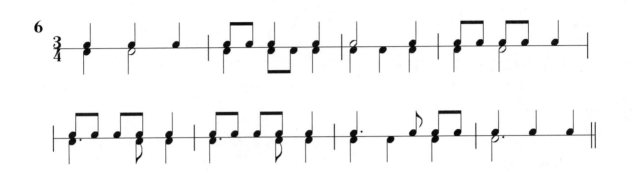

Rhythm Unit

II

1. Compound Meters

For this Unit, review in Chapter 4:

1. Upbeat (anacrusis)
2. Repeat signs
3. Rests
4. Tied notes

1 Compound Meters

Compound meters are simple meters ($\frac{2}{8}$ $\frac{3}{8}$ $\frac{4}{8}$) multiplied by 3. For example,

$$\frac{6}{8} \qquad \frac{9}{8} \qquad \frac{12}{8}$$

Recall that in simple meters, the beat is represented by an undotted note that divides evenly into 2. In compound meters, on the other hand, the basic beat is represented by a dotted note that divides evenly into 3.[1]

Note: It is the *top* number of the meter signature that determines whether the meter is simple or compound.

The compound meters are shown in example RHY-L, along with the note value of the basic beat and the note that represents one-third of the basic beat.

RHY-L   **Compound meter**

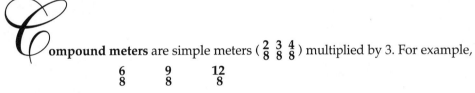

COMPOUND DUPLE METERS	COMPOUND TRIPLE METERS	COMPOUND QUADRUPLE METERS
$\frac{6}{4}$ = 2 / 𝅗𝅥. = 6 / ♩	$\frac{9}{4}$ = 3 / 𝅗𝅥. = 9 / ♩	$\frac{12}{4}$ = 4 / 𝅗𝅥. = 12 / ♩
$\frac{6}{8}$ = 2 / ♩. = 6 / ♪	$\frac{9}{8}$ = 3 / ♩. = 9 / ♪	$\frac{12}{8}$ = 4 / ♩. = 12 / ♪
$\frac{6}{16}$ = 2 / ♪. = 6 / ♬	$\frac{9}{16}$ = 3 / ♪. = 9 / ♬	$\frac{12}{16}$ = 4 / ♪. = 12 / ♬

---

[1] After the initial division, however, there is even division.

Example RHY-M shows a comparison of simple and compound meters.

RHY-M **Simple meter and compound meter**

In compound meters, each of the three divisions of the beat can subdivide. To ensure accuracy of the rhythm in such cases, we can count *one and, two and, three and,* and so on, as shown in example RHY-N.

RHY-N **Counting in compound meter**

Example RHY-O contains examples of pieces in compound meters.

RHY-O

"Vive l'amour" (college song)

Let ev- 'ry good fellow now fill up his glass, Vi- ve la com-pag- nie,   And

drink to the health of our glo-ri-ous class,   Vi- ve la com - pag- nie.

Vi-ve la, vi-ve la, vi-ve l'a-mour,   Vi-ve la, vi-ve la, vi-ve l'a-mour,

Vi-ve l'a-mour,   Vi-ve l'a-mour,   Vi-ve la com- pag- nie!____

"Beautiful Dreamer" (Stephen Foster)

Beau-ti- ful dream- er,   wake un- to me, _____

Star-light and dew drops are wait-ing for   thee;_____

Gone   are the cares   of   life's bus- y   throng,_____

Beau- ti- ful Dream-er   the queen of   my   song._____

"**Memory,**" from *Cats* (Andrew Lloyd Weber)

Mid – night,___ not a sound from the pave- ment.___ Has the moon lost her

me – mory?___ She is smil-ing a – lone._____ In the

etc.

Aural Skills II-1 is recommended here.

Unit Review

Review Questions

1.   What is meant by *compound meter*?

2.   In simple meters, the basic metric unit is divided evenly by 2. How is it divided in *compound meters*?

Aural Skills

Other Aural Skills Exercises are located in the Instructor's Manual. The following can be done by the student alone.

1.   Try to think of familiar tunes that are in compound meter. Write the rhythms of these tunes in musical notation to verify your decision.

Directions: In each of the following exercises, count aloud, clap the rhythm, and accent appropriately.

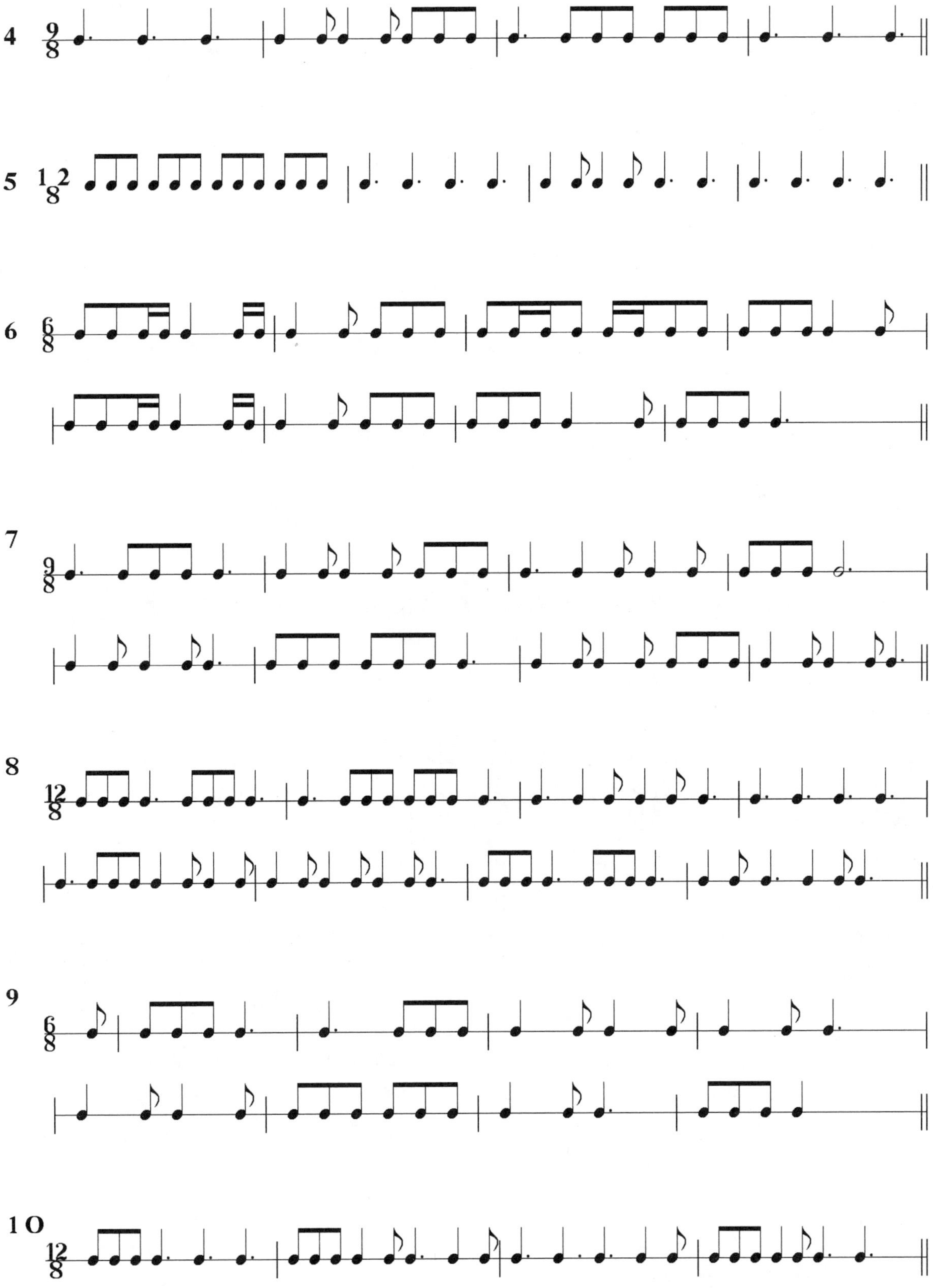
4
5
6
7
8
9
10

1 1

1 2

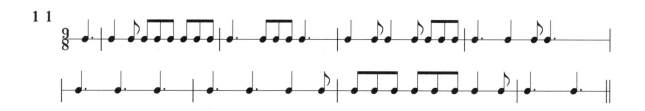

The following exercises are for two hands (or two different pitches at the piano).

1

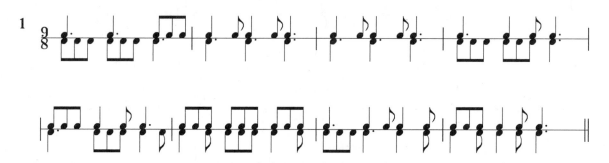

2

3

4

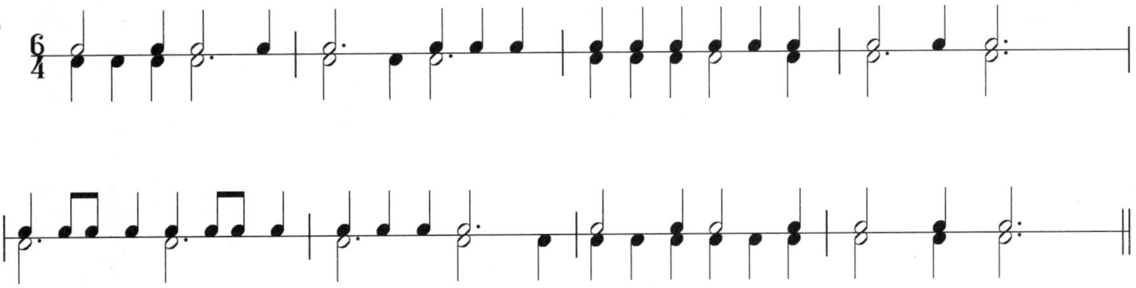

5

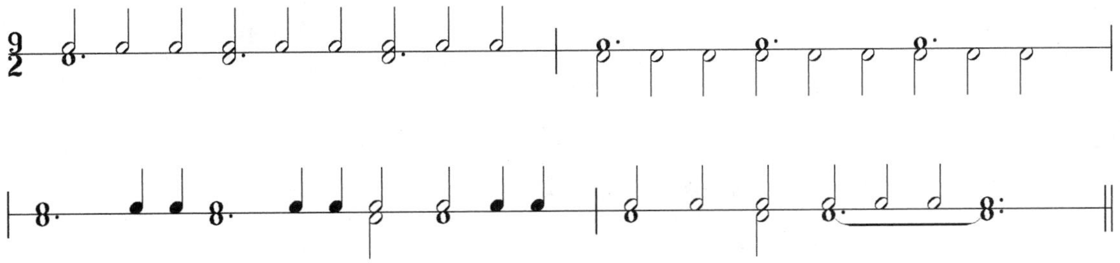

6

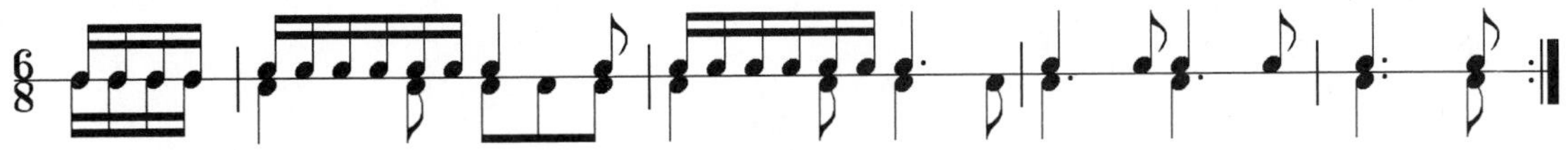

Rhythm Unit

1. Subdivisions of the Beat
   in Simple Meters

For this Unit, review in Chapter 4:

1. Note values: 16ths and 32nds

For this Unit, review in Chapter 2:

1. Tempo indicators

1 Subdivisions of the Beat in Simple Meters

*I*n the preceding units, we examined rhythms in which the beat was divided into halves. The beat can be subdivided further into quarters, eighths, sixteenths, and so on. Example RHY-P shows the division of the beat into quarters, in *simple meters.*

RHY-P   **Division of the beat into fourths in simple meters**

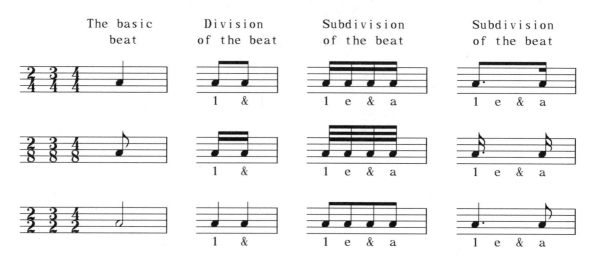

The following example indicates one way of counting when the beat is divided into quarters.

RHY-Q   **Counting method for subdivided beats in simple meters**

1 e & a 2e &a 3e&a 4e &a   1e&a 2e&a 3e&a 4e &a   1e&a 2e&a 3e&a 4e&a   etc.

RHY-R   **Pieces in simple meters with subdivided beats**

"This Old Man" (English)

This old man,   He played one,   He played nick-nack   on   his   thumb;

Nick-nack, paddy whack, Give the dog a bone, This old man came roll-ing home.

"Listen to the Mockingbird" (Alice Hawthorne)

1. Lis-ten to the   Mock-ingbird,   Lis-ten to the   Mock-ingbird,   The
   2. Mock-ingbird,   Lis-ten to the   Mock-ingbird,   Still

Mock-ingbird still sing-ing o'er her   grave;   Lis-ten to the

sing-ing where the   weep-ing wil- lows   wave._____

Aural Skills III-1 is recommended here.

Unit Review

Review Questions

1. When a *quarter-note beat* is divided in half, the half value is represented by what note value?

2. When an *eighth note* is divided in half, the half is represented by what note value?

3. When a *quarter note* is subdivided into fourths, what note values are used?

4. How do we show a *quarter note* that is divided into ¾ + ¼?

Aural Skills

Other exercises can be found in the Instructor's Manual. The following can be done by the student.

1. Practice writing the rhythm for the piece titled "The Battle Hymn of the Republic" (words by Julia Ward Howe; music by William Steffe).

2. Practice writing the rhythm for any other piece that you think has the beat divided into fourths; for example:

"Oh, My Darling Clementine" (Percy Montrose)

"Winter Wonderland" (words by Dick Smith; music by Felix Bernard)

"Dixie" (Bobby Platter)

"Chances Are" (words by Al Stillman; music by Robert Allen)

"Alouette"(French-Canadian folk song)

Directions: In each of the following, count aloud and clap the rhythm. Be careful to emphasize the primary accent in each measure and, to a lesser degree, the secondary accent, if there is one.
Note: This section also contains tied notes and rests.

2

3

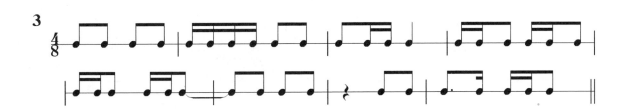

4

5

6

7

8

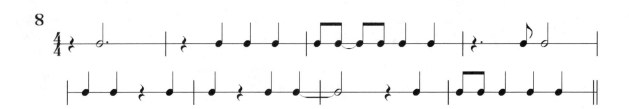

9

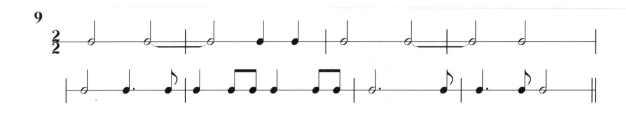

1 0

1 1

The following exercises are for two hands.

1

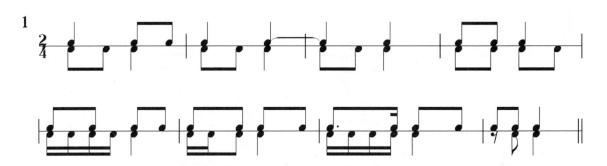

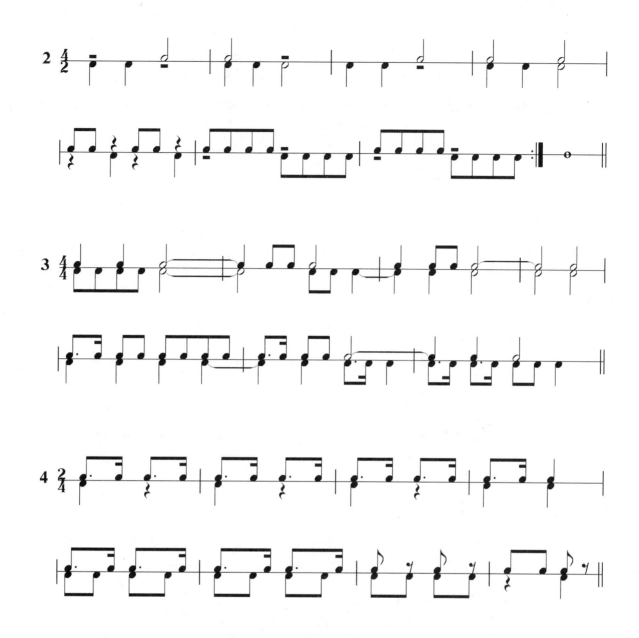

The following exercises review meters and rhythms from Units I, II, and III.

2

3

4

5

Rhythm Unit

1. Subdivisions in Compound
   Meters

For this Unit, review in Unit II:

1. Compound meters

Also review in Chapter 2:

1. Fermata

1 Subdivisions in Compound Meters

*I*n compound meters, the beat is represented by a dotted note which divides evenly into 3's, each of which can be subdivided.

RHY-S   **Division of a note value into fourths in compound meters**

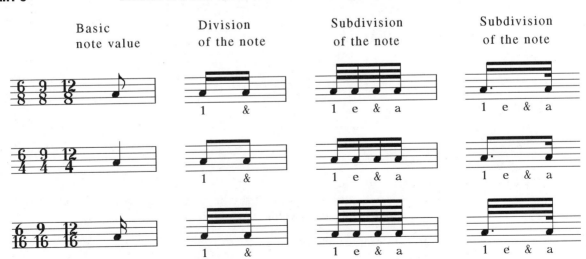

Example RHY-T shows one way to count notes divided into fourths in compound meter so that each note value receives its precise amount of time.

RHY-T   **Counting method for subdivided beats in compound time**

1 e & a 2 e & a 3 e & a   4 e & a 5 e & a 6 e & a   1e&a2e&a3e&a   4e&a5e&a6e&a

RHY-U   **Pieces in compound meter with subdivided notes**
Note: There is not an abundance of pieces in compound meter, and there are fewer still with subdivided notes. Simple meters, particularly $\frac{4}{4}$, are by far the most commonly used meters, especially for popular music. Compound meters are sometimes encountered in "musicals" and more often (though still not frequent by comparison) in classical music.

"Believe Me If All Those Endearing Young Charms" (Thomas Moore)

Be - lieve me if all those en - dear-ing young charms Which I

gaze on so fond-ly to - day, _____ Were to change by to-mor-row and

fleet in my arms, Like fai-ry gifts fad - ing a- way._____ etc.

Aural Skills IV-1 is recommended here.

Unit Review

Review Questions

1. What is a helpful way to count rhythm so that each beat and each part of the beat gets its precise value:

    a.   In simple meters?

    b.   In compound meters?

2. What is the difference between simple *division* and *subdivision* of the beat?

Aural Skills

Aside from the instructor-assisted Aural Skills Exercises, which are located in the Instructor's Manual, the student can do the following, either alone or with a colleague.

1. If you are familiar with the following pieces (all of which are in compound meters), try to write the rhythm for at least the first few phrases.

   a. " Greensleeves" ("What Child Is This?") (English traditional)

   b. "Home on the Range" (American traditional)

2. If you can recall other tunes that are in compound meter, try to write the rhythm and determine whether or not the beat is divided or subdivided.

   Directions: In each of the following, count and clap the rhythm. Be careful to observe the accents.

The following exercises are for two hands.

The following exercises review meters and rhythms from Units I, II, III, and IV.

5

Rhythm Unit

V

1. Division of the Beat into Halves and Quarters

2. Triplets

1 Division of the Beat into Halves and Quarters

*I*n the preceding units, we saw how the beat in simple meters can divide into halves and into quarters. For example:

2 Triplets

Subdivisions of the beat into three parts (though more characteristic of compound meters) is also possible in simple meters. The group of notes resulting from the division of the beat into three equal parts in simple meter is called a **triplet.**

Triplets can produce effective rhythmic variation, but if used too extensively, they can give the rhythmic feel of compound meter.

Note: A more comprehensive definition, one that truly distinguishes the triplet from what is the normal division of the beat in compound meters, is *three in the time of two.*

Triplets are grouped and usually are labeled with an arabic numeral, as shown in example RHY-V.

RHY-V   **Triplets**

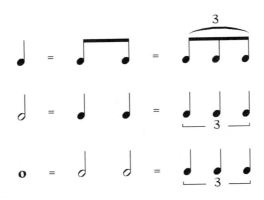

Example RHY-W shows four different divisions of the beat in four *simple duple* meters. Notice that the note values for a triplet are *those of the next smaller value than the beat it fills.*

RHY-W   **Beat division into halves and triplets**

There are various counting methods for ensuring the accurate performance of the triplet. One method is shown in example RHY-X. Note that the triplet can also appear in a "2 plus 1 division," and it may also include a rest.

RHY-X   **Counting method for triplets**

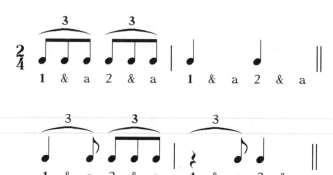

Labeling the triplet with a bracket (or a curved line) and the number 3 facilitates the distinction between it and groups of three found in compound time (for example, $\frac{6}{8}$). A comparison is shown here.

RHY-Y   **The triplet in simple meter and triple division of the beat in compound meter**

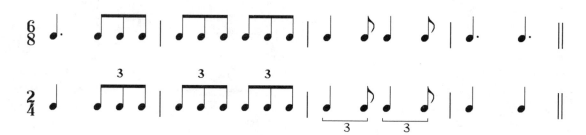

The following are examples of pieces containing triplet divisions of the beat.

RHY-Z   **Three different versions of triplets**

"Chariots of Fire" (Vangelis)

"For Me and My Gal" (George W. Meyer)

The bells are ring-ing_____ For Me and My Gal,_____

The birds are sing-ing_____ For Me and My Gal,_____ etc.

"Born Free" (John Barry)

Born free,_____ as free as the wind blows,_____ As free as the

grass grows, Born free to fol-low your heart.

Unit Review

Review Questions

1. What is meant by the term *triplet*?

2. What distinguishes the triplet from the regular division of the beat in *compound meter*?

3. What is a method for counting triplets so that each part of the triplet gets exactly the same amount of time (and so that the undivided beats always get their full value)?

Aural Skills

Other exercises, which require the instructor's assistance, are located in the Instructor's Manual. The following may be done by the students without the instructor's assistance.

1. Hum the tune "Chariots of Fire" by Vangelis and see if you can feel the triplet division of the beat.

2. See if you can write the rhythm of this piece.

3. Can you think of any other tunes that contain triplets?

Directions: Count aloud and clap all the following rhythms. These exercises contain divisions of the beat into halves, triplets, and quarters.

6

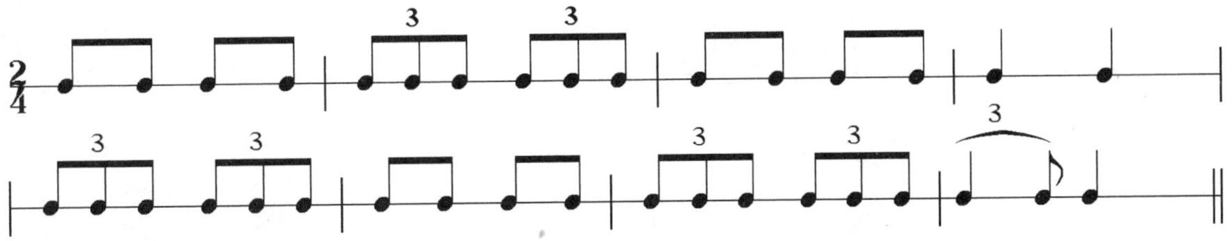

7

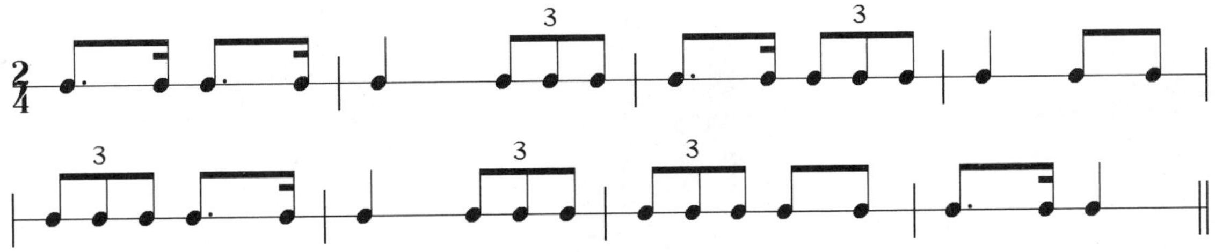

8

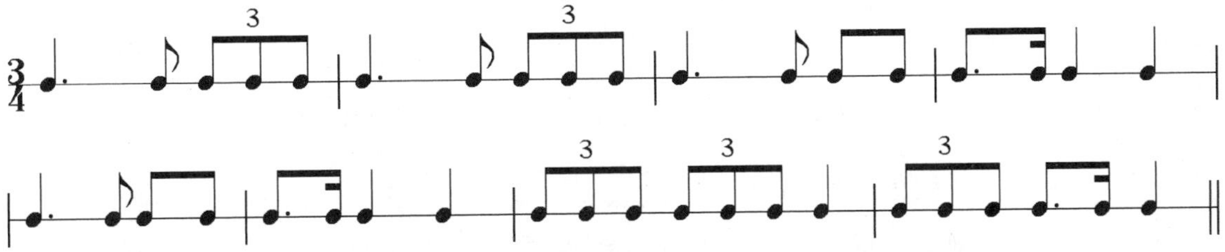

9

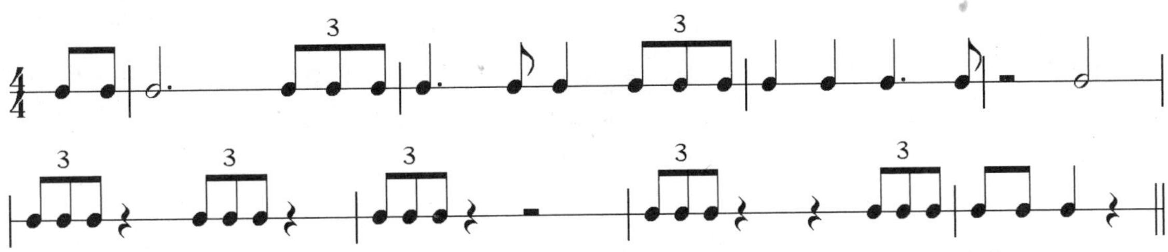

10

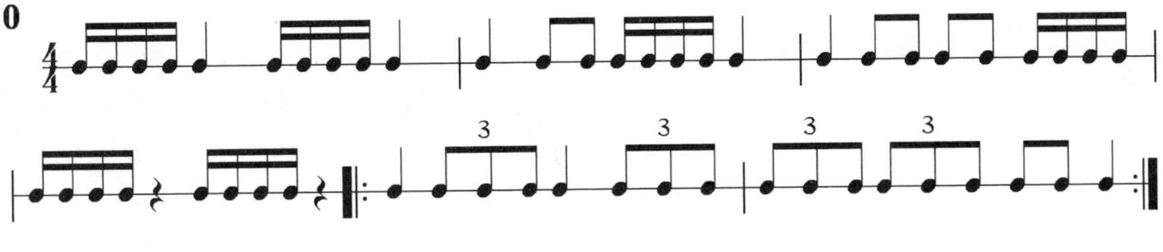

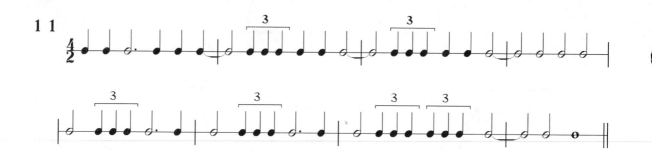

The following exercises are for two hands (or two pitches at the keyboard).

The following exercises review meters and rhythms from all preceding units.

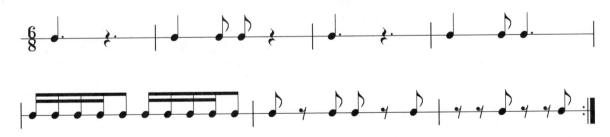

2

3

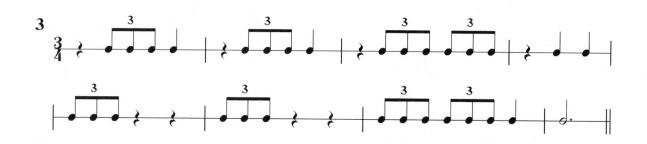

4

5

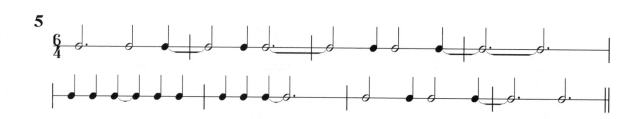

Rhythm Unit

1. Syncopation

2. Hemiola

1 Syncopation

$\mathcal{T}$he term **syncopation** means *a displacement of the regular accent*. It is the placement of an accent on what would normally be a weak beat in a measure. In European American music, the strongest accent normally is on beat 1—the *downbeat*. In example RHY-AA, we show the normal accent in three simple meters and in one compound meter. (*Note:* We have actually notated the accents here, but generally these normal accents are merely understood by the performer.)

RHY-AA **Normal accent in simple and compound meters**

We can *syncopate* a rhythm in various ways, as shown in example RHY-BB.

RHY-BB   **Various types of syncopation**

1.   Place an accent on a normally weak beat:

2.   Accent the second half of a beat:

3.   Lengthen the value of the normally weak beat (frequently done by tying it to the next note):

4.   Put a rest in place of the normally accented beat:

5.   Combine items 2 and 4:

2   Hemiola

The term **hemiola** comes from a Greek word meaning "a whole and a half," which indicates the 3:2 ratio. It is a type of syncopation implying a shift in the normal rhythmic arrangement of the beats in a measure. A good example is the division of $\frac{6}{8}$ into 2 + 2 + 2 instead of the usual 3 + 3.

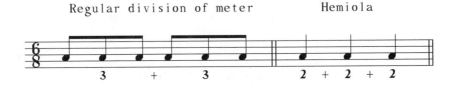

Phrase from *West Side Story* (Leonard Bernstein)

I   want   to   live   in   A —   mer — i — ca

Aural Skills VI-1 is recommended here.

Example RHY-DD shows three pieces, each of which contains syncopated rhythms.

"Michael, Row the Boat Ashore" (folk song)

Mi – chael,   row   the   boat   a – shore,   Hal – le – lu –   jah!

Mi – chael,   row   the   boat   a – shore,   Hal – le – lu –   jah!

"Jacob's Ladder" (traditional)

We   are   climb-ing   Ja-cob's   lad-der.   We   are

climb-ing   Ja-cob's   lad-der,   We   are   climb-ing

Ja-cob's   lad-der,   Sol-diers   of   the   cross.____

"People" (Jule Styne and Bob Merrill)

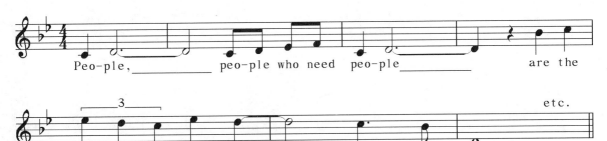

Peo-ple,_____   peo-ple who need   peo-ple_____   are the

luck – i – est   peo – ple_____   in   the   world.

etc.

Unit Review

Review Questions

1. What is *syncopation*?

2. What is *hemiola*?

3. Is there any difference between syncopation and hemiola? If so, what is it?

4. What is the most effective type of syncopation?

Aural Skills

Exercises noted in the unit can be found in the Instructor's Manual. The following can be done by the student alone.

1. Try to write the rhythm of the following pieces:

   a. "When the Saints Go Marching In" (traditional)

   b. "Standin' in the Need of Prayer" (spiritual)

   c. "Go Down, Moses" (spiritual)

   d. "Born Free" (words by Don Black; music by John Barry)

   Directions: The following rhythmic exercises contain syncopated rhythms as well as regular rhythms. Count and clap each. Use a metronome, if possible.

13

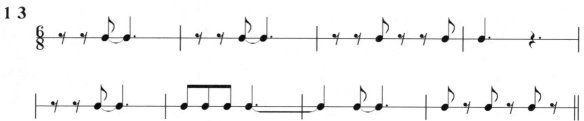

14

15

16

The following exercises are for two hands.

The following rhythms are a review of Units I–V.

5

6

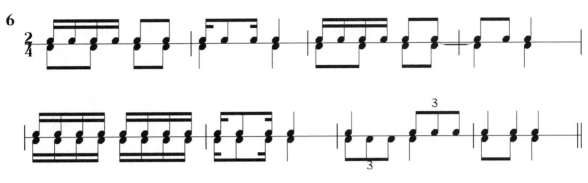

7

8

9

10

Rhythm Unit

1. Asymmetrical Meters

1 Asymmetrical Meters

*A*symmetrical meters are those in which the measure cannot divide equally into twos, threes, or fours. Examples are $\frac{5}{4}$ and $\frac{7}{8}$. In $\frac{5}{4}$, the division might be either 2 + 3 or 3 + 2, or even 2 + 2 + 1. In $\frac{7}{8}$, it might divide into 3 + 4, 4 + 3, 3 + 2 + 3, and so on.

RHY-EE   **Asymmetrical meters**

Note: It is difficult to tap your foot or snap your fingers to the beat in asymmetrical meters because the accents keep shifting location. In other words, the accents do not occur at regularly recurring intervals.

A technique used by some composers to achieve an asymmetrical rhythm is referred to as "multimeter." Here, asymmetrical meter is achieved through frequent changes in meter, thus avoiding a predictable repetition of an accent pattern.

RHY-FF   **Multimetered music**

Example RHY-GG shows two examples of asymmetrical rhythms. The first uses the same meter throughout; the second is *multimetered*.

RHY-GG

Czechoslovakian Folk Song

"Valley of the Dolls" (Andre Previn)

Got-ta get off,   Gon-na get,   have to get   off from this ride,____

Got-ta get hold,   Gon-na get,   need to get   hold of my pride._____

Aural Skills VII-1 is recommended here.

Unit Review

Review Questions

1. What is the difference between *symmetrical* and *asymmetrical* meters?

2. Is it possible to use a symmetrical meter but still produce an asymmetrical rhythm?

3. What are some of the asymmetrical meters?

4. What is *multimeter*?

Aural Skills

1. Listen to some twentieth-century music by composers such as Arnold Schoenberg and Charles Ives in order to begin to hear the sound of asymmetrical meters and rhythms.

2. Write some symmetrical and some asymmetrical rhythms for the class to perform.

Directions: Clap the following examples, which include a variety of asymmetrical meters and rhythmic patterns.

6

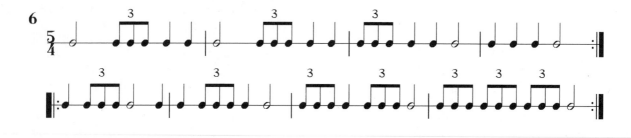

7

8

Fine

9

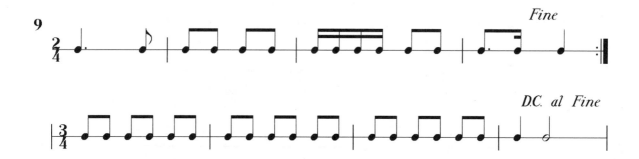

D.C. al Fine

10

1 1

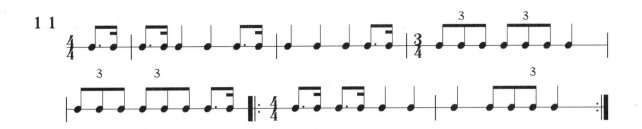

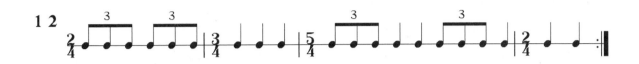

1 2

The following exercises are for two hands.

1

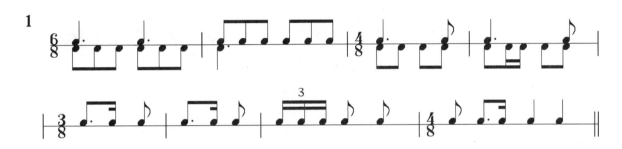

2

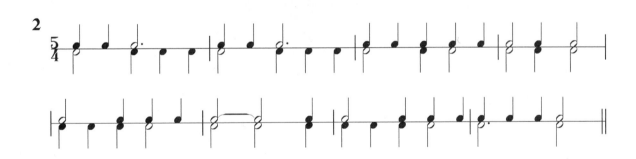

3

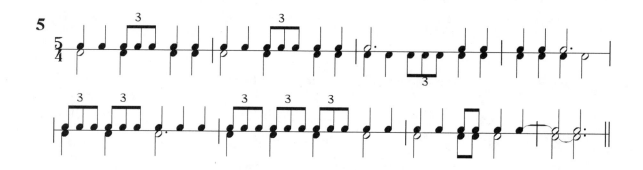

Part Three

APPENDICES

Answers to Chapter Drills

(Chapters 2–14)

Chapter 2

1. Indicate whether the second pitch is A (higher than), B (lower than), or C (same as) the first.

1 _B_   2 _A_   3 _C_   4 _A_   5 _C_   6 _B_   7 _B_   8 _A_   9 _C_   10 _A_

2. Indicate whether the pitches are A (ascending), B (descending), or C (static).

1 _A_   2 _B_   3 _A_   4 _C_   5 _B_

3. Indicate the number of times the highest pitch appears.

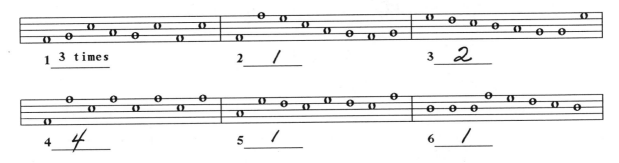

1 _3 times_   2 _1_   3 _2_

4 _4_   5 _1_   6 _1_

4. Indicate whether the pitch arrangment is A (conjunct), B (mildly disjunct), C (extremely disjunct), or D (static).

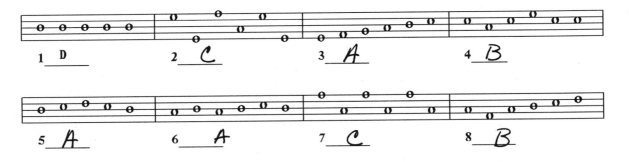

1 _D_   2 _C_   3 _A_   4 _B_

5 _A_   6 _A_   7 _C_   8 _B_

5. Consider each entire line of notes separately and indicate whether the melody is A (motivic) or B (through-composed).

1 A _____

2 B _____

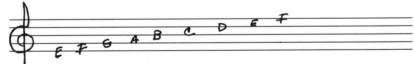

3 A _____

Chapter 3

6. Identify and define the following symbols:

1. TREBLE CLEF
   (all pitches above middle c)

2. TREBLE STAFF

3. WHOLE NOTE (= 2 d) o

4. FORTE – LOUD f

5. SHARP (raise pitch 1/2 step) ♯

6. OCTAVE (play one octave higher or lower) 8va

7. BASS STAFF

8. CRESCENDO <
   (Gradually getting louder)

7. Practice drawing the treble clef sign and the bass clef sign on the staff.

8. Draw the treble clef and write in the names of the lines and spaces.

9. Draw the bass clef and write in the names of the lines and spaces.

10a. Add the appropriate symbols to make a grand staff of the following two staffs.

10b. Starting with the lowest pitch, write in the name of each line and space on the staff.

11. Write the letter names of the treble staff lines: _E G B D F_

12. Write the letter names of the treble staff spaces: _F A C E_

13. Write the letter names of the bass staff lines: _G B D F A_

14. Write the letter names of the bass staff spaces: _A C E G_

15. Draw a grand staff and draw a note to show each location of pitch A.

16. Place the treble clef on the staff and write the notes on the staff (in *any* location).

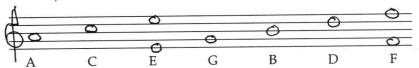

| A | C | E | G | B | D | F |

17. Place the bass clef on the staff and write the notes (in *any* location).

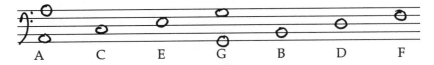

| A | C | E | G | B | D | F |

18. In each of the following exercises, write the letter name of the note.

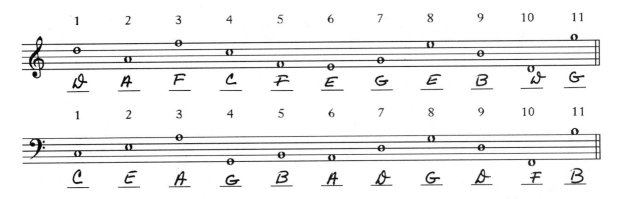

19. Show where the following would be played on the keyboard by writing the *number* of the pitch on the appropriate white key.

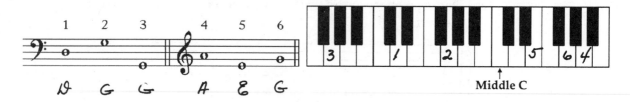

D   G   G   A   E   G

20. Write the name of each ledger line or ledger space.

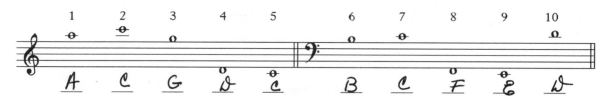

A   C   G   D   C   B   C   F   E   D

21. Show where each note would be played on the keyboard (sharps, flats, double sharps, and double flats).

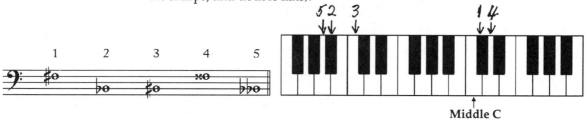

22. Give an enharmonic name for each of the following pitches.

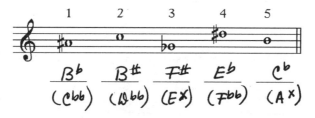

B♭   B♯   F♯   E♭   C♭
(C♭♭) (A♭♭) (E✗)   (F♭♭) (A✗)

23. Beside each note, lower it one half step. Do *not* change the letter name. Add or delete accidentals as needed.

Chapter 4

1.   Name the type of note(s).

HALF   EIGHTHS   WHOLE   16ths   32nd   8th

2.   Directly beside the note, correct any errors in stem direction or location.

3.   Give the number of values requested that could be contained in the given note.

No.:   Eighths   Quarters   32nds   Quarters   Eighths   Quarters
         8   2   4   4   2   2

4.   Name the type of rest and draw the equivalent note value beside it.

HALF   WHOLE   8th   16th   QUARTER

5.   Write one note that equals the combined value of the notes given.

6. Write one note only that completes each measure in the meter given.

7. Write one rest only that completes the measure in the meter given.

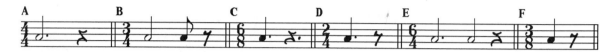

8. Write four different measures of rhythm for each of the two meters given.

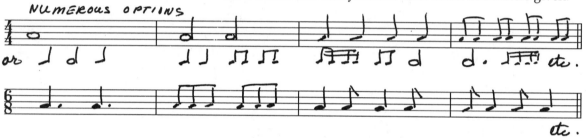

9. Write the number of beats each dotted note/rest should receive.

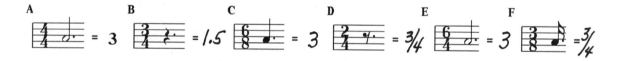

10. Write the total value (number of beats) of each tied note.

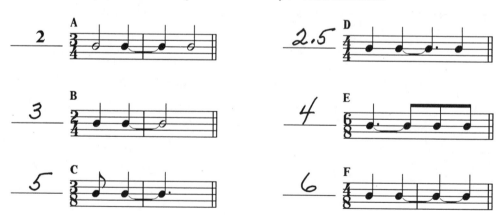

11. Place bar lines where appropriate for the meter indicated.

12. Provide the appropriate time signature for the following four measures.

13. What is meant by each of the following symbols?

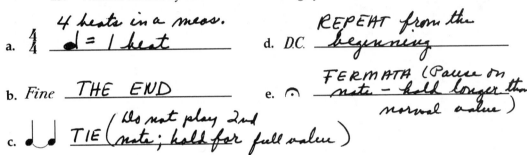

a. 4/4   4 beats in a meas. ♩ = 1 beat

b. *Fine*   THE END

c. ♩‿♩ TIE (Do not play 2nd note; hold for full value)

d. *D.C.*   REPEAT from the beginning

e. ⌢   FERMATA (Pause on note – hold longer than normal value)

14. In each of the following examples, give the numbers for the measures in the order in which they should be played.

a.

A =   1 2 3 4 5   3 4 5 6

b.

B =   1 2 3 4A   1 2 3 4B

1. Write each scale indicated here, ascending only. Start each on C and use sharps as needed. (You may find it a help to write the scale in letter names first, then place the notes on the staff.)

a. DIATONIC SCALE (Major Mode—half steps between 3 and 4 and 7 and 1)

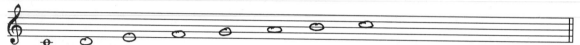

b. CHROMATIC SCALE

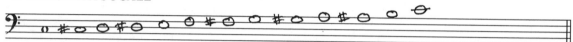

c. PENTATONIC SCALE

OR

d. WHOLE-TONE SCALE

e. OCTATONIC SCALE (Start with either a whole step or a half step.)

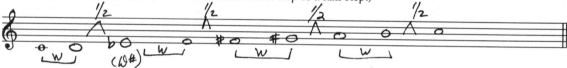

f. TWELVE-TONE ROW (Do not omit or duplicate any pitch.)

g. SYNTHETIC SCALE (Use seven pitches only.)

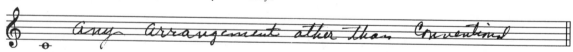

h. WRITE ANOTHER SYNTHETIC SCALE (Start on any pitch and use eight pitches.)

2. Identify the *type* of scale in each of the following exercises. To determine which type scale is being used, do a *pitch inventory*, from A through G, writing down each pitch that appears in the scale, as shown in the first exercise.

Chapter 6

1. Using the following steps, write the major scales indicated:

    a. Above the staff, write the letter names for the entire octave.

    b. Number each letter (starting with 1 and proceeding through the octave).

    c. Mark the proper location of the half steps.

    d. Enter the appropriate sharp(s) or flat(s).

    e. Put the scale and the key signature on staff.

2. Give the name of the major key for each key signature given.

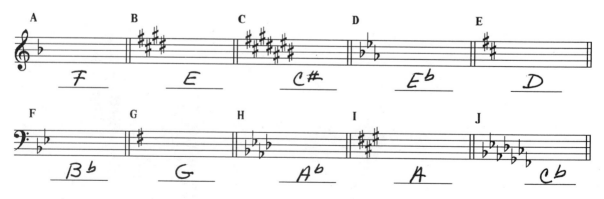

3. Practice writing the key signatures for 7 sharps and 7 flats, first in the treble clef and then in the bass clef. (Be sure to add your clef signs.)

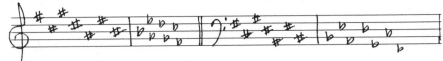

4. Indicate the number of sharps or flats that each major key has.

a. _2#_ D   d. _2♭_ B♭   g. _6#_ F♯

b. _3♭_ E♭   e. _5#_ B   h. _6♭_ G♭

c. _5♭_ D♭   f. _1#_ G   i. _1♭_ F

5. Give the name of the major key that has the number of sharps or flats indicated.

a. _F♯_ 6 sharps   d. _B♭_ 2 flats   g. _E_ 4 sharps

b. _E♭_ 3 flats   e. _C#_ 7 sharps   h. _A♭_ 4 flats

c. _C_ 0 sharps/flats   f. _F_ 1 flat   i. _D_ 2 sharps

6. Practice drawing the Circle of Fifths.

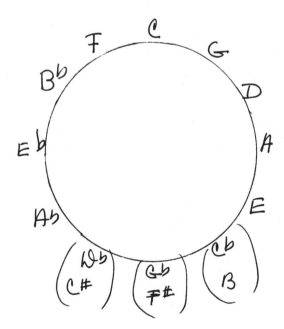

7. Place the appropriate key signature in the appropriate location on the staff, and enter the correct tonic (key center) for each. (Watch the clef signs.)

F MAJOR   D-FLAT MAJOR   E MAJOR   C-SHARP MAJOR

A-FLAT MAJOR   D MAJOR   C-FLAT MAJOR   F-SHARP MAJOR

8. Give the scale-degree name for each of the following pitches in the key indicated.

a. _SUBMEDIANT_   A in C major

b. _MEDIANT_   F♯ in D major

c. _LEADING TONE_   B in C major

d. _SUPERTONIC_   F in E♭ major

e. _SUB DOMINANT_   B♭ in F major

f. _DOMINANT_   D in G major

g. _TONIC_   F in F major

h. _SUBMEDIANT_   D in F major

i. _LEADING TONE_   C♯ in D major

j. _SUPERTONIC_   C in B♭ major

Chapter 7

1. Which minor key is indicated by the following key signatures?

2. Give the major and minor keys for each of the following signatures.

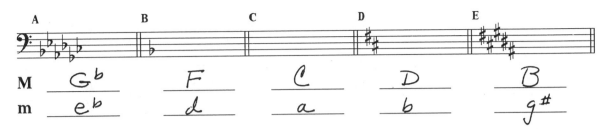

M   G♭   F   C   D   B

m   e♭   d   a   b   g♯

3. First give the name of the minor key represented by the signature; then beside each give the appropriate key signature for the parallel major.

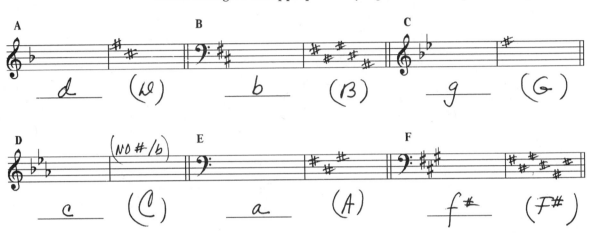

d   (D)   b   (B)   g   (G)

c   (C)   a   (A)   f♯   (F♯)

4. Based on the key signature and the key tone (tonic) provided, give the correct key and mode (M or m).

E   d   C   e   c   D

A   a   g   f   F   F♯

5. Give the appropriate key and key signature. (Just give the number of sharps or flats.)

   a. RELATIVE of G major   e minor   1 #

   b. PARALLEL of A major   a minor   NO #/b

   c. RELATIVE of f minor   Ab MAJOR   4 b

   d. PARALLEL of f minor   F MAJOR   1 b

   e. PARALLEL of G major   g minor   2 b

6. Write the three forms of the e minor and the f minor scales (ascending and descending). Be sure to use a key signature and add accidentals where necessary. (Add clef signs, starting with treble and alternating with bass.)

e natural minor

e harmonic minor

e melodic minor

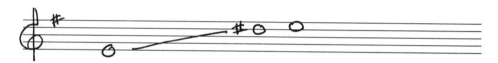

f natural minor

f harmonic minor

f melodic minor

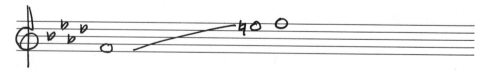

7. Write the following scales.

g harmonic minor

f sharp natural minor

a flat harmonic minor

B major's relative minor (Melodic form)

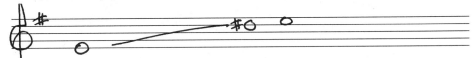

E major's parallel minor (Harmonic form)

f minor's relative major

8. Practice drawing the Circle of Fifths for major and minor keys. (Be sure to show all the enharmonic keys.)

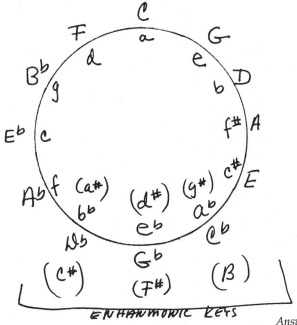

ENHARMONIC KEYS

9. Place the appropriate key signature in the proper location on the staff, and enter the correct tonic (key center) for each.

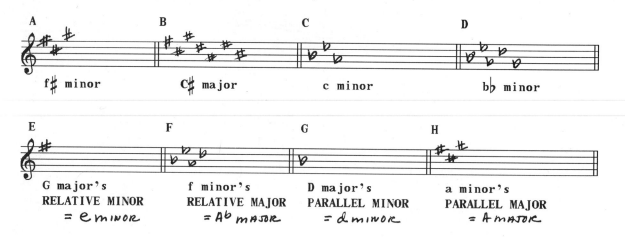

A   f♯ minor

B   C♯ major

C   c minor

D   b♭ minor

E   G major's
RELATIVE MINOR
= e minor

F   f minor's
RELATIVE MAJOR
= A♭ major

G   D major's
PARALLEL MINOR
= d minor

H   a minor's
PARALLEL MAJOR
= A major

Chapter 8

PITCH INVENTORY
(always start
with letter A):

Ⓐ	A♯/B♭	B	Ⓒ	C♯/D♭	Ⓓ	D♯/E♭	Ⓔ	Ⓕ	F♯/G♭	Ⓖ	G♯/A♭
1	2	3	4	5	6	7	8	9	10	11	12

MELODY A = F major (F G A B♭ C D E F

MELODY B = C CHROMATIC (C C♯ D D♯ E F F♯ G G♯ A A♯ B)

Chapter 9

1. Indicate whether the interval is melodic (M) or harmonic (H).

A. H B. M C. H D. M E. M F. H G. M H. H

2. Give the size of each interval.

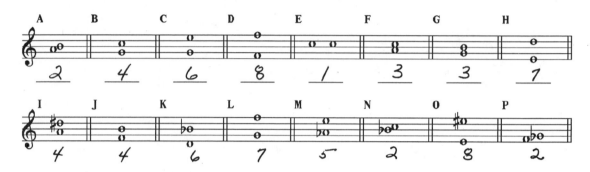

A. 2 B. 4 C. 6 D. 8 E. 1 F. 3 G. 3 H. 7

I. 4 J. 4 K. 6 L. 7 M. 5 N. 2 O. 8 P. 2

3. Write a second note above the given note (using an accidental if necessary) to create the size and quality indicated.

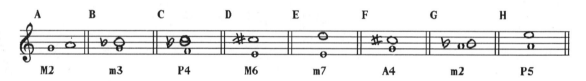

A. M2 B. m3 C. P4 D. M6 E. m7 F. A4 G. m2 H. P5

4. Alter the second pitch, with an accidental as needed, to write the quality of the interval requested. Write answers above the staff in letter names.

A. C# B. A♮ C. E♮ D. B♭ E. F# F. F# G. D♭ H. G♭

M3 M2 P8 m3 M6 M7 P4 m2

5. Identify the size and quality of each interval; then, in the empty measure beside it, invert each and identify the size and quality of the inversion.

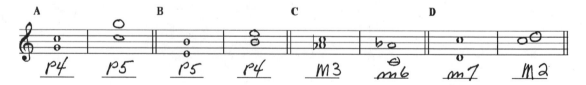

A. P4 P5 B. P5 P4 C. M3 m6 D. m7 M2

6. Reduce the compound intervals to simple intervals and identify their size and quality.

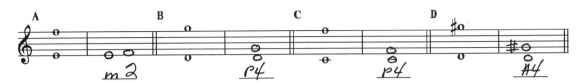

7. In the following melody, indicate the size of each melodic interval.

HYMNE (Vangelis)

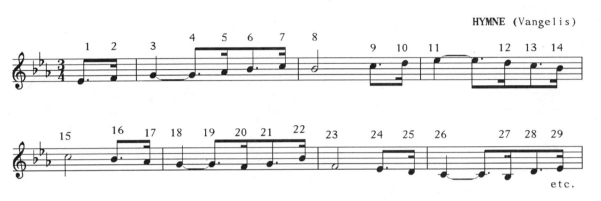

etc.

Between Beats	Size	Quality	Between Beats	Size	Quality
1 & 2	2	M	15 & 16	2	M
2 & 3	2	M	16 & 17	2	M
3 & 4	1	P	17 & 18	2	m
4 & 5	2	m	18 & 19	1	P
5 & 6	2	M	19 & 20	2	M
6 & 7	2	M	20 & 21	2	M
7 & 8	2	M	21 & 22	3	m
8 & 9	2	M	22 & 23	4	P
9 & 10	2	M	23 & 24	2	M
10 & 11	2	m	24 & 25	2	m
11 & 12	2	m	25 & 26	2	M
12 & 13	2	M	26 & 27	2	M
13 & 14	2	M	27 & 28	3	M
14 & 15	2	M	28 & 29	2	m

Chapter 10

1. Spell tertian chords using the following roots:

   a. F   *F A C*   e. A   *A C E*

   b. B   *B D F*   f. C   *C E G*

   c. D   *D F A*   g. G   *G B D*

   d. E-flat   *E♭ G B*   h. F-sharp   *F♯ A C*

2. Using the note provided as the root, write the chords in the quality indicated.

3. Identify the chords by letter name and give the quality.

4. Using the note provided as the 3rd of the chord, write the complete chord in the quality indicated.

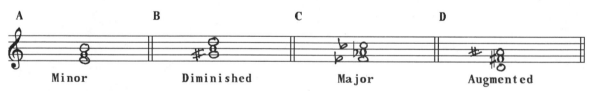

5. Using the given note as the 5th, write the complete chord in the quality requested.

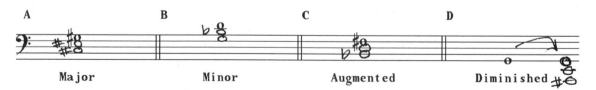

6. Write the major chords in the two keys indicated.

A. D MAJOR   B. f minor

    I   IV   V   III   VI   VII

7. Write the chord indicated by the roman numeral in the mode and key specified.

MINOR KEYS   MAJOR KEYS

A   B   C   D   E   F   G   H

    i   VI   III+   ii°   IV   vi   V   vii°

8. Give the roman numeral for each chord in the specified key; give the scale-degree name for each chord. (Indicate key first.)

MINOR KEYS

A   B   C   D

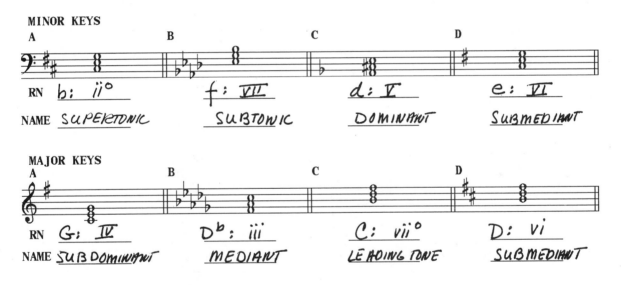

RN b: ii°   f: VII   d: V   e: VI

NAME SUPERTONIC   SUBTONIC   DOMINANT   SUBMEDIANT

MAJOR KEYS

A   B   C   D

RN G: IV   Db: iii   C: vii°   D: vi

NAME SUBDOMINANT   MEDIANT   LEADING TONE   SUBMEDIANT

9. Write the chords specified by the "pop" music symbols.

A   F   B   G7   C   g m   D   d°

10. Write the chords and inversions in the key specified and the position indicated.

A   B   C   D   E

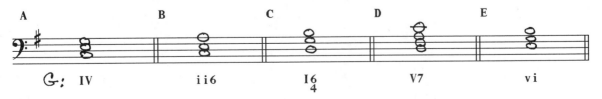

  G: IV   ii6   I6/4   V7   vi

Chapter 11

(A)

HARMONIC RHYTHM: 1 2 3 4 5 6 7 8

POLLY WOLLY DOODLE (American)

Lively

Oh, I went down South for to see my Sal, Sing Pol-ly wol-ly doo-dle all day;

KEY/MODE: F

CHORDS (RN) I   I   I   V6

My Sal she is a spun-ky gal, Sing Pol-ly wol-ly doo-dle all day.

V6   V6   I6/4 V6 I

(B)

HARMONIC RHYTHM 1 2 3 4 5 6 7 8 9 10 11 12 13 14 15 16

JACOB'S LADDER (Traditional)

Andante

We are climb-ing Ja-cob's lad-der, We are climb-ing Ja-cob's lad-der,

SUSP

KEY/MODE: E♭

CHORDS (RN) I   I   I   I   V6   V6   ii   V6

APP

We are climb-ing Ja-cob's lad-der, Sol-diers of the cross.

I   I   IV6/4 V6   I   V7 1st inv.   I   I

(C)

Chapter 12

1. In the following five arrangements of the first four measures of "Joy to the World," determine the following:

   a. Which type of texture is used?

   Example A: *HOMOPHONIC*

   Example B: *HOMOPHONIC*

   Example C: *MONOPHONIC*

   Example D: *HOMOPHONIC*

   Example E: *POLYPHONIC*

   b. Starting with the "thinnest," list the five examples in order of density.

   (1) *C* (2) *D* (3) *E* (4) *A* (5) *B*

Chapter 14

1. Analyze the following musical examples for the form. Diagram your phrase, period, and overall formal analysis as shown in this chapter.

EXAMPLE A: *PHRASE*

EXAMPLE B: *CONTRASTING PERIOD (4 + 4*

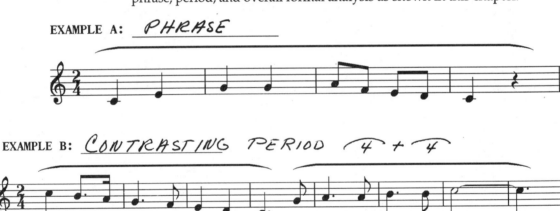

EXAMPLE C: *TERNARY* *(3-PART SONG FORM)*

A = 4 + 4 CP
B = 4 + 4 CP
A = 4 + 4   Fine

D.C. al Fine

EXAMPLE D: CONTRASTING PERIOD

EXAMPLE E: CONTRASTING DOUBLE PERIOD

Style Periods in Music History

Melodic Emphasis: 3000 B.C.–A.D. 900	
3000–500 B.C.	Ancient
500 B.C.–A.D. 300	Greek/Roman
A.D. 300–900	Medieval

Harmony and Notation Developing and Evolving: 900–1600	
900–1150	Romanesque
1150–1400	Gothic
1400–1600	Renaissance

Common Practice Period: 1600–1900 (Notation Standard)
Tertian Harmony • Tonality • Metrical Rhythm • Equal Temperament • Instrumental and Vocal

1600–1750	Baroque
1750–1800	Classical
1800–1900	Romantic

Contemporary: 1900–2000
Quartal • Quintal • Secundal Harmony (as well as Tertian)
Atonality • Bitonality • Polytonality • Neotonality (as well as Tonality)
Ametric Rhythm (as well as Metric)
Experimental and Electronic Music • Jazz

Dynamics and Tempo Indicators

Dynamics

Degrees of Sound-Volume

Pianissimo (pp): Very soft

Piano (p): Soft

Mezzo piano (mp): Medium soft

Mezzo forte (mf): Medium loud

Forte (f): Loud

Fortissimo (ff): Very loud

Changing Dynamics

Crescendo (cresc): Gradually getting louder

Decrescendo (decresc.): Gradually getting softer

Diminuendo (dim.): Gradually getting softer

Sudden Changes in Dynamics

Forzando (fz): Strong accent or emphasis

Rinforzando (rf, rfz): Pronounced accent or stress

Sforzando (sf, sfz): Forced tone, very strong accent

Tempo

Common Tempo Terms with Metronome Indicators

Largo: Very slow (quarter note = 42–66)

Lento: Slow (quarter note = 52–108)

Adagio: Slowly, leisurely (quarter note = 50–76)

Andante: Moderately, walking tempo (quarter note = 56–88)

Moderato: Moderately (quarter note = 66–126)

Allegro: Fast, lively (quarter note = 84–144)

Vivace: Very lively, animated (quarter note = 80–160)

Presto: Very, very rapid (quarter note = 100–152)

Other Tempo Terms

Andantino: A little faster than *Andante*

Animato: Animated, spirited, quickening

Allegretto: A little less fast than *Allegro*

Prestissimo: As fast as possible

Changing Tempo Terms

Accelerando (accel.): Gradual increase in speed

A tempo: Resume original tempo

Poco a poco animato: Little by little getting faster

Rallentando (rall.): Gradually slowing down

Ritardando (rit.): Gradually slowing down

Style

Ben marcarto: Well accented, energetic

Brio: Vigor, spirit

Cantabile: Singing style

Con moto: With motion

Dolce: Sweetly

Funebre: Somber

Giocoso: Humorously, playfully

Grazioso: Gracefully

Legato: Smoothly, connected

Maestoso: Majestically

Marcia: Marchlike

Pastorale: Peacefully

Religioso: With religious feeling

Scherzando: Playfully, jokingly

Sostenuto: Sustained tones or slightly slower

Staccato: Disconnected tones

Conducting Patterns

The following diagrams show patterns used to mark the beats in simple meters. The conductor of larger instrumental or vocal ensembles (orchestras, bands, choruses, and the like) can keep all the musicians together (in time and rhythm) by performing these patterns. The patterns are performed with the right arm, leaving the left arm free to cue instruments and to indicate dynamics.

It is helpful to conduct your own rhythms when practicing the exercises located in Part II of this text (the seven units on Rhythm). (Remember to note the *downbeat* as contrasted with the *upbeat*.)

two-beat pattern

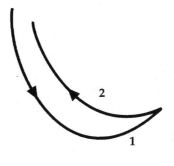

three-beat pattern

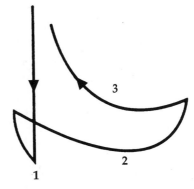

four-beat pattern

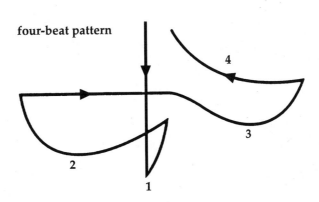

Chord Symbols

Versions of the C Chord

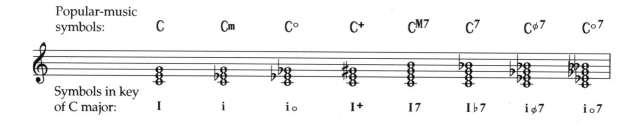

Popular-music symbols:	C	Cm	C°	C+	C^M7	C^7	C^∅7	C^°7
Symbols in key of C major:	I	i	i°	I+	I7	I♭7	i∅7	i°7

All Chords in Key of C Major

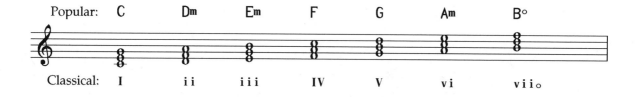

Popular:	C	Dm	Em	F	G	Am	B°
Classical:	I	ii	iii	IV	V	vi	vii°

All Chords in Key of c Minor

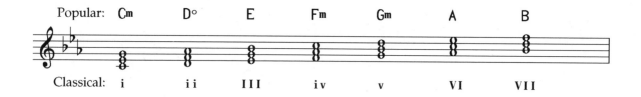

Popular:	Cm	D°	E	Fm	Gm	A	B
Classical:	i	ii	III	iv	v	VI	VII

Other Popular-Music Chord Symbols

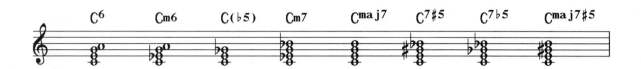

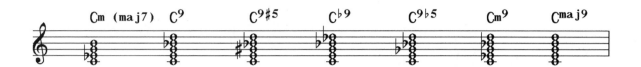

Harmonic Series

itch is determined by *frequency,* that is, the number of vibrations occurring per second. Every pitch is a composite of the *fundamental* (the object vibrating as a whole) and *overtones* (the object vibrating in parts). The two, referred to as the sound's *partials,* combine to produce what is called a *harmonic series.*

The fundamental is the strongest vibration and is what determines the basic pitch we hear. It is the composite, however (the total harmonic series), that determines the quality of the sound, the *timbre,* which enables us to distinguish between sounds.

The following example shows the harmonic series for pitch C (the fundamental and its fifteen overtones).

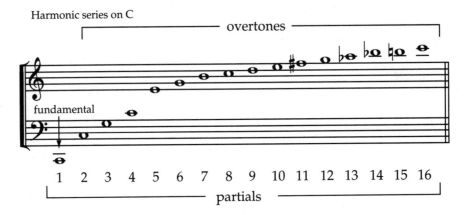

The following table[1] illustrates a string vibrating as a whole, producing the fundamental, and in its various parts, producing the overtones.

OVERTONE SERIES

Harmonics Generated by a Fundamental
(Great C*)

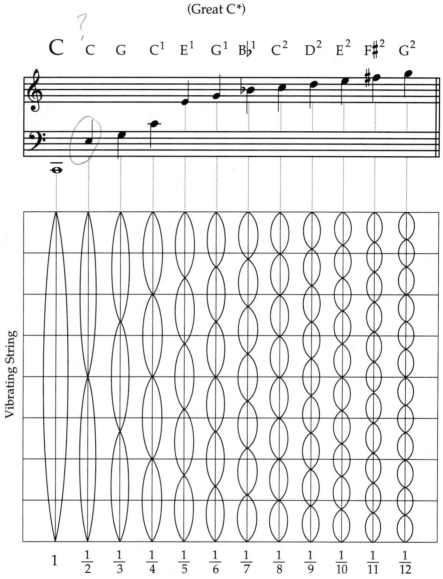

[1] Table from *Music Theory Dictionary* by Dr. William F. Lee. Reprinted by permission of Charles Hansen.

* Harmonics are generated by any given note serving as the fundamental producing the same intervallic relationship.

Acoustical Instruments

Strings

Bowed/Plucked

Violin
Viola
Cello
Bass

Plucked

Harp	Banjo
Guitar	Ukulele
Lute	Mandolin

Lute

Violin

Banjo

Ukulele

Mandolin

Classical Guitar

Bass

Cello

Viola

Harp

Adapted from *The World Book Encyclopedia*. © 1994 World Book, Inc. By permission of the publisher.

Woodwinds

Piccolo
Flute
Oboe
Clarinet
English horn

Bass clarinet
Bassoon
Contrabassoon
Saxophone

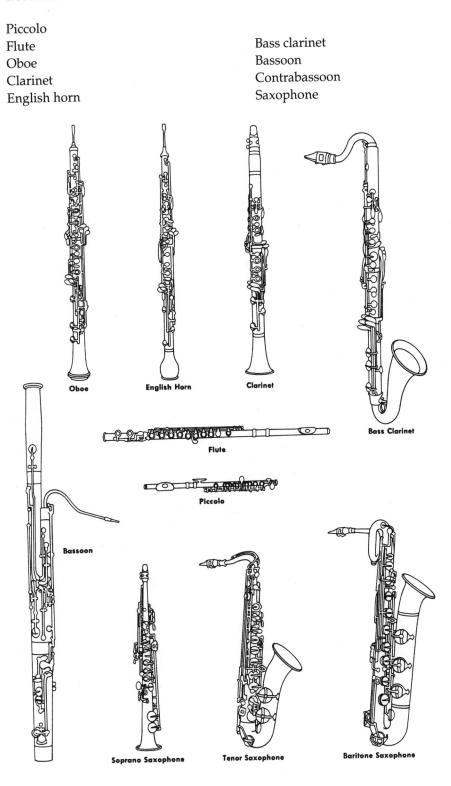

Adapted from *The World Book Encyclopedia*. © 1994 World Book, Inc. By permission of the publisher.

Brass

Trumpet
Cornet
Bugle
Flugelhorn
French horn

Baritone
Euphonium
Trombone
Tuba
Sousaphone

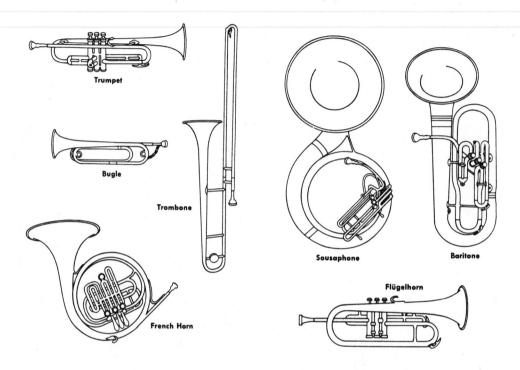

Trumpet

Bugle

Trombone

French Horn

Sousaphone

Baritone

Flügelhorn

Adapted from *The World Book Encyclopedia*. © 1994 World Book, Inc. By permission of the publisher.

Percussion

Pitched

Marimba
Xylophone
Vibraphone
Bells
Chimes
Celesta
Timpani

Nonpitched

Snare drum
Bass drum
Bongos
Cymbals
Triangle
Gong
Tamborine
Others

Kettledrum

Snare Drum

Bongo Drums

Bass Drum

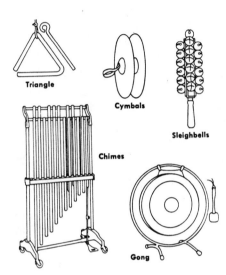

Triangle

Cymbals

Sleighbells

Chimes

Gong

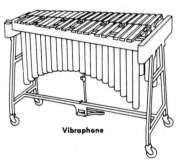

Vibraphone

Adapted from *The World Book Encyclopedia*. © 1994 World Book, Inc. By permission of the publisher.

Keyboard Instruments

Piano
Harpsichord
Clavichord
Organ

Other

Accordion
Harmonica
Bagpipes

Electronic Instruments, Materials, and Concepts

*T*he *oscillator* makes possible the production of new sounds and the variation of waveforms. Most oscillators produce five standard waveforms: sine wave, saw tooth, triangle, square, and pulse.

Mixers are used, in a variety of ways, to alter sounds produced by oscillators. *Reverb* units are used to liven up sounds, provide echo effects, and so on.

Filters enable us to further shape the harmonic content—in other words, to alter the spectrum—by isolating or eliminating overtones and harmonics. *Equalizers* can increase some of the harmonic content (overtones).

A *noise generator* makes it possible to simultaneously produce all audible frequencies, creating what is known as *white noise*.

With a *tape recorder*, we can control the envelope by isolating or eliminating any component of the sound, that is, the attack, internal dynamics, and decay. We can also reverse the direction of the sound so that we hear the decay first, thus permitting the sound to get stronger instead of weaker.

With *tape loops* and *signal processors*, we can obtain continuous repetition, echo effects, and a myriad of other alterations and new timbral effects. This is now more generally achieved digitally.

The *synthesizer* is a one-unit electronic device (with or without a keyboard) that can produce and control all aspects of sound generation relative to spectrum and envelope.

A *sampler* is like a synthesizer, except that it can contain recorded acoustical sounds in digital form. There are hybrids of samplers and synthesizers that allow us to simultaneously play synthesized and sampled acoustical sounds as well as to electronically modify those sounds.

A *sequencer* is basically an analog or digital microcomputer or dedicated system that can record, store, and transmit sequences of musical values to a sound-producing device such as a synthesizer or a sound sampler.

The *computer* has greatly enhanced the control of sound. Just as the computer has increased efficiency in the logging, storing, disseminating, and reuse of information in general, so it has in music. The computer can increase the efficiency of electronic music instruments.

In *computer sound synthesis*, the composer specifies for the computer each detail of the desired sound, such as the frequency spectrum, the envelope, dynamics, duration, and so on, all of which can be retrieved and used to generate a musical work of art.

Another valuable tool for the composer of electronic music is *MIDI* (an acronym for Musical Instrument Digital Interface). MIDI has provided an international standard that enables us to link various electronic components. It has enhanced the versatility of computers and has changed how we use them.

See sources on electronic musical instruments and electronic music composition for more detailed lists and information pertaining to the following:

Sound-Producing Equipment

Oscillator

White noise generator

Sound-processing equipment

Mixer

Ring modulator

Filter

Equalizer

Reverb

Sound Controllers

Envelope generator

Sequencer

Keyboard

Sound Storage

Tape recorder

The following distinctions pertaining to music—acoustic and electronic—are taken from *Introduction to Electro-Acoustic Music* by Barry Schrader (Englewood Cliffs, N.J.: Prentice Hall, 1982).

Acoustic music: Music produced by naturally resonating bodies

Electro-acoustic music: Any music that is produced, changed, or reproduced by electronic means

Musique concrète: Any electro-acoustic music that uses acoustic sounds as source material

Electronic music: Music in which the sound source has been electronically produced

Computer music: A type of electronic music in which the computer is used to generate sound material

Careers in Music and
Music-Related Areas*

Arts Business Management, Concert

Management
Concert manager
Booking agent
Business agent
Hiring contractor

Concert Production

Manager
Agent
Arts manager
Lighting technician

Sales and Distribution

Branch manager
Sales manager
Sales secretary/coordinator
Salesperson
Singles specialist
Inventory specialist
Merchandiser
Distribution manager
Distribution purchasing & inventory control
Distribution clerk

Promotion

National promotion director: singles, albums,
    R&B, country
Regional promotion manager
Local promotion manager
Promotion secretary/coordinator

Artist Development

Artist development manager
Tour manager
Special projects coordinator
Tour publicist
Media placement specialist
Advertising specialist
Product manager

Recording

Producer
Artist & repertoire person
Recording artist
Arranger
"Side-man"—studio musician
Recording engineer
Mixer
Graphic artist
Promoter

Publishing

Editor
Arranger—copyist
Composer & lyricist
Autographer
Graphic artist
Wholesale distributor
Retailer
Copyright expert
Proofreader
Music grapher
Music engraver
Artist & repertoire person

* *Source:* Curriculum Development Branch, Bureau of Occupational and Adult Education, U.S. Office of Education.

Production-Performance Management

Symphony orchestra manager
Chorus manager
Stage manager

Sound, Technical Equipment Operators

Acoustician
Sound equipment operator

On-Site Recording & Broadcasting

Broadcast director
Broadcast engineer
Announcer
Recording engineer

Music Technical Services

Acoustician
Instrument building & maintenance
Music instrument repair
Electronic musical instrument
Piano tuner
Organ tuner
Road crew for traveling group ("roadies")

Broadcasting

Broadcast director
Programmer
Announcement & disc jockey
Record librarian

Accounting Services

Accountant
Data processor
Computer programmer

Professional Associations & Organizations

Instrument Manufacture

Instrumentalists

Solo performer
Accompanist
Orchestral & band musician
Free-lance work

Vocalists

Solo concert career
Opera
Professional chorus
Free-lance solo work with professional &
    amateur groups
Club work, entertainment
Broadway show
Dinner theater
Recording session

Conductors

Composers

Composer
Arranger
Librettist
Lyricist

Studio Recording

Record producer
Artist & repertoire person
Recording engineer
Sound person

Retailing/Wholesaling

Inventory management
Purchasing
Sales
Advertising
Management
Accounting
Regional supervisor

Legal & Financial Services

Music copyright lawyer
Copyright expert
Performing & broadcast rights organization

Library Services

Institutional (public, university, college,
    conservatory)
Performing organization
Music theater
Opera

Music Therapy

Hospital
Clinic
Correctional institution

Writers about Music

Musicologist
Music critic
Program annotator
Album note writer

Teaching

Public school
> Supervisor
> Director
> Teacher

College conservatory
Community music school
Private school
Music store

Government Services

Museum Services

Curator, historical
Instrument collection

Glossary

NOTE: Terms in *italics* are defined elsewhere in the Glossary.

Accent: Special emphasis placed on certain notes, usually to make a tone louder. (Many different types of accents exist, but they are not addressed in this text.)

Accelerando: Indicates a gradual increase in *tempo*.

Accidentals: Symbols placed before notes to indicate some alteration: *sharps, flats, double sharps, double flats, and naturals.*

Acoustics: The physics (science) of sound.

Allegro: Indicates a fast or lively *tempo*.

Alphabet: In music, letters used to specify *pitch*. The music alphabet is *A B C D E F G.*

Alto clef: A *clef* that indicates the location of middle C on the *staff*. (Evolved from the script for the letter C.)

Anacrusis: The technical term for *upbeat*.

Andante: Indicates a slow, walking *tempo*.

Antecedent phrase: The first of two phrases in a musical *period*; followed by the *consequent phrase*.

Anticipation: A *nonchord tone* that precedes the harmony to which it belongs; approached by step or skip.

Appoggiatura: A *nonchord tone* that is approached by a skip and left stepwise; usually occurs on a strong beat.

Asymmetrical meters: Meters in which the measure cannot divide equally into twos, threes, or fours (for example, $\frac{5}{4}$ $\frac{7}{8}$).

Atonal: Having no *tonal center*.

Augmented triad: A *chord* made up of a major 3rd and an augmented 5th.

Authentic cadence: Dominant-to-tonic harmony (V–I); can be *perfect* or *imperfect*, based on the voicings of each chord.

Bar: Synonymous with *measure*.

Bar lines: Vertical lines drawn through the staff to designate division of rhythm into *measures*.

Bass clef: A *clef* that identifies the fourth line of the *staff* as the position of the F below middle C. (Evolved from the script for the letter F.)

Bass staff: The *staff* designated by the use of the *bass clef*; indicates that all lines and spaces specify pitches below middle C.

Beat: The recurring patterns of strong and weak *pulses*, with the first note of each group being accented. The patterns are established by the *meter*.

Binary form: Two-part song form consisting of two complementary but independent periods or sections, each ending with a strong cadence and each capable of standing alone.

Blues scale: The *scale* used in jazz, rock, blues, and so on. The diatonic scale with lowered 3rd, 5th, and 7th is the popular and the traditional version, although other versions exist.

Brace: A bracket that is used to join the treble and bass staffs to create the *grand staff.*

Cadence: A pause or closure identified by rhythmic/melodic/harmonic formulae located at the end of musical phrases, periods, sections, and entire pieces.

Changing tones: Nonchord tones that are a combination of an *upper* and a *lower neighbor* but without the chord tone appearing between the two.

Chord: Three or more pitches played simultaneously (as opposed to *interval*, which is two pitches only).

Chord inversions: Chords in which the root is not presented as the lowest-sounding pitch. In 1st inversion, the 3rd is the lowest-sounding pitch; in 2nd inversion, the 5th is the lowest-sounding pitch. Unlike intervals, chords do not change their quality when inverted.

Chord names: A chord is named (a) by its *root,* (b) by its *scale-degree name,* or (c) by the roman numeral applied to the respective scale degree on which it is built.

Chord quality: Major, minor, diminished, augmented—determined by the type of 3rd and the type of 5th.

Chord tone: Any pitch that is part of the current harmony (as opposed to *nonchord tone*).

Chromatic scale: A scale consisting of pitches in consecutive half-step order, within an octave.

Circle of Fifths: A visual depiction of the pattern of descending fifths, read counterclockwise; serves as an aid to memorization of key signatures, among other purposes.

Clef: A symbol placed at the beginning of the staff to designate specific pitch names. In current use are *treble* (G); *bass* (F); *alto,* and *tenor* (C).

Common time: $\frac{4}{4}$ meter.

Components of music: Sound and time. (Some authorities include space and silence.)

Compound intervals: Intervals larger than an *octave* (9ths, 10ths, and so on).

Compound meter: A meter in which the basic beat is represented by a dotted note, which divides evenly into threes, ($\frac{6}{8}$ $\frac{9}{8}$ and so on).

Conjunct motion: A type of melodic motion that proceeds by stepwise movement (as opposed to *disjunct motion*).

Consequent phrase: The second phrase in a musical *period;* preceded by the *antecedent phrase.*

Consonant intervals: Intervals that are heard as "agreeable" or "reposeful": unisons, octaves, 3rds, 6ths, perfect 4ths, and perfect 5ths (as opposed to *dissonant intervals*).

Contour: The overall shape of the *melody*.

Counterpoint: A type of *texture*, practically synonymous with *polyphony*, implying the simultaneous performance of two or more independent melodies; the term also is used to refer to a systematic study of the art of writing polyphonic textures.

Crescendo: Gradually becoming louder.

Cut time: $\frac{2}{2}$ meter ($\frac{4}{4}$ halved).

Da Capo: An indication that the piece is to be repeated from the beginning (abbrev. D.C.).

Dal Segno: An indication that the section so marked should be repeated.

Decrescendo: Gradually becoming softer.

Diatonic scale: A seven-tone scale consisting of five whole steps and two half steps); seven arrangements *(modes)* are in use.

Diminished triad: A chord made up of a minor 3rd and a diminished 5th.

Disjunct motion: A type of melodic motion that proceeds by *intervals* larger than a whole step (as opposed to *conjunct motion*).

Dissonant intervals: Intervals that contain "tension" or that are heard as "restless" and in need of resolution: 2nds and 7ths; augmented 4ths; diminished 5ths).

Dominant: The fifth degree of the *diatonic scale*.

Dot: A sign placed after a note that lengthens the note's value by one-half.

Double bar: Two vertical lines drawn through the staff to designate the end of a composition or the end of a particular section of a composition.

Double dots: A sign placed after a note that lengthens the note's value by one and a half.

Double flat: A symbol (♭♭) placed before a note indicating that the pitch is to be played one whole step lower.

Double period: The combination of two interdependent *periods*; there are two types: parallel and contrasting.

Double sharp: a symbol (✖) placed before a note indicating that the pitch is to be played one whole step higher.

Downbeat: The first beat of a measure; frequently used to refer to the first accented beat of a composition, that is, the first beat 1 in the piece.

Duple meter: A meter in which the measure contains two beats.

Duration: The length of a sound; one of the four *properties of sound*.

Dynamics: The aspect of musical expression resulting from variation in the *intensity* of the sound (loudness/softness).

Eighth note: A note type equivalent to one half the value of a *quarter note*. Written as a black notehead with a stem and a flag.

Elements of music: The organizational components for composing music; generally included are *melody, rhythm, harmony, form, texture, timbre, tempo,* and *dynamics.*

Enharmonic: A term referring to pitches that sound the same but that have different names, for example, C-sharp/D-flat. (Names are determined by musical context.)

Escape tone: A *nonchord tone* that is approached stepwise and left by a skip, usually in the opposite direction.

Fermata: A symbol indicating a pause or hold of the note over/under which it is placed; the length of the pause or hold is at the discretion of the performer and is based upon the musical context.

Fine: The end.

Flag: A curved line attached to the note stem that indicates a value smaller than the *quarter note*.

Flat: A symbol (♭) placed before a note to indicate that the pitch is to be played one half step lower.

Form: The design and structure of a composition.

Forte (*f*): Dynamic indicator meaning loud.

Fortepiano (*fp*): Dynamic indicator meaning suddenly loud and then soft.

Fortissimo (*ff*): Dynamic indicator meaning very loud.

Frequency: The number of vibrations occurring per second in a vibrating object; determines the *pitch* of the sound.

Grand staff: The combination of the treble and bass staffs, joined by a *brace* (bracket), with middle C (B and D) lying between the two. Used for piano literature, choral music, and so on. Also referred to as the great staff.

Half cadence: A cadence based on dominant harmony; incomplete closure. Also called a semicadence.

Half note: A note type equivalent to half a *whole note*, two *quarter notes*, and so on. Written as a white notehead with a stem.

Half step: The distance from one pitch to the very next (when the *octave* is divided into twelve equal parts). Also referred to as a semitone.

Harmonic interval: The distance between two pitches that are sounded simultaneously.

Harmonic minor scale: A diatonic minor scale with accidentals to provide a raised seventh scale degree (to provide a *leading tone* to the *tonic*).

Harmonic rhythm: The rate of chord change (or harmonic change) in a piece.

Harmony: In general, the simultaneous sounding of pitches; more specifically, the arrangement of chords (within a harmonic context) in a piece.

Hemiola: A type of *syncopation* implying a shift in the normal rhythmic arrangement of the beats.

Homophony: A type of *texture* in which one line of melody is most notable and is accompanied by chords; in this type of texture, the primary emphasis is vertical, but there is a horizontal effect as well.

Imperfect authentic cadence: A *cadence* in which one or both of the cadence chords (V I) is not in root position or in which the tonic does not appear as the highest-sounding note in the final chord.

Intensity: The relative loudness or softness of a sound, determined by the amount of energy causing the vibrations; one of the *properties of sound*.

Interval: The distance between two pitches. If two pitches occur successively, the interval is melodic. If two pitches occur simultaneously, the interval is harmonic.

Interval inversion: The reversal of the original positions of the two pitches in an interval. Except in perfect intervals, the *interval quality* is affected by inversion: Major becomes Minor, and vice versa; diminished becomes augmented, and vice versa; perfect remains perfect. The *interval number* always changes: A 2nd becomes a 7th, and so on.

Interval number: A measurement of interval size (2nd, 3rd, and so on). determined by the distance from one pitch to another based on the number of letter names encompassed by the two pitches.

Interval quality: A measurement of interval size determined by the number of half steps between the two pitches. Interval qualities are major, minor, diminished, and augmented (2nds, 3rds, 6ths, 7ths); and perfect, diminished, and augmented (unisons, 4ths, 5ths, octaves).

Inversion: Presentation of melodic material in the opposite direction.

Keyboard: The white and black keys on the piano. (Standard acoustic pianos have 88 keys.)

Keys: The white and black levers on keyboard instruments; also, the names (tonal centers) of the various transpositions of the major and minor scales.

Key signatures: Sharps or flats placed at the beginning of each staff to indicate which pitches are to be sharped or flatted throughout; likewise indicates the tonal center, or key.

Leading tone: Scale degree 7; one half step below the *tonic*.

Ledger lines: Segments of lines added above or below the staff to designate pitches that are higher or lower than those available on the staffs themselves.

Legato: A style of performance in which the notes are played in a smooth and connected manner; indicated by a curved line *(slur)* over the respective notes.

Lines: Lines of the treble clef are E G B D F; of the bass clef, G B D F A.

Major mode: A *diatonic scale* with half steps between scale degrees 3 and 4 and 7 and 8. Also called the major scale.

Major triad: A chord consisting of a major 3rd and a perfect 5th.

Measures: Metric units usually determined by the *meter* and designated by *bar lines*.

Mediant: Scale degree 3; midway between *tonic* and *dominant*.

Melodic interval: The distance between two pitches that are heard successively.

Melodic minor scale: A diatonic minor scale with accidentals used to raise the sixth and seventh degrees ascending but not descending, thus providing a *leading tone* to the *tonic* when approaching in that direction.

Melody: A series of pitches (with a rhythm) that conveys a musical idea or thought. Sometimes referred to as the "tune."

Meter: The system of regularly recurring patterns of strong and weak beats (pulses) of equal duration. The patterns usually are marked off by a constant and regular accent. The meter is designated at the beginning of the composition by a *meter signature*.

Meter signature: Indicates the beat pattern being used; consists of an upper and a lower number. Also called a time signature.

Metronome: A mechanical or electric device used to accurately perceive the suggested *tempo* of a piece. Composers can indicate specific tempo by indicating M.M. data at the beginning of a composition or at various places throughout.

Mezzo forte (*mf*): Dynamic indicator meaning medium loud.

Mezzo piano (*mp*): Dynamic indicator meaning medium soft.

Middle C: The centermost C key on the keyboard; the ledger line located directly between the *treble* and *bass staffs*.

Minor mode: A *diatonic scale* with half steps between steps 2 and 3 and 5 and 6. Three versions of this mode are possible: *natural*, *harmonic*, and *melodic*. Also called the minor scale.

Minor triad: A chord consisting of a minor 3rd and a perfect 5th.

Moderato: Indicates moderate *tempo*.

Modes: Various arrangements of the whole steps and half steps in a *diatonic scale*. Seven arrangements are in general use: Ionian (major), Dorian, Phrygian, Lydian, Mixolydian, Aeolian (minor), and Locrian.

Modulation: A change of *tonal centers* within a piece.

Monophony: A type of *texture*, consisting of a single line of unaccompanied melody.

Motive: A short rhythmic/melodic idea that serves as a unifying cell for a composition.

Motivic melody: A melody (or an entire composition) based on a *motive*.

Music: The art of "sound organized in time."

Mutation: A change of *modes* within a piece.

Natural: A symbol (♮) placed before a note indicating that a previous alteration has been canceled.

Natural minor scale: A *diatonic scale* with half steps located between steps 2 and 3 and 5 and 6.

Neighboring tones: Nonchord tones that are approached stepwise and left stepwise but in the opposite direction. Two types are upper and lower neighboring tones.

Nonchord tones: Pitches that do not belong to the chord (harmony) with which they are heard. Also called nonharmonic tones.

Notation: A set of symbols enabling composers to indicate specific information pertaining to the various *elements of music* in their compositions.

Note: A notational symbol placed on the *staff* to designate pitch; various types indicate durational values.

Note types (note names): Various types of notes, specifying relative durational values (whole, half, quarter, eighth, sixteenth, thirty-second, sixty-fourth).

Octatonic scale: An eight-pitch scale arranged in alternating whole steps and half steps (or alternating half steps/whole steps).

Octave: The distance from one pitch to another with the same name. (Consists of twelve equal half steps.)

8va: A symbol (standing for *ottava*) used to indicate that the notes are to be played an *octave* higher (or an *octave* lower) than written; useful for the avoidance of many ledger lines.

Parallel major/minor scales: Scales that have the same *tonal center* but a different configuration of whole steps and half steps (and a different key signature).

Passing tone: A nonchord tone that is approached and left stepwise, in the same direction; may occur on accented or unaccented beats of the measure.

Pedal point: A nonchord tone that is sustained throughout one chord change, and frequently more; may occur in any voice.

Pentatonic scale: A five-tone scale, traditionally arranged with two skips of one and a half steps, although other arrangements are possible. (Jazz musicians distinguish between major pentatonic and minor pentatonic, and so on.)

Perfect authentic cadence: A cadence in which the dominant chord proceeds to the tonic chord; both chords (V I) are in root position and the tonic is the highest note of the final chord.

Perfect intervals: An interval category consisting of unisons, octaves, 4ths, and 5ths.

Period: A musical form consisting of two interdependent phrases; there are two types: parallel and contrasting. (Occasionally, three-phrase periods are encountered in the literature.)

Phrase: The smallest form in music; usually four measures (although fewer or more measures are encountered in the literature); length designated by a *cadence.*

Pianissimo (*pp*): Dynamic indicator meaning very soft.

Piano (*p*): Dynamic indicator meaning soft.

Pitch: The relative highness or lowness of a sound; determined by the number of *frequencies* produced by the vibrating object; one of the *properties of sound.*

Plagal cadence: A cadence consisting of a progression of subdominant harmony to tonic.

Polyphony: A type of *texture* in which two or more independent melodies are heard simultaneously; practically synonymous with *counterpoint,* although the latter has additional connotations.

Popular-music chord symbols: Letter names plus suffix symbols used to specify harmony in most popular music, including jazz, popular songs, folk songs, and rock.

Primary triads: The tonic, dominant, and subdominant triads (I, IV, V) in any key.

Properties of sound: Pitch, intensity, duration, timbre.

Pulse: The recurring patterns of strong and weak *beats,* with the first note of each group being accented. (It is what we tap our foot to when we listen to metered music.)

Quadruple meter: A meter in which the measure contains four beats.

Quartal chords: Chords built in intervals of 4ths.

Quintal chords: Chords built in intervals of 5ths.

Quarter note: A note type equivalent to two eighth notes. Written as a black notehead with a stem.

Range: The distance from the lowest to the highest note in a melody or piece.

Register: A specific part of the total range of an instrument or a voice (high register, middle register, low register, and so on).

Relative major/minor scales: Scales that share the same key signatures but have different *tonal centers*.

Repeat signs: Various types of notational symbols that indicate the material to be repeated; for example, double dotted/double bars, D.C. al Fine, and so on.

Rest: Notational symbol that indicates silence. Rest values are identical with those of various *note types*.

Rhythm: The *time* or the temporal aspect of music, or the time relationships in music; indicated by length of pitches and affected by accents.

Root: The pitch on which a *tertian chord* is built.

Rounded binary form: A song form with two distinct sections, each usually ending with a strong cadence; differs from *binary form* in that the *A* section is heard again but as part of the *B* section.

Scale: An arrangement of pitches in consecutive ascending/descending order, within the octave.

Scale-degree names: The names of the numbered positions of pitches in the scale: *tonic* (1), *supertonic* (2), *mediant* (3), *subdominant* (4), *dominant* (5), *submediant* (6), *leading tone* (7) (*subtonic* = lowered 7). (Chords built from these scale degrees use the same names.)

Secundal chords: Chords built in intervals of 2nds. Sometimes called "cluster chords."

Sequence: A variation technique in which melodic material is presented either higher or lower than the original; not to be confused with *transposition*.

Sharp: A symbol (♯) placed before a note indicating that the pitch is to be raised one half step.

Simple interval: Any interval of an *octave* or less (as opposed to *compound intervals*).

Simple meter: Meter in which the basic beat divides evenly in halves.

Sixteenth note: A note type equivalent to two thirty-second notes, or half the value of an eighth note. Written as a black notehead with a stem and two flags.

Slur: A curved line used to indicate phrasing, as well as *legato* performance style.

Sound: A component of music; the sensation perceived by the mind when sound waves reach the ear; also, the sound source itself.

Spaces: Spaces of the treble clef are F A C E; of the bass clef, A C E G.

Staccato: A style of performance in which the notes are played in a detached (short/crisp) manner; indicated by a dot placed above or below the respective notes.

Staff: A type of grid consisting of five parallel lines and four spaces on which notes are placed to indicate pitch.

Subdominant: Scale degree 4; one whole step below the *dominant*.

Submediant: Scale degree 6; midway between *tonic* and *subdominant*.

Subtonic: Scale degree 7; one whole step from the *tonic*.

Supertonic: Scale degree 2; one whole step above the *tonic*.

Suspension: A nonchord tone that is held over from the previous harmony and then moves to resolution after the new chord has been sounded. Suspensions usually resolve downward to the chord tone; when resolving upward, they are generally referred to as *retardations*.

Syllable names: Syllables that designate pitches: Do, Re, Mi, Fa, Sol, La, Ti in major; Do, Re, Me, Fa, Sol, Le, Te in minor. Used as an aid in sight singing.

Syncopation: A displacement of the regular accent in traditional meters in Western music.

Synthetic scale: Any predetermined pitch pattern, individually designed; that is, not one of the traditional scales.

Tempo: The speed or pace of the music.

Tenor clef: A *clef* that indicates the location of middle C. (Evolved from the script for the letter C.)

Ternary form: Three-part song form in which the first two sections (*A* and *B*) are followed by a repeat of *A*.

Tertian chord: A chord built in intervals of 3rds.

Tertian harmony: Harmony based on chords built in intervals of 3rds.

Texture: The density of the music, dependent upon the number and nature of the musical events happening simultaneously; the particular "weave" of the music (analogous to fabric), heard as thin, thick, and so on.

Through-composed: Describes a melody that simply evolves without being based on a *motive*.

Tie: A curved line joining two adjacent notes of the same pitch, indicating that the second is not to be resounded but should be held for the total value of the two combined.

Timbre: The unique quality or "tone color" of a sound; one of the *properties of sound*.

Time: A component of music; the interval between one event and the next.

Time signature: See *Meter signature*.

Tonal center: The keynote, or *tonic*, of a piece (or scale). Serves as "home base," or the focal point of the composition.

Tonality: The establishment of *key* or *mode*. Implies that the tones are arranged to emphasize one pitch as the *tonal center* (key center) and to establish a hierarchy among the other pitches as determined by their intervallic relationship to the tonal center.

Tone row: An arbitrary arrangement (not one of the standard or traditional patterns) of a series of pitches, usually twelve, that serves as a pitch pattern for a composer's individual composition. Also called series.

Tonic: Scale degree 1; the *tonal center* of a tonal composition.

Transposition: The process of moving the tonal center to a new location while maintaining all the interval relationships in the piece (or scale).

Treble clef: A *clef* that identifies the second line of the *staff* as the position of the G above middle C. (Evolved from the script for the letter G.)

Treble staff: The *staff* designated by the use of the *treble clef*; indicates pitches above middle C.

Triad: A chord with three pitches.

Triple meter: Meter with three beats per measure.

Triplet: Subdivision into three parts (heard as three in the time of two).

Unison: The name given to two notes of the same pitch. Also referred to as prime.

Upbeat: Any note(s) that occurs before the accented beat *(downbeat)* in a piece. Also called the *anacrusis*.

Whole note: A note type equivalent to two half notes. Written as a white note-head without a stem.

Whole step: The equivalent of two half steps, or the distance from one pitch to another (with one pitch intervening) when the *octave* is divided equally into twelve half steps. Also referred to as a whole tone.

Whole-tone scale: A six-note scale in which all steps are whole steps.

Index of Music Examples

This list includes only examples of pieces or excerpts of pieces. It does not include graphic displays. NOTE: **WKBK** = Workbook; **SB** = Scorebook; **RHY** = Rhythm Units; **DRLS** = Drills in Chapter Reviews.

Jacob's Ladder—Traditional (**DRLS—Chapter 11**), (**RHY-VI**)

Jingle Bells—J. S. Pierpont (**WKBK 3-34**)

Joy to the World—George Frideric Handel (**8-J**)

Joy to the World (with "Jingle Bells") (**12-G**)

Kum Ba Ya—Nigerian Melody (**WKBK 6 11-b**)

L'Arabesque—J. F. Burgmueller (**WKBK 11-5**)

Les Demons s'amusent—Vladmir Rebikov (**5-N**) (*4 measures*)

Listen to the Mockingbird—Alice Hawthorne (**RHY-III**)

Little Duple Tune—J.D. (**WKBK 11-2**)

Little Folk Song—Robert Schumann (**WKBK 8-3b**)

Little Suite "Morning Song"—Cornelius Gurlitt (**WKBK 11-14**)

London Bridge—English Traditional (**WKBK 3-6a**)

Long, Long Ago—Thomas H. Bayley (**WKBK 4 22-f**)

March of the Tin Soldiers—Gurlitt (**WKBK 12-1d**)

Marriage of Figaro, The—Wolfgang Mozart (**SB**)

Me and Bobby McGee—Kris Kristofferson and Fred Foster (**WKBK 3-34**)

Melody embellished and simplified (**8-M**)

Melody with meter change (**8-O**)

Melody with register change (**8-P**)

Melody with rhythmic change (**8-N**)

Memory, from *Cats*—Andrew Lloyd Weber (**RHY-II**) (*4 measures*)

Merrily We Roll Along—Traditional (**6-E**), (**RHY-I**)

Michael, Row the Boat Ashore—Spiritual (**RHY-VI**) (**WKBK 4-21f**)

Mikrokosmos, No. 78—Béla Bartók (**WKBK 8-13d**)

Mikrokosmos, No. 136—Béla Bartók (**WKBK 8-7**)

Minuet in G Major—Johann Sebastian Bach (**WKBK 8-1**)

Moldau, The (theme)—Bedřich Smetana (**WKBK 8-13a**) (*8 measures*)

Nonchord Tone March, The—J.D. (**WKBK 11-4**)

Nonchord Tone Waltz, The—J.D. (**WKBK 11-6**)

O Come, O Come Emmanuel—Gregorian Chant (**WKBK 4-21a**), (**WKBK 6-16d**)

Octatonic Melody—J.D. (**5-T**)

O Dear! What Can the Matter Be—English Trad. (**WKBK 3-6c**), (**WKBK 4-22b**)

Ode to Joy—Ludwig van Beethoven (Symphony No. 9) (**14-G, 14-S**)

O Hanukkah—Jewish Folk Song (**5-R**)

Oh! Susanna—Stephen Foster (**14-I**), (**WKBK 4-22e**)

One Grain of Sand—Appalachian Lullaby (**SB**)

One More River—Traditional (**WKBK 11-8**)

On Top of Old Smokey—American (**5-D**)

Original NCT Melody—(**DRLS—Chapter 11**)

Pentatonic Waltz, The—J.D. (**8-E**)

People—Jule Styne and Bob Merrill (**RHY-VI**) (*7 measures*)

Polly Wolly Doodle—American (**DRLS—Chapter 11**)

Polyphonic texture—J.D. (**12-F**)

Prayer—Gebet (**WKBK 12-1b**)

Prelude, No. 20, in c Minor—Frédéric Chopin (**SB**)

Prelude, Op. 28, No. 7, in A Major—Frédéric Chopin (**SB**)

Rage Over the Lost Penny—Ludwig van Beethoven (**WKBK 4-24**)

Red River Valley—Traditional (**WKBK 11-10**)

Rejoice, O My Soul—Robert Schumann (**WKBK 22-c**)

Row, Row, Row Your Boat (round) (**12-E**)

Russian Melody (**WKBK 7-14d**) (*6 measures*)

S. Basin Street (**WKBK 11-17**)

Santa Lucia—Neapolitan Song (**WKBK 14-7d**)

Satin Doll—Duke Ellington (**11-M**) (*8 measures*)

Scarborough Fair—English Folk Song (**SB**)

Seventeenth-century round (**WKBK 6-16a**) (*4 measures*)

Shalom Chaverim—Israeli Song (**11-C**)

Sidewalks of New York, The—Blake (**WKBK 6-11a**)

Silent Night—Franz Gruber (**WKBK 14-1d**)

Silesian Folk Song (**WKBK 6-16c**) (*4 measures*)

Simple Song—J.D. (**WKBK 14-1c**)

Skip to My Lou—Game Song (**WKBK 14-1e**)

Song of Ivan—Aram Khachaturian (**WKBK 7-14c**) (*4 measures*)

Spanish Folk Song (**WKBK 6-8a**)

Standing in the Need of Prayer—Spiritual (**SB**)

Star-Spangled Banner, The—J. S. Smith (**8-K**)

Summer's Gone—J.D. (**WKBK 12-1a**)

Swedish Folk Song (**WKBK 7-14e**) (*5 measures*)

Symphony No. 5—Ludwig van Beethoven (**8-K**) (*motive only*)

Symphony No. 5—Ludwig van Beethoven (**12-A**) (*10 measures*)

This Old Man—English (**RHY-III**), (**WKBK 14-1a**)

Time in a Bottle—Jim Croce (**SB**)

Tom Dooley—American Folk Song (**13-A**)

Tone-Row Waltz, The—J.D. (**8-F**)

Valley of the Dolls—André Previn (**RHY-VII**) (*10 measures*)

Valsette—Zoltán Kodály (**5-W**), (**WKBK 8-9**)

Victimae—Gregorian Chant (**WKBK 12-1c**)

Village Waltz— Louis Kohler (**WKBK 11-15**)

Vive l'amour—College Song (**RHY-II**)

Water Is Wide, The—Folk Song (**SB**)

Wayfaring Stranger—American (**WKBK 7-14a**) (*4 measures*)

We Shall Overcome—Civil Rights Song (**WKBK 14-3a**)

We Three Kings of Orient Are—John H. Hopkins (**SB**)

When I Grow Too Old to Dream—Sigmund Romberg (**WKBK6-11b**)

When Johnny Comes Marching Home Again— P. S. Gilmore (**14-K, 14-O**)

When the Saints Go Marching In—Traditional (**14-K**)

Where Have All the Flowers Gone?—Peter Seeger (**WKBK 14-3b**)

Whole-Tone Waltz, The—J.D. (**8-D**)

Wild Rider, The—Robert Schumann (**WKBK 8-3a**), (**WKBK 11-3**)

William Tell Overture—Antonio Rossini (**WKBK 14-7b**)

Yankee Doodle—American (**14-Q**)

Subject Index